Y

Year Zero

An Inside View of the Scottish Parliament

MIKE WATSON

For Clare

© Mike Watson, 2001

Polygon at Edinburgh
An imprint of Edinburgh University Press Ltd
22, George Square, Edinburgh

Typeset in Bembo
by Pioneer Associates, Perthshire, and
printed and bound in Great Britain by
MPG Books Ltd, Bodmin, Cornwall

A CIP Record for this book is available from the British Library

ISBN 1 902930 26 6 (paperback)

The right of Mike Watson
to be identified as author of this work
has been asserted in accordance with
the Copyright, Designs and Patents Act 1988.

Contents

	Acknowledgements	vii
	List of interviewees	ix
	Preface	xi
1	Winners and losers	1
2	The new and the not-so-new politics	15
3	Anything but Westminster ...	27
4	Hard pressed	38
5	The people speak	65
6	Events	79
7	Turf wars	112
8	Scotland under the microscope	138
9	In committee	162
10	And now what?	187
	Postscript	201
	Bibliography	204
	Index	205

Acknowledgements

Several people have been instrumental in this book reaching fruition, some of them without even realising it.

Gemma Swart played a central role in its completion. We first discussed it as a project in August 1999 and her encouragement and suggested themes at that time led to my original drafts. For various reasons, little progress was made until the beginning of 2000, at which time I questioned whether the time required both for research and writing could be found in the face of competing demands on time (not least from the Parliament itself).

It was only in April that the proposal was sent to EUP and I am extremely grateful that they agreed to publish within what were very tight deadlines.

The major share of the research was carried out by Gemma. Trawling through hundreds of newspapers and microfiches took up a sizeable portion of her time, which in itself was constrained by daily travel between home in Edinburgh and her job in Glasgow. But newspaper coverage of events form the core of the book and these were identified, prioritised and contextualised by Gemma.

That done, she remained a source of ideas and constructive criticism on both style and content, culminating in her advice on the choice of illustrations. As she also shared the interviews with me and helped with proof reading too, it can be seen that her efforts were immense, as is my appreciation of them.

The supporting cast also played important roles. Gerry Hassan was influential in his initial encouragement and subsequent suggestions. Nicola Carr was supportive throughout and contributed helpful additions to the initial draft. The advice of her colleague James Dale and Sarah Burnett with copy-editing was crucial in producing the finished article.

In various ways, Patricia Harris, Ann Henderson, Neil McGarvey, Derek Munn, Elizabeth Quigley, Donald Reid and Clare Thomas all contributed as the deadlines bore down.

I am grateful to the *Daily Record*, *The Herald* and *The Scotsman* for permission to use their photographs. Further illustrations were provided with the assistance of Alan Smart, the Parliament's head of broadcasting.

The Scottish Parliament Information Centre (SPICe) was invaluable in filling gaps which remained as the writing approached its conclusion. The assistance which they provided was a collective effort, but I hope their colleagues will forgive me if I record special thanks to Jean Smith, Francesca McGrath and Megan Hunter.

Finally, I want to record my thanks to the twenty-five interviewees who readily made themselves available and spoke enthusiastically and candidly of their experiences. Their contributions give the book a dimension which I hope will enable it to act as a record in years to come of how the Parliament's first year felt and looked from within.

List of interviewees
(information correct at 30 September 2000)

Malcolm Chisholm is the Labour MP and MSP for Edinburgh North and Leith.

Sarah Davidson is secretary to the Scottish Parliament Holyrood Progress Group. She was clerk to the Scottish Parliament Audit and Finance committees from May 1999–May 2000.

Brian Donohoe is the Labour MP for Cunninghame South.

Frank Doran is the Labour MP for Aberdeen Central.

Lord James Douglas Hamilton is a Conservative list MSP for Lothians, the Conservative Party business manager and a member of the Parliamentary Bureau of the Scottish Parliament.

Patricia Ferguson is the Labour MSP for Glasgow Maryhill and a Deputy Presiding Officer of the Scottish Parliament.

Douglas Fraser is the political editor of the *Sunday Herald*.

Maria Fyfe is the Labour MP for Glasgow Maryhill.

Sam Galbraith is the Labour MP and MSP for Strathkelvin and Bearsden and Scottish Executive Education minister.

Kenny Gibson is an SNP list MSP for Glasgow and shadow minister for Local Government.

List of interviewees

Donald Gorrie is the Liberal Democrat MP for Edinburgh West and a Liberal Democrat list MSP for Central Scotland.

John Home Robertson is the Labour MP and MSP for East Lothian and Scottish Parliament deputy Rural Affairs minister.

Andy Kerr is the Labour MSP for East Kilbride and convener of the Scottish Parliament Transport and Environment committee. He was Labour's campaign manager for the Ayr by-election.

Dave King is the political correspondent of the *Daily Record*.

Johann Lamont is the Labour MSP for Glasgow Pollok.

Jack McConnell is the Labour MSP for Motherwell and Wishaw and Scottish Executive Finance minister.

Maureen MacMillan is a Labour list MSP for the Highlands and Islands.

Duncan McNeil is the Labour MSP for Greenock and Inverclyde and a deputy Labour business manager.

Pauline McNeill is the Labour MSP for Glasgow Kelvin and a vice-convener of the Scottish Parliamentary Labour Party.

Tricia Marwick is an SNP list MSP for Mid Scotland and Fife, SNP business manager and a member of the Parliamentary Bureau of the Scottish Parliament.

Brian Monteith is a Conservative list MSP for Mid Scotland and Fife and is Conservative spokesperson on Education, Culture and Sport.

Margaret Smith is the Liberal Democrat MSP for Edinburgh West and convener of the Scottish Parliament Health and Community Care committee.

Brian Taylor is political editor of BBC Scotland.

Ian Welsh is the chief executive of Kilmarnock Football Club. He was the Labour MSP for Ayr from May–December 1999.

Andrew Wilson is an SNP list MSP for Central Scotland and shadow Finance minister.

Preface

I can hardly claim to be a dispassionate observer capable of objective assessment of Scotland's Parliament. That is based on more than the fact that I am a member of it. Having campaigned for twenty years to bring it into being, I am naturally intent on making the Parliament a success, although I hope that does not mean I view our redrawn political landscape entirely through rose-tinted spectacles.

The Scottish Parliament was a long time in coming – as was the demand for it. It is ironic that the efforts of those who strained their every sinew to deny Scotland home rule were probably just as important as those of the many involved in the struggle to bring it about. Had the Tories acted more sensibly and more sensitively in their governance of Scotland between 1979 and 1997, then the Parliament might yet be some years distant.

Returning to Scotland at the end of 1979 after five years in the Midlands of England, my political activism thereafter was shaped by that year's double defeat. The rigged referendum and the installation of the Thatcher government seemed less sinister viewed from Derby than Dundee. Distance had had a numbing effect which quickly wore off as I absorbed the Scottish political environment. For some in the Labour Party in Scotland, the referendum had proved the more bitter pill. That is not to suggest there was a lack of realism, given the requirement that Labour regain power at UK level before devolution's return to the agenda. The mood of the moment was that it must await the next general election, failing which the one after that.

There was certainly no expectation that almost two decades would elapse before the people of Scotland were again offered a voice on the constitutional question. The years in between witnessed the slow incline towards the Parliament which developed through the efforts of many people inside and outside political parties. Within Labour the argument was hard-won, although there remained after the referendum in 1997 – as is still the case today – those who believe that the United Kingdom is endangered by the loosening of its constituent parts. My own belief has long been that the denial of that process was potentially much more damaging.

The anti-climax of the 1992 general election threatened to stall the progress made through the Scottish Constitutional Convention in preparing for Scotland's parliament. The lack of willingness of the Labour leadership at Westminster to exploit the leverage which the party's fifty-six Scottish MPs possessed thereafter was a disappointment to me and many others across the political spectrum; for a while enthusiasm for a return to the fray was difficult to summon. Would it really take just one last push?

Memories of 1979 made the double victory of 1997 all the sweeter. Labour's return to government and the decisive endorsement of the people of Scotland in the referendum which followed formed what I thought would be the high-water mark of my political activity. The ending of my association with Westminster – and the manner of it – left me without expectation of achieving a place in Scotland's first democratic legislature. Gaining first the confidence of Labour Party members in Cathcart and then the support of the people of that constituency moved that watermark yet higher.

Witnessing the establishment of the Scottish Parliament would have been reward enough after many setbacks over the previous two decades; to be a part of it was the source of fulfilment greater than any other event in my life.

That may explain my motivation in attempting to record the Parliament's first year. How it looked, how it felt, how it was. I wanted that to involve more than simply my own experiences, perceptions and assessments. There are 129 of us and no one member's

Preface

opinion is of greater value than another. So this is not *the* view of year zero, it is simply a collection of views.

I hope it might form a useful addition to the millions of words written about our Parliament in its short life thus far. Millions more will follow in years to come, as the Scottish Parliament develops into an institution which will make a real difference to the lives of our people and from which our country can take genuine pride.

Whatever it achieves in future its principal legacy is, I believe, already established: it exists.

Mike Watson
September 2000

Two weeks after this book was completed, Donald Dewar died. Rather than attempt to reflect that tragic event in the narrative, I felt it would be more appropriate to leave it as written, a snapshot of the period between May 1999 and July 2000, and record my feelings on the loss of the First Minister as a postscript.

Mike Watson
November 2000

1 Winners and losers

7 May 1999: Dawn was breaking over the cavernous SECC, as the last Glasgow results were announced. But most people there were too exhausted to do anything other than stagger homewards, knowing they would be back in five hours for the Glasgow City Council count.

Scotland's new electoral system meant that the final results from other parts of the country would not be known for up to twelve more hours. Calculating the fifty-six regional list members who would join the seventy-three MSPs elected for individual constituencies proved complex, but meanwhile the atmosphere in Glasgow's Scottish Exhibition and Conference Centre was electric, more reminiscent of a football match than politics, with chanting, singing and taunting of opponents.

Labour Party members were ecstatic that we had won all ten city seats, particularly Govan where we had braced ourselves for defeat. Despite the SNP's manifest disappointment at not capturing that seat, they were still pleased at having secured four of the city's seven list seats. With one seat each, the Conservatives and Liberal Democrats may not have had anything to shout about, but for most of their supporters it must have felt like it. If few Tories could recall the name of their last successful parliamentary candidate in Glasgow in 1979, it is a safe bet that not a single LibDem was even aware that their party had not had cause to raise a cheer at a parliamentary election count in the city since 1910.

The additional member system (AMS) had also seen Glasgow return one of the Scottish Parliament's three 'one-off' MSPs, none of whom would have been elected under the old system. The Scottish Socialist Party had gained 6.4 per cent of the vote across the city, sufficient to secure a seat for its leader, Tommy Sheridan. But while all elections are about winners and losers, this one was about winners, losers – and winners. Each of the city's list members had contested individual constituencies and, with the exception of the SNP's Nicola Sturgeon in Govan, all would be honest enough to admit (in retrospect at least) that they anticipated securing a place at Holyrood only as a list member.

The system is such that the outcome of each constituency contest has a knock-on effect not just on other parties, but on list candidates of all parties. This meant that some may not have anticipated the huge disappointment which came with being left out in the cold. I spoke with two list candidates, both of whom lost out as a result of the outcome in Govan. Brian Fitzpatrick was top of Labour's list and would have been elected had his colleague Gordon Jackson failed to defeat Sturgeon. Because Labour captured all ten city constituencies, the party did not qualify for a list seat. My SNP opponent in Cathcart was Maire Whitehead, who was also number five on the SNP's list for the city. Had Sturgeon, who was number one on the SNP list, succeeded in Govan, she would not have required a list place, meaning that Whitehead would have taken the SNP's fourth list seat. So Fitzpatrick and Whitehead were left high and dry, and witnessing their reactions that morning brought home to me the propensity of AMS to determine electoral and political fortunes by the narrowest of margins.

By the following afternoon, the allocation of all 129 seats was known, Labour having secured the largest number with fifty-six, followed by the SNP with thirty-five, the Tories with eighteen and the LibDems with seventeen. The remaining three places were taken by Sheridan, Robin Harper of the Scottish Greens and Dennis Canavan, the Labour MP who had stood against his own party to win resoundingly as an independent. As widely predicted, not even Labour had been able to reach the magical figure of sixty-five seats, which would have opened the door to power as the first devolved government of Scotland.

14 May 1999: *Driving to Dunkeld for the Labour group's post-election bonding session, I listened to* Good Morning Scotland *as Donald Dewar and Jim Wallace announced the basis on which the partnership had been formed.*

It had been obvious since the election of the last MSP was declared on 7 May that the only possible outcome of the first Scottish Parliament elections was a coalition between Labour and the Liberal Democrats. In theory, a LibDem–SNP link-up would have been possible in certain circumstances, but in this case it was simple arithmetic rather than political considerations which made that a non-runner – it would have yielded only fifty-two seats, well short of a majority.

So peacetime coalition government – *A Partnership for Scotland*, according to the title of the joint statement by Donald Dewar and Jim Wallace which announced it – arrived in the UK for the first time since 1922.

Was a coalition inevitable? Could Labour, having secured less than 40 per cent of first votes, have used that as a step ladder from which to reach out and grab 100 per cent of the power in Scotland's new democracy? Certainly, in constitutional terms there was nothing to prevent Donald Dewar from declaring his intention to do just that, as indeed Alun Michael, his counterpart in the National Assembly of Wales, proceeded to do from an even smaller vote base. It appears that no serious thought was given in Wales to working with the Liberal Democrats, or even perhaps Plaid Cymru, a party that has a much softer edge to it than the SNP, to the extent that it does not even have a policy in favour of independence.

Doubtless, Dewar did consider soldiering on alone, taking total command over appointments to the cabinet and the details of his programme for government. However, given his hugely influential role in delivering the devolution settlement for Scotland and his consequent responsibility for the proportional voting system, I suspect he did not consider it for long.

Scotland's Parliament had been delivered on the basis of new politics and a break from the Westminster system. The additional member system (AMS) makes it unlikely that any one of Scotland's four main parties will ever gain an overall majority. That provision was not included lightly in the Scotland Act, and some political commentators have argued that it was designed specifically to prevent an SNP majority at a future Scottish Parliament election opening the door to Scotland's separation from the rest of the UK. Indeed, that view has been expressed to me by SNP MSPs who themselves believe this to be the case, but, if so, it represents a powerful example of Labour cutting off its nose to spite its face. There can be few examples of a party in power at national level legislating to introduce a sub-national level of government which it would be unlikely ever to control. Whatever accusations might be levelled at the Labour Party in terms of the devolution settlement, self-interest should not be among them.

As recently as March 2000, it was possible to hear Clydesdale MP Jimmy Hood (at a Scottish Labour conference fringe meeting) criticising the Blair government for having 'given away' power in Scotland and calling for a return to the first-past-the-post system which, he said, had 'served Labour well in the past'. There was some truth in this, although Labour in Scotland – the party as well as voters – gained little from that system in the years 1951–64 or 1979–97.

However, having gone to some lengths to ensure that the Scottish electorate understood a two-vote system which none had previously experienced, it would have been indefensible if Dewar had then opted for an outcome which replicated precisely that which would have resulted under the old system. Nevertheless, just such a position was advocated by some members of the Scottish Parliamentary Labour Party (SPLP), as the Labour group at Holyrood is known. This arose during a SPLP meeting on 19 May, when MSP John McAllion criticised the leadership for deciding to press ahead with coalition talks with the Liberal Democrats without first at least discussing the matter in order to gain group approval. In McAllion's view, such approval should have been withheld and Dewar should then have taken Labour into government from a minority position. Nor was the Member for Dundee East alone in such a position, although it was clear he was supported by only half a dozen others. What I found surprising about McAllion's position was that he is a long-standing member of the pressure group Labour Campaign for Electoral Reform, which advocates a more proportional voting system for the House of Commons, and he had been in the vanguard of the group's efforts to ensure that AMS was adopted for the Scottish Parliament. Having secured the introduction of a system for which he had long argued, McAllion seemed strangely unwilling to come to terms with its consequences.

Patricia Ferguson, now one of the Deputy Presiding Officers, was sympathetic to McAllion's aim, but did not think it a practical proposition. 'I would have preferred that we go it alone, but I knew that was not an option. If we had done so, we would have had to treat each issue on its merits, and we would never have got as much legislation passed in the first year as we have,' (interview, August 2000). Her Glasgow colleague Pauline McNeill reached the same conclusion, although by a different route: 'Quite simply, the partnership was a necessity, to enable us to get the work through the Parliament. And besides, I and other Labour Party members had worked with Liberal Democrats over the years in the Campaign for a Scottish Parliament, so we knew we had certain things in common,' (interview, June 2000).

It was to be expected that, as members of the opposition, SNP MSPs would not share this view of the political landscape, but, in fact, opinions varied. Tricia Marwick was unequivocal: 'Labour could have governed as a minority, although obviously they would not have got their own way all of the time. But it would have been a better Parliament because of it – there would have been better arguments and better debates. People who voted in the election did not expect the party with the lowest number of MSPs would end up having a role to play in the Executive,' (interview, June 2000). Her use of the word 'arguments' is open to interpretation.

Marwick's colleague Andrew Wilson saw the issue differently: 'It is basic political science that there would be a coalition. There are pros and cons with a minority administration or a coalition; a coalition brings a stability to the government's ability to push its agenda but the question for the LibDems is 'at what price?' We have to look very hard to see where their policy has had any impact,' (interview, June 2000).

Tory leader David McLetchie contemptuously dismissed the partnership when it was formed as a 'backstairs deal' and has rarely missed an opportunity since to criticise its existence, but his colleague Brian Monteith adopted a more pragmatic position: 'The partnership was inevitable because the two parties had sown the seeds before the election. The surprise for me was the extent to which the LibDems allowed themselves to become a hostage to fortune – they were hung out to dry on tuition fees, which may explain why, initially at least, the partnership was clearly an uncomfortable one,' (interview, July 2000).

The LibDems' Donald Gorrie has never disguised his view. 'I would have preferred it if Labour had formed a minority administration. Above all else, I want the Parliament to succeed and I thought it would find its feet better with a minority government as it would need to negotiate issue by issue and this would increase the inclusiveness of the Parliament,' (interview, July 2000).

In Greenock and Inverclyde, Labour's Duncan McNeil had other reservations. 'With a strong Liberal Democrat opposition during the election campaign, they were not a natural ally. In my case, they were the political enemy, and an enemy who stood to be a cabinet minister (Ross Finnie) if the coalition went ahead. But I realised partnership was the best way of making the Parliament work for the next four years,' (interview, June 2000).

The overwhelming majority of Labour members supported the aim of securing an agreement with the LibDems, although there was some concern that we had not been kept as well informed as our putative partnership colleagues. The LibDems held daily group meetings at which progress was reported and the views of the group sought. No similar arrangement existed for Labour members, leaving us dependent on journalists (or LibDem MSPs) for news of developments. The leadership had clearly made the assessment that most Labour members expected a coalition to be the outcome and that the talks should therefore proceed to a conclusion before they reported back. This did not cause a great deal of disquiet, perhaps because the group was not yet a cohesive unit, with many members yet to become acquainted with one another.

Meanwhile from 10 May, negotiations took place on forming a coalition. From the start, the item at the top of the agenda was the issue which had dominated the election campaign – the future of student tuition fees. Labour was led by Donald Dewar, supported by former Scottish Office ministers Henry McLeish, Sam Galbraith, plus Sarah Boyack and Tom McCabe, both of whose inclusion raised eyebrows within the SPLP as they had not hitherto been seen as part of the 'inner circle'. The LibDems were led not by an MSP but by MP Michael Moore, who had been their election campaign manager. Parliamentary representation came from Jim Wallace, Ross Finnie and Nicol Stephen, who were joined by Denis Robertson Sullivan, the party's Scottish treasurer.

Sullivan believes his party sold itself short at the negotiations, largely because Jim Wallace regarded coalition as something which *had* to happen, as a consequence of the voting system. He also identified another factor at play: 'Finnie and Stephen were Wallace's *confidantes* and they knew that, if agreement was reached, all three would be in government. This coloured their judgement and also meant that Wallace did not attempt to negotiate as Dewar's equal,' (interview, July 2000).

Gorrie expressed his support for this view with characteristic bluntness: 'Donald Dewar needed Jim Wallace more than Jim Wallace needed Donald Dewar – but Wallace didn't realise it. He never seriously considered the possibility of not reaching an agreement with Labour,' (interview, July 2000). Sullivan would not go that far, however. 'Having a new Parliament and a new political system meant you had to offer reassurances to the public, which meant stable government for the first four years. But Labour's team were at one with Wallace in taking it as read that there would be an agreement and I felt their approach (to us) was patronising as a result.'

Negotiations continued until agreement between the parties was reached late on the evening of 13 May. Before finalising acceptance, the LibDem team called their parliamentary group to a meeting to endorse it. Sixteen of the seventeen MSPs were there (Sir David Steel chose not to attend) and there was a vigorous debate on the principle as well as the content of the agreement. Margaret Smith (Edinburgh West) recalled the pressure of that occasion: 'I felt the weight of the party and our members was on my shoulders – the outcome would have a fundamental impact on Scottish politics. Ultimately, the fact that my party had been out of government for more than seventy years was what swayed it for me – not just to be in power, but to be able to have an effect, tempering some aspects of Labour's agenda with Liberal Democrat policies,' (interview, July 2000).

It had been agreed that a two-thirds majority (of the group as a whole) would be required for acceptance, which meant that if six members were opposed, there could be no deal. Donald Gorrie recalls: 'I was seeking to convince my colleagues to vote "no" and at one stage there were five of us against. Eventually, however, the leadership chipped away two of these and the final vote was thirteen to three in favour of acceptance.' The other opponents were John Farquhar Munro and Keith Raffan.

That sequence of events explains why Gorrie uttered his infamous 'Labour liars' jibe after the meeting, although he claims it was taken out of context. 'I was very frustrated at having lost the argument and was pretty cheesed off at the Labour spinning that had gone on. So when I emerged from the meeting I said to journalists that I regarded Labour as a bunch of liars, although what I meant to say was that it was their spin doctors who were liars – which I still believe is the case.'

At least the LibDem MSPs were consulted. As previously mentioned, the first I and other Labour members heard of the detail of the agreement was via our radios the following morning. Nevertheless, all of us, meeting that day in Dunkeld, thought that Labour had got the best of the bargain. And since that was patently the case, most Liberal Democrats were less than overwhelmed.

Both Sullivan and Gorrie believe their party sold itself short in the agreement. 'The speed with which negotiations were conducted and concluded suited Labour and we should have stood our ground. We should have secured concessions on proportional representation for local government (on which we should at least have guaranteed an inquiry) and a firmer commitment on the abolition of tuition fees. I also urged my colleagues to seek a *primus inter pares* arrangement between Dewar and Wallace, but this was not taken up,' says Sullivan (interview, July 2000).

Gorrie goes further: 'We should have got more out of it; all in all, we negotiated a bad deal. In other comparable situations, for instance between the SPD and the Greens in Germany, ministerial appointments are divided on a basis which gives the junior partner more than its share, based on the number of members which it has. We got fewer than our share and should have had at least one, if not two, more ministers' (interview, July 2000).

The document signed by Donald Dewar and Jim Wallace which

sealed the coalition, *A Partnership for Scotland*, ran to just twenty-three lines. Its second paragraph outlined its basic aims: 'We are determined to serve the people of Scotland by working together in partnership in the Parliament and in Government, building on the co-operation and success we achieved in the Scottish Constitutional Convention.'

Reference to the Convention reflected the fact that co-working between the parties had not begun on 10 May 1999. In fact, the partnership really dated as far back as March 1989, when the Convention met for the first time. The body had been driven by the Scottish Labour Party and the Scottish Liberal Democrats, although many other people had also played essential roles in the conclusions which it reached in its final report in November 1995. The signing of *A Partnership for Scotland* was different in one crucial way, because instead of outlining what the signatories *hoped* would happen, it set out in clear terms what *would* actually happen.

If *A Partnership for Scotland* covered less than a page, the document which accompanied it was much more substantial. *A Programme for Government* outlined the principles which were to guide the partnership in developing and implementing policies over the four years the agreement was intended to last. To nobody's surprise, item one was headed 'Student Finance'. Other items covered each of the Scottish Executive departments and there was a final section entitled 'Working Together', which explained how collective decision-making – an entirely new concept in Scottish politics – would be achieved. That section also provided that, subject to the approval of the Parliament, the leader of the Scottish Liberal Democrats should be the Deputy First Minister.

It was an historic agreement and one which had been concluded rather more quickly than might have been the case – a similar situation following the 1997 general election in New Zealand took seven weeks to resolve. The new electoral system having elected the new Parliament, the partnership paved the way for the new government of Scotland, in a new and untried style. Yet some commentators chose to characterise it as a compromise which meant 'business as usual'. This represented a peculiar assessment of events, because the opposite was true. Compromise was what the people of Scotland voted for, and that is precisely what they got as a result of the new proportional politics.

Questions were raised as to just what – ministerial cars apart – the LibDems had achieved in the negotiations. That was a classic example of rushing to judgement, as the subsequent abolition of tuition fees was to demonstrate. Columnist Iain Macwhirter painted a vision of life without the partnership: 'If the media has been hard on the coalition deal-making, just imagine how it would have treated a minority government staggering from crisis to crisis for the next four years. Instead of one unseemly fix, it would have been a fix before every vote. Jim Wallace may well have laid his party's interests aside in the interest of Scottish democracy,' (*Sunday Herald*, 16 May 1999).

Meanwhile, the Parliament had not awaited the outcome of the negotiations before opening its doors.

New faces

12 May 1999: Looking round the Parliament, I saw beaming faces around the chamber and in the gallery. Expectation was almost tangible in both; I had a strong sense that we could not let down the people who had invested their faith in us.

12 May 1999: Donald Dewar leads a group of Labour MSPs to the Assembly Hall for the Parliament's historic first sitting since 1707 (source: *Daily Record*)

Winners and losers

On 12 May, the new MSPs took the oath of allegiance to the Queen, not all Labour members showing much more conviction than the Nationalists. One SNP member, Winnie Ewing – the Parliament's oldest member at sixty-nine – had the distinction of taking the chair and declaring famously that 'the Scottish Parliament, adjourned on the twenty-fifth day of March 1707, is hereby reconvened'. Well, almost, since the Parliament would have been unrecognisable to those present at the adjournment some twelve generations earlier.

Indeed, the newly-elected members were noticeably different even from those elected to the House of Commons at the general election two years previously. For a start, forty-eight women were elected, representing 37.2 per cent of the Parliament as a whole. This ranked the Scottish Parliament third in Europe, behind Denmark and Sweden (were the Welsh Assembly a parliament, it would take that position since 40 per cent of its number are women). By comparison, women constitute a mere 16.7 per cent of Scotland's representation at Westminster.

The main reason for the increase was the Labour Party's operation of a system of pairing constituencies, which ensured that an equal number of men and women were selected (although the same could not be said for its list nominees). However, from that point on, the outcome rested with the electorate, but a pleasant quirk of fate resulted in Labour's fifty-six members being split equally by gender, although Ian Welsh's resignation (see Chapter 5) put the women in the majority. Of the other parties, the SNP did well using encouragement rather than a mechanism (fifteen female MSPs, or 43 per cent) while the Tories and the LibDems, who deliberately avoided giving women any preferential treatment, predictably ended up with a mere three and two respectively.

Another noticeable feature of the Parliament's make-up is its age profile. At the time of the election, eight were in their twenties and twenty-nine in their thirties. The average age of an MSP elected on 6 May 1999 was 45.2, with little difference between men (45.7) and women (44.3).

At the younger end, these figures contrast starkly (in percentage terms) with the House of Commons. Despite this, the mean age is not that different, with Scottish MPs averaging forty-nine years of age. The same cannot be said for class, however, with just 1.6 per cent of

MSPs having worked in the traditional 'blue-collar'/industrial sector, compared to 19.4 per cent of Scotland's MPs (Cavanagh et al. 2000). So, while the Scottish Parliament scores highly in terms of female representation, it is less representative of the working class and ethnic minorities (there are only white faces at Holyrood).

The number of younger members can be seen as something of a double-edged sword. On the one hand, a more youthful profile means members come with less experience of life in general and politics in particular. Some see this as an advantage, meaning younger members are prepared to develop the style of the Parliament as they would like it, refusing to be hidebound by experiences elsewhere, be it the House of Commons or local authorities. On the other hand they are, by definition, less experienced and could be said to lack the *gravitas* to take on the important task of producing a Parliament which quickly establishes itself as an institution of which the people of Scotland can feel proud.

The Labour MSP Johann Lamont believes that the benefits of life experience outweigh those of youth. 'Working for twenty years in the real world as I did means it would be impossible for me to divorce myself from people. I couldn't talk or act differently than I've been doing for those twenty years. Many young people don't have that, especially if they decide university debating is the ideal preparation for being an MSP. The problem with those who take that route is that they mix with their own kind all the time and bring a managerial focus to the Parliament,' (interview, August 2000).

My own feeling is that, provided they come to the Parliament having spent some time in what Johann Lamont rightly calls the 'real world', the younger members bring a freshness, an enthusiasm and an energy to the Parliament. These are qualities which I found generally lacking at Westminster, other than in the most recent arrivals who were in no position to influence anything – indeed, they were positively discouraged from seeking to do so. It is also easier to harness that sort of energy when the Parliament is starting out and is capable of being moulded to the shape which fits and works best. Being trapped in the past, Westminster is virtually an immovable object where the words 'can do' are alien to the whole ethos. In the Scottish Parliament, there is a feeling that, if something is not working as was intended, the obvious answer is to change it for the better.

For example, when it was discovered that there was no means of committees meeting when the convener was not there (because the election of deputy conveners had not then been agreed within the Parliamentary Bureau), standing orders were altered. This was one of a number of changes to standing orders in October 1999 and further changes were made in autumn 2000.

A feature of the cabinet is the number of members in their thirties. It was a major news story when Prime Minister Jim Callaghan appointed the thirty-eight-year old David Owen to his cabinet in 1977, and even Tony Blair has not yet offered a seat at the cabinet table to anyone under forty-one. Yet Donald Dewar appointed Jack McConnell (38), Sarah Boyack (37), as well as Wendy Alexander and Susan Deacon (both 35) not just to the cabinet, but to senior posts. At the junior level there was Alasdair Morrison (29) and Angus MacKay (34), Jackie Baillie (35) and Frank McAveety (36). Of these, only McAveety, McConnell and MacKay (at council level) had previously held elected office, which makes their achievement in reaching a high level of performance in the chamber as well as within their portfolios all the more commendable.

Lower down the scale, many of the Parliament's best performers are among the younger element. Other thirtysomethings such as Kenny Gibson, Fiona Hyslop, Andy Kerr, Pauline McNeill, Tavish Scott and Tommy Sheridan have already made their mark as effective speakers/debaters as well as being confident television performers. Youth (relatively speaking) has been given its head in Holyrood and it seems to me that will produce two distinct benefits. The first is that the youth of Scotland (which, like that age group anywhere else has a tendency to view politics with disdain, as something which does not involve them and is not, therefore, *for* them) are more likely to perceive the Parliament as being relevant if they witness among its membership people closer to them, in age at least.

The younger feel to Holyrood also gives it a different look to that of its big brother on the Thames. A major aim in the establishment of the Parliament was that it should be distinct from Westminster. The voting system played a major part in achieving that and the age profile further contributes to it. In general, the younger members are less willing to be dragged into a confrontational exchange in the chamber than some of the older ones. Viewing it from the gallery or on television, the public see a chamber in which most members are determined to make their points in a robust manner, but with an absence of the rancour and childish point-scoring which all too often characterise the House of Commons.

The Parliament's first day saw the unopposed election of Sir David Steel as the Presiding Officer and on the following day elections took place for the post of First Minister. Donald Dewar was elected with seventy-one votes; his opponents were the leaders of the two opposition parties, Alex Salmond (who collected thirty-five votes), and David McLetchie (eighteen votes), plus the Parliament's only independent member, Dennis Canavan (three votes).

As might be expected, all SNP members gave their support to Salmond, but another course had been suggested in the group. Two of their MSPs thought that, given the inevitability of Dewar's election, it would have made a gesture of national unity to back him, or at least not to oppose him. 'He was going to win and it would have helped to let the people see that our Parliament was different from Westminster,' said one. 'But this view did not prevail and as the allowances fiasco broke, the idea of promoting such positive gestures became less and less possible,' (interview, June 2000).

The following week, the First Minister (following consultation with the Deputy First Minister, as provided for in 'Working Together') announced his appointments of eleven cabinet ministers and the same number of junior ministers, two of each being Liberal Democrats. Together they formed the Scottish Executive, the government of Scotland, for Scotland, in Scotland.

The new Scottish political landscape, having been shaped by the people, was about to have depth and colour added by its Parliament and its government.

2 The new and the not-so-new politics

> **9 May 1999**: Today the Labour group met for the first time. We had our photograph taken outside the Assembly Hall on the Mound; very reminiscent of the first day at secondary school – not least because I was able to name only about half of my new colleagues.

On 7 May, politics in Scotland had neither shape nor form. The people had spoken, and those of us fortunate enough to have benefitted from their patronage could contemplate four years in the Parliament; but doing precisely what? The Scotland Act had set out ground rules, but the newly-elected representatives had no precedent on which to base the construction of the Parliament. It made for an exciting and challenging first few weeks.

It would not be accurate to suggest that we were faced with blank sheets of paper on our arrival. The Consultative Steering Group (CSG) had issued its main report in December 1999 and this in effect constituted a blueprint for the Parliament's first, tentative steps. But it is doubtful whether many, if indeed any, of the new MSPs had had the opportunity of dipping into it. We had all been much too heavily involved in the process of ensuring we actually got there to be concerned about what might face us if and when we did.

The CSG had been established by Henry McLeish in his role as Devolution Minister shortly after the September 1997 referendum which paved the way for the Parliament. Its membership was drawn from all of the four main parties and also included many Scots who were members of no party but had valuable experience to offer in drawing up proposals in such areas as the committee structure, the finance functions, the legislative process and the standing orders under which the Parliament would operate.

Of more immediate practical use was the heavy ring-binder which was handed to each member on our first day at the Parliament. Entitled *A Guide to The Scottish Parliament*, its nine sections included helpful information on how to navigate your way around the complex of five buildings which formed the Parliament's temporary home. It also revealed the roles of strange-sounding directorates like clerking, corporate services and communications, and provided contact numbers for some of the key staff. More than 200 staff are employed by the Parliament under Paul Grice, who is effectively the chief executive, although he carries the rather grander title of Clerk of the Parliament.

Politicians being politicians, the jockeying for positions began almost immediately. The cabinet and junior ministerial appointments (or disappointments, as they turned out to be for many Labour members, this one included) having been completed by 19 May, much of the attention turned to the committees. Those with local authority experience had an advantage in being able to draw on knowledge of the horse-trading long established within the portals of our municipal chambers. For those like myself with ambitions to secure one of the convenerships, the feverish discussion was not restricted to what particular committee remit would be of most interest (or perhaps influence), but concerned which committees Labour would have at its disposal. This was because detailed and fractious negotiations were underway between the business managers of the four main parties as to which party would have the right to nominate the convener for each of the Parliament's sixteen committees. The CSG had not specified a number, and the choice of sixteen was partly a result of the fact that this made an acceptable division between the four main parties somewhat simpler.

Simpler, but not simple. The method used to divide the committees up was known as the D'Hondt system, devised apparently by a Belgian lawyer (with a wry sense of humour, it would appear) for use in the European Parliament. The Parliamentary Bureau decided that, as far as possible, the division of conveners should be in the same proportion as seats in the Parliament. Nevertheless, this involved an inordinate amount of wrangling, to the extent that agreement was not finalised until the middle of June, with the announcement of the names of conveners delayed until 17 June, a full six weeks after election day.

Some weeks earlier, Labour backbenchers had been invited by Tom McCabe, our business manager, to indicate three committees on which we had an interest in serving. Some of the less experienced group members may have mistaken this for an indication that they would be accommodated as far as was practicable; if so, events would disabuse them of any such notion, with the purpose of the exercise not immediately apparent when the announcements were made.

Having long been interested in higher education, my personal preference was for a place on the Enterprise and Lifelong Learning committee. As an enthusiast for the European Union, my second choice was the European committee and my third the Social Inclusion, Housing and Voluntary Sector committee, which would be relevant to my constituency work (although there is not meant to be a direct relationship between the two).

Harbouring hopes of securing a convenership, I approached the Enterprise Minister, Henry McLeish, and laid my cards on the table. He reacted positively, but could not offer any assurances. In the belief that Donald Dewar would ultimately have the say as to who went where, I also approached his Special Adviser, John Rafferty, as well as Wendy Alexander, the newly-appointed Communities Minister and one of Dewar's closest political allies. Both also offered encouragement, as a result of which I made no moves in respect of any other committee.

> **9 June 1999:** *Having heard there was still no agreement on the committee appointments, I approached Henry McLeish again for his take on things, while also seeking his continued support for my nomination as convener of ELL. To my dismay, he informed me almost casually that it now looked unlikely the ELL committee would fall within the gift of the Labour Party.*

I was concerned that, should this prove to be the case, I would by then have missed the boat in terms of securing one of the other major subject committees, for which I assumed other colleagues would have been lobbying as I had done. The only consolation to be taken from that discussion was that Henry confirmed that I was in the frame for one of the convenerships.

The operation of the convoluted D'Hondt system meant that Labour had the choice of the first two committees, with the SNP then getting one; the two main parties then repeated the process before the LibDems and the Tories received one apiece. And so the system continued until, of the total of sixteen, Labour had eight, the SNP four and the Tories and LibDems two each.

My concern was that the party leadership had identified Finance and Local Government as their two priorities while, armed with this knowledge, the SNP had made Enterprise and Lifelong Learning their first choice. Unless that position altered, they would have the right to nominate its convener. This came as a severe disappointment to me and I approached our business manager Tom McCabe, aiming to establish what my options were. I decided to make a pitch for the Social Inclusion committee, which seemed to be the only one of the major committees for which I had not heard colleagues openly say they were lobbying. I telephoned him at home on the evening of 13 June and was taken by surprise when he said, 'We had you in mind for the Finance Committee. Would you be interested?'

Recognising the importance of the committee which Labour had opted for as its first choice in the allocation, I replied that I certainly would be interested, although Tom did not disguise the fact that nothing had yet been finalised and until then I must keep the information to myself.

I had not identified the Finance Committee in my initial response to Tom's circular for two reasons. First, I had no particular expertise or experience in the field, and secondly, I assumed that there were several senior colleagues who had gained such expertise as a result of their service in local government.

Labour members were finally informed of the make-up of the various committees at our weekly meeting on 16 June. Papers listing the proposed membership of each committee, along with Labour conveners and lead members (on those committees where we would not have the convenership) were handed out as we entered the room. It was the first notice we had had of the proposals and as I took my seat my colleague Andy Kerr (who was to be our nomination as convener of Transport and Environment) came over: 'A nice piece of negotiation,' he said in congratulating me. I merely smiled, modesty preventing me from admitting that the Finance convenership had actually landed in my lap.

The group meeting was rather a tetchy affair, with a considerable number of members dissatisfied at the proposals. Their mood was not eased when it was announced that the Party's nominations had to be submitted that very day, with the result that anyone unhappy with the committees allocated to them had until 4.00 pm to arrange a swap with a colleague. To the best of my knowledge, no such swaps took place which, given that the meeting did not end until almost 2.00 pm, is hardly surprising.

As a colleague remarked to me, the system adopted was reminiscent of the selection of the Pope. When the puffs of white smoke emerged from the fifth floor of Parliament HQ, only those involved knew the basis on which members had been appointed to the various committees, with the nominations of conveners and lead members no more evident. As I had been appointed to the Social Inclusion committee, I had achieved my third choice, but neither of my first two. Some colleagues had done less well, such as Janis Hughes, who had spent her working life in the NHS as a nurse, yet was denied the place she particularly wanted on the Health committee. Former Westminster minister Malcolm Chisholm, who had sought a place on Finance (and must have been a candidate for convener), was given a place on Health, which he had requested, but ended up with no convenership.

There was considerable concern (and in some cases anger) within the group over the lack of transparency in this process, although the only two spokespersons during the election campaign who had not been appointed to frontbench posts (Kate Maclean and John McAllion) were both given convenerships. John's abilities and experience entitled him to harbour hopes of convening a more senior committee than Public Petitions, but with typical candour he conceded he had not expected to be given one at all.

I had an indication of the task in hand when the Finance committee met for the first time on 22 June. The SNP had nominated its shadow finance minister, the youthful, bright and energetic Andrew Wilson, as well as the party's deputy leader (now leader)

John Swinney, who for some years had been (and remained) their Treasury spokesperson in the House of Commons. As the LibDems and Tories had also appointed their finance spokespersons (Keith Raffan and David Davidson), I realised that I was on a steep learning curve and had better use the summer recess to bring myself up to speed on the intricacies of annually managed expenditure, departmental expenditure limits and the Barnett formula.

The committee had been allocated Sarah Davidson as our senior clerk, but as a result of the under-staffing caused by the increase of committees to sixteen, she had to double up as clerk to the Audit Committee. This was not a satisfactory state of affairs, and it was to take almost a year before extra staff were appointed. When Sarah departed in May 2000 to become secretary to the Holyrood Progress Group, her replacement on *both* committees was her deputy, Callum Thomson.

A less-than-perfect start

Although the committees had taken some time to get off the ground, the Parliament itself had been sitting since 12 May. A major dilemma facing it was how should it fill the eight weeks until formal powers were transferred to it on 1 July? The answer was a great deal of what might be termed 'essential housekeeping', work which had to be done but which was as unattractive for the Parliament and its members to undertake as it was for the public and the media to watch. That is not to say that the coverage which the media produced – in full knowledge of the limitations unavoidably placed on the Parliament in its opening weeks – was responsible, understandable or in any way acceptable.

In fact, the chamber did hold debates on some important subjects during this period, such as those on the transfer of powers from Westminster on 2 and 3 June; on the outline of the legislative programme for the year ahead on 16 June; and on the important (and hotly-contested) matter of whether the Holyrood building project should continue, on 17 June. However, this period of limbo has become best remembered for the debate on the level at which Parliamentary allowances for members should be set.

> **8 June 1999:** *My first speech in the Parliament and I wish it had been a more auspicious occasion. This was not the new politics, it was too reminiscent*

of the squabbling style of the House of Commons, something I had hoped would not be seen in our shiny new Parliament.

This was a debate which should never have taken place, and the unpleasant taste which it left in the mouth and the undignified spectacle which it produced should have been avoided. Essentially, the disagreement concerned the perception of the role of list MSPs by those who were directly elected to represent a single constituency. Crudely, that is code for SNP on the one hand and Labour on the other, and each was determined to protect their own position, if possible at the expense of the other.

Traditionally, there has been little love lost between the two parties, their members and their elected representatives. The result is that relations have stabilised at the level where the two have a political association akin to that of Celtic and Rangers. This is not to suggest there are any of the pseudo-religious overtones associated with Glasgow's big two clubs, but the analogy is valid at the political level in that the traditions of Labour and the SNP are as far removed, and their aims as mutually exclusive.

The matter of allowances had been discussed by the SPLP, with a majority clearly in favour of denying list MSPs any allowance to pay for a constituency office, on the spurious grounds that they did not have a constituency. The fear was expressed that SNP list members would establish their own office in the individual constituency which they intended to contest at the 2003 election, and would then, free from constituency casework, wage a full-time political campaign over the ensuing four years against the Labour incumbents.

This ignored the fact that we had three list MSPs of our own, and needless to say Rhoda Grant, Maureen Macmillan and Peter Peacock felt their position was being given no consideration in this debate. It also ignored the fact that, as with constituency MSPs, list members would be obliged to attend Parliament and its committees three days a week and could not simply indulge themselves in the role of roving propagandist.

I was a member of the minority of the SPLP which believed that this was an issue not worth bringing into the open. First, it was one which we could not win, because it suggested that there were two classes of MSP, a position which was not sustainable under any interpretation of the Scotland Act. Secondly, it ignored the fact that the list members had responsibility for several constituencies and could not simply concentrate on one; if they did, then this could be exposed relatively easily and used against them.

No consensus could be reached in the group, but Tom McCabe was charged with the task of attempting to achieve the most advantageous arrangement in his discussions with the other party business managers. This was not an easy task but it was certainly attempted. Had he been successful, the whole issue of allowances could simply have been brought to the Parliament for rubber-stamping and would probably not have attracted much notice from the media. But reaching agreement proved impossible, largely because the partnership parties had reduced the amount of public money which the opposition parties received to run their parliamentary offices. This was estimated to have cost the SNP around £250,000 a year and naturally caused considerable resentment.

Whatever its causes, the lack of an agreement between all the parties on members' allowances meant that the matter had to be debated and then voted on in the Parliament. Ultimately, the partnership had enough votes to carry a watered-down scheme, allowing list MSPs their full staffing allowance, but a reduced office allowance. Where there was more than one list member from a political party in a region, then the office allowance for one MSP would be available to share between them. For example, in Glasgow, instead of each of the four SNP MSPs having an office, there could be only one.

The debate itself was of a poor standard and extremely bad-tempered, with some Labour members attacking their own direct opposite numbers. I myself became embroiled in an attack on the SNP's business manager Mike Russell, who argued that all MSPs were the same, when clearly we were not. I cited as an example the fact that, were I to find my way to an early grave, there would be a by-election in Cathcart to decide who my replacement should be. Should a similar fate befall Mike Russell, his place would simply be allocated to the next person on the SNP's list for South of Scotland. Equally, fifteen of the list members had not contested a seat in the election and had therefore arrived in the Parliament having done nothing more than curry favour within their own parties. That was not to say that list members were lesser beings, merely to illustrate that it was factually incorrect to claim that all MSPs are 'the same'.

Reading my contribution to that debate a year later makes me cringe, but it does provide an example of how simplistic it was to expect that the new politics (still largely undefined beyond 'consensus') could hit the ground running. The debate on 8 June 1999 certainly represented a serious stumble on the path to meeting those expectations. It sent out a message that MSPs were serving our own interests first, when we had expressly been sent there to look after the interests of the people of Scotland.

Predictably, the hostile press coverage of the issue did not play well with the voters. Speaking to constituents in Cathcart, it became clear that apologies were needed. The whole episode – the rancour and petty squabbling associated with decisions which were of no importance or interest to anyone but MSPs – was deeply damaging to our attempts at establishing the reputation of MSPs and indeed of the Parliament itself. The price paid by both for these issues being aired in such a clumsy manner in the chamber was high; indeed, more than a year later it is still referred to regularly by those inside the political tent and – more importantly – those outside.

17 June 1999: Decision time for the Holyrood Project in the chamber. The issue had hotted up, fuelled by exaggerated press reports, and there were fears that some LibDems might defect with Donald Gorrie and cost us the vote, which would have been a disaster.

Nine days later, the Parliament debated the future of the Holyrood building project and this was an altogether more impressive demonstration of the new institution in action. This issue is considered in some detail in Chapter 6, but the standard of speeches and the behaviour of MSPs in the chamber was much more attuned to Scotland's optimism for its Parliament.

That said, the opposition parties (as well as some LibDems) sought to tarnish the partnership in general and the Labour-controlled Scottish Office (as was) under Donald Dewar in particular, with accusations that the real extent of the projected costs associated with the project were being concealed. This related to the fact that, at the time of the debate, the projected costs stood at £105 million, a considerable increase on the original estimate of £50 million. This projection would double again over the following nine months, but Andrew Wilson, the SNP's finance spokesperson, defended the criticism which his party launched during the debate on 17 June 1999: 'It is the role of the opposition to voice concern where we believe it is justified, and the whole Holyrood project was handled badly by the Executive. There were inconsistencies and information was withheld from the Parliament. The vote in June 1999 was made on the basis of misinformation and could have been different if the facts had been known,' (interview, June 2000).

Donald Gorrie went further: 'The vote in June 1999 was very close and had the extent to which the project was out of control been exposed, I have not the slightest doubt that the majority would have been reversed and Holyrood would have been no more,' (interview, July 2000).

Evidence to back up SNP claims of information being withheld – energetically supported in the Parliament by the Tories – has never been produced and they were denied during the debate by Donald Dewar, as they have been since.

The first legislative programme: radical or dull?

The day prior to that debate, the First Minister had outlined the partnership's inaugural legislative programme which, over the following twelve months, would translate into the first acts of the Scottish Parliament. In doing so, Donald Dewar acknowledged some of the criticism which had characterised the Parliament's turbulent – but powerless – first weeks: 'This Parliament is in charge of a wide sweep of domestic policy, which will touch on the lives of every man, woman and child in the land. This is fundamental, radical change. I emphasise that this is just the start . . .'

The programme which he went on to outline contained eight bills, with proposals ranging from reforming centuries-old laws involving the system of land ownership and feudal tenure to relieving traffic congestion in cities and raising standards in education. This contrasted starkly with what had gone before, as Maria Fyfe, MP for Glasgow Maryhill since 1987, was well qualified to observe: 'When I saw that list of bills for the first year, it brought home to me the effect which the Scottish Parliament would have on the lives of Scots. Eight new acts of parliament relating specifically to

The new and the not-so-new politics

Scotland was probably as many as I have seen in my entire time at the House of Commons! We usually get Scottish legislation rolled up into one big act every five years and this was such a change,' (interview, August 2000).

The SNP were critical of the fact that there was no mention of housing, although this complaint overlooked the fact that a consultation exercise begun in 1998 had not yet been completed. A commitment was made by Communities Minister Wendy Alexander that this would inform the preparation of a housing bill for the Parliament's second year.

Nonetheless, the programme of bills attracted some criticism from journalists who thought it dull and unlikely to catch the public's imagination. It is difficult to imagine what might have been included in order to have that effect. Perhaps a bill to re-introduce public flogging; or one to allow every citizen the right to a day off work or school on their birthday? Really, such criticism was more a feature of the mindset into which most of the political press had sunk, with criticism the automatic reaction to anything which the Executive or the Parliament did. This was a classic example of the half-full/half-empty dichotomy and I was not alone at that time in believing that most of the journalists covering events in and around the Parliament needed to get out a bit more.

By this stage, it seemed the Parliament and all who were part of it were caught in a situation akin to *zugzwang*, a chess position where the player must make a move, yet whatever choice is made leads to defeat. It is not difficult to imagine what the media reaction would have been had the Executive announced a legislative programme which was designed, first and foremost, to be populist.

There were few voices of reason at the time, although reviewing the parliament's first year, Peter Jones of the *Economist* had this to say of the first legislative programme: '[It] lacked a populist edge. Including a bill to abolish the warrant sale method of debt recovery would have filled that part and would have avoided the embarrassing mess the Executive got into in April 2000. The virtue of dullness, however, lay in providing a programme on which the new Parliament and new politicians could cut their teeth without getting into too much party political controversy,' (Hassan and Warhurst, p. 61).

A retrospective view also enabled Peter MacMahon to comment, 'The legislative programme for the first full session . . . does contain some measures which the First Minister can point to as demonstrating the worth of having a Parliament . . . with land reform taking pride of place. We can already see there are matters which will come before the Parliament which should provoke political debate, giving rise, it is to be hoped, to some of the healthy passion which has so far been missing in the wood-panelled chamber,' (*The Scotsman*, 1 September 1999).

Those words were written as the Parliament's first summer recess drew to a close and it began to settle down, its members determined to proceed with the serious business of legislating for Scotland. To my relief, the political press also seems to have settled down, although there have been occasions where they have resorted to the kind of hyperbole produced as a matter of course in the opening weeks.

Clearly, the Executive, the opposition parties and individual members from all parties have to earn the respect of the nation. However, the same should not apply to newspaper editors and political journalists, and what rankled most among my colleagues was that the press made neither allowance for nor acknowledgement of the fact that we were starting from scratch in May 1999.

3 Anything but Westminster . . .

> **12 May 1999:** *The Scottish Parliament met for the first time today and I had to pinch myself to be sure it was real. I had imagined I might react by standing up and shouting 'Yeee-es!' but actually I just sat there and drank it in. It's been a long time coming, and there can never be another day like this, ever.*

One of my earliest memories of the campaign to achieve a Scottish Parliament dates back to the early 1980s and one of many conferences on the subject organised by the Labour Co-ordinating Committee, a left pressure group within the Labour Party. The discussion featured a number of party activists who would later win election to the House of Commons, although at that time none had any direct experience of it. Nevertheless, there was unanimity in the belief that the Commons chamber was scarcely different from the student debating societies which had recently provided many of us with our introduction to public speaking and political activity. At the student level it was acceptable; at the level where those involved – or at least some of them – were ostensibly running the country, it was not.

Even at that stage, there was agreement that Scotland's new legislature should be more powerful than the Scottish Assembly which had been backed, if somewhat half-heartedly, by those voting in the

1979 referendum. The discussion turned to what this new legislature might look like and one of my young activist colleagues uttered the words, 'Anything but Westminster.' This won immediate approval from a group confident that not only could we do much better in a Parliament in Scotland, we *had to* do better.

Some of those people are colleagues in the Scottish Parliament today. Two of them agree with my assessment that the Parliament has been successful in forging a distinct identity from Westminster, while still having some way to travel.

'I had voted "no" in the referendum because I came from the strand on the left which saw the politics of nationalism as a diversion from more central aims in terms of economic policy, feminism, anti-racism. I came to see the Parliament as a vehicle for democratic change in Scotland and as offering more opportunities for women to get elected to a position where they could influence that change. It was a reaction to Thatcher's centralising of power. It highlighted the need to achieve a political outcome that involved more people than was the case at Westminster,' recalls Johann Lamont (interview, August 2000).

'Those of us who cast our first adult vote in the 1979 referendum were shaped by the event and its outcome and developed a passion for Scottish politics which remains to this day. By the early 1980s, however, we wanted more than an assembly – we wanted a real parliament able to tackle social justice across Scotland, with its own identity and political dynamics,' adds Jack McConnell (interview, September 2000).

When the Scottish Constitutional Convention was established in March 1989, it was in recognition that the demand for constitutional change had reached the level where a broad cross-section of Scottish society accepted the need for our own legislature. The report that led to the establishment of the Convention stated, 'Scotland faces a crisis of identity and survival. It is now being governed without consent.' And it continued:

> Scotland, if it is to remain Scotland, can no longer live with such a constitution and has nothing to hope for from it. Scots have shown it more tolerance than it deserves. They must now show enterprise by starting the reform of their own government.
> (both quotes from *A Claim of Right for Scotland*, July 1988)

In the Convention's final report, published in November 1995, it stressed the need for distinctiveness in the new legislature:

> The working arrangements for Scotland's Parliament set out here describe a legislature that is very different from the Westminster model. The Convention expects that the Parliament will . . . differ from Westminster in a less procedural, and more radical, sense.

The devolution white paper, *Scotland's Parliament* (July 1997), led to Henry McLeish's Consultative Steering Group (CSG) being established shortly after the referendum of September 1997. Over the years, a great many people made their contribution to the re-establishment of Scotland's Parliament. On 12 May 1999, their efforts were finally rewarded.

Eight years in the House of Commons taught me that nothing moves quickly in that place. The practices operated there do so because they always have done (or so it seems). Only since the 1997 general election has the House discarded the practice of MPs being required to wear a hat to raise a point of order during a vote. Given that few MPs actually wear hats these days, a Member was permitted to place a piece of paper on top of his or her head in order to be heard!

Perhaps Westminster's greatest anachronism is the Parliament's hours, starting at 2.30 pm and finishing at 10.00 pm on an early night, often going on until well after midnight. Some marginal adjustments were made in the mid-1990s, with Wednesday mornings being given over to Members' debates, and now Tuesday and Thursday mornings are also used for such debates, although outside the main chamber. But the whole nature of the place remains one that stresses a macho culture of grinding down the opposition or laying 'ambushes' at 2.00 am in the morning, in the name of holding the government to account.

In 1989, after my first month as an MP, I was asked by a journalist for my impressions of the House of Commons. I replied that it seemed to me to be a cross between a public school and a gentlemen's club, a view influenced by a telling-off I had received from a crusty old Tory for running in a corridor. Each time I return, that feeling is reinforced.

The most surprising thing of all is that many MPs actually believe that the spectacle of Prime Minister's questions creates a good impression among voters. In my experience, when the electorate watches at all, it does so with incredulity, finding the baying and cat-calling reminiscent of a children's playground.

The Scottish Parliament had to do better, had to produce a modern, flexible, responsive legislature. I believe it has succeeded in this.

There are some basic factors creating a different atmosphere in the chamber on the Mound, the most obvious being the seating arrangements. The semi-circular style means that there is no echo of the face-to-face confrontation of the House of Commons or the House of Lords. Although, strictly speaking, the SNP and the Tories are directly opposite each other, in parliamentary terms they are not in opposition to each other; rather, both of these parties are in opposition (although the nationalists are the official opposition) to the Labour/LibDem Partnership, which sits in the centre of the chamber.

It is difficult to be precise as to what causes the different feel to the chamber compared to either chamber at Westminster. Certainly, the atmosphere is more consensual, although as a Labour member this may have something to do with the fact we are in partnership with another party. Or perhaps it is psychological, in that the chamber just *seems* less confrontational, with members at desks, unlike the House of Commons, where springing to your feet and sounding off certainly feels more natural.

There is also the more informal nature of the chamber on the Mound. Addressing members of other parties involves not just the use of their name, but often their first name; sometimes only their first name, although in times of raised voices and tempers this may not hold. It is noticeable that some of the fifteen MSPs who are also MPs occasionally slip back into Westminster ways by beginning a reference with 'the member for . . .', which is perfectly acceptable, but seems old-fashioned and out of place.

An electoral system that produced a different political balance is clearly a factor, although members of the opposition parties may not feel this to the same extent. After all, to them there are merely the government and the opposition; the fact that the government happens to encompass two parties is not of great significance. However, the fact that the LibDems can be accused of being, for example, 'Dewar's poodles' sometimes gives an extra edge, although rarely with the rancour so often apparent at Westminster.

Indeed, it is the Conservative Party that seems least willing to let go of the old ways, producing some of the most withering – and personal – criticism of the partnership, not least from its surly leader, David McLetchie. He has a habit of deriding the term 'new politics', and no less the partnership it has produced, clearly driven by the fact that he has no time for consensus and craves a return to the two-party system epitomised by Westminster. In this, he may be overlooking the fact that, but for the new voting system, in May 1999 the Tories would have had as many MSPs as the Natural Law Party.

The hours of the Parliament have produced a dramatic, indeed stark, contrast to the amount of time the House of Commons spends in session. Self-evidently, this has also had a major effect on the amount of time available to discuss issues. Although this was a cornerstone in making the Parliament more attractive for parents of school-age children to seek election, there are also disadvantages. Basically, there is insufficient time available either to cover all of the work which the Parliament has before it or to allow MSPs the time to make meaningful contributions when given the opportunity to speak.

It should be borne in mind that, unlike its European equivalent, the Scottish Parliament does not deal in set-piece speeches, it actually debates issues. It does so in a manner similar to the House of Commons, although in a much-truncated form: in most debates in the Scottish Parliament, backbench speakers are allocated only four minutes. Despite this, members are usually willing to accept interventions because they are conscious that there is little point in simply reading out pre-written speeches. I have found it noticeable that interventions are used in a different manner to the House of Commons. If you are making a speech in the Commons, unless the intervention comes from a colleague, you can be sure that it is not designed to be helpful (come to think of it, not all colleagues are necessarily helpful either). It is either designed to break the speaker's rhythm, particularly in the case of ministers or frontbench spokespersons, or to score a political point. Whilst the former is not unknown and the latter certainly not uncommon in the Scottish Parliament, it is much more likely that the point made by the member intervening will be germane to the subject being debated and probably directly related to the point just made by the speaker.

The decision as to whether or not to accept an intervention, just as much as how it is dealt with, is part of the skill that regular debating helps develop. The major problem in coping with interventions is once again the time available. The Presiding Officer and his deputies rarely allow additional time to reflect the fact that interventions have been accepted. When a speaker waves away an attempt to intervene with the comment 'Sorry, I don't have time,' he or she is usually stating the fact of the matter. It is difficult enough to develop an argument in four minutes; it is frustrating to be told to finish when the reason for an over-run is your willingness to enter into the spirit of standard debating practice.

Pressures on time are always likely to be present and the frustration is something which MSPs will simply need to get used to, but the problem takes on a more serious nature when it comes to consideration of bills, particularly at stage three. This is the final part of the process of passing legislation and involves what is termed a 'running whip'. This means that, unlike the usual 5.00 pm slot for decision time, voting is unpredictable, as a result of amendments being considered and debated; it also means that MSPs must remain in the chamber throughout the session. The flaw in this process is that, because of the unpredictability, members moving amendments in the early part of the session are likely to get their four minutes while those later on almost certainly will not; this is despite the fact that the session is usually extended beyond the normal finishing time.

The problem was highlighted at stage three of the Standards in Scotland's Schools Bill on 7 June 2000. As the afternoon progressed, members moving amendments were told to restrict themselves to three minutes, and then to one minute. The nadir was reached when the Deputy Presiding Officer, George Reid, implored Cathy Jamieson to 'say only two sentences in moving the amendment'. Cathy tried her best, but could not reduce it to less than seven. This could have its humorous side, were it not that the Parliament is engaged in passing legislation for the betterment of the people of Scotland. Proper scrutiny is an essential part of that process and it should not be squeezed out by an arbitrarily imposed time limit.

There is no further stage at which amendments inadequately dealt with can be considered, and following stage three, a bill requires only royal assent to become law.

Some means of timetabling legislation to allow for full consideration will have to be found, and it seems to me there are just two alternatives: where additional time is required, the conclusion of the third stage should be delayed and extended to a further day; or the Executive should accept that it cannot deal with the number of bills intended in the timescale envisaged. Neither will be easily achieved, but it is no doubt a matter to which the Procedures committee will turn its attention.

Some of the most unpleasant and unwarranted criticism levelled at MSPs in the Parliament's initial period concerned speeches made in the chamber. For journalists to lambaste the standard of speaking or debating merely signified that they had little of substance with which to occupy themselves. It was sadly typical that many of those reporting events should place style above substance. Their major criticism was that some of the MSPs – usually the younger ones or those who had not previously held elected office – read set speeches rather than indulging in flowing oratory, liberally sprinkled with quotes and wisecracks. This tended to ignore the fact that what a politician says should be more important than how he or she says it. It also ignores the fact that ministers (who are, in theory at least, among the more able performers in the Parliament) almost always read speeches or statements, yet are not condemned for it. Indeed, some are noticeably less comfortable on their feet than backbenchers, but levels of expertise will vary in any legislature. Having witnessed some dreadful performances in the House of Commons from MPs who had been there for many years, I am in no doubt that MSPs have no need to apologise for their oratorical prowess.

John Home Robertson, who still sits in both Parliaments, agrees and defends his new colleagues. 'I've been generally impressed with the standard of MSPs across all the parties. They certainly stand comparison with their Westminster counterparts and they're getting better as they gain experience,' (interview, July 2000).

The chamber is not just about debates and speeches, it is also the place where the Scottish Executive is held to account, through the media of First Minister's questions and open question time. Or is it?

In theory, yes; in practice, not really. Questions to ministers form a ritual which has become a part of parliamentary life in the UK. It is one aspect of Westminster which has been adopted in an almost identical form, and therein lies the problem. I frequently recount an occasion when I was an MP and a family from the constituency visited the House of Commons while on holiday in London. I showed them around the Palace of Westminster and gave them tickets for Prime Minister's questions. After it was over, I asked if they had enjoyed it. 'Up to a point,' one of them replied. What could she mean? 'Well, it's not Prime Minister's answers, is it?'

The Consultative Steering Group (CSG) had in mind a system of questions which would be, in effect, a grown-up version of Westminster's:

> Oral and written Parliamentary Questions (PQs) will provide an important means for individual members to obtain information from the Executive and to hold the Executive to account. The time provided . . . should not be used for political points scoring. PQs should be used genuinely to elicit information.

The theory has not been translated into practice, although it would make for a duller spectacle if it had. Questions have the benefit of offering an alternative to the speech-making which otherwise occupies the chamber and it lets the public – whether in the gallery or watching on television – see their ministers being questioned by the opposition. It is valid and not without value at those levels, but it cannot be argued that it genuinely holds the Executive to account. Political points scoring is the aim of all parties and it is difficult to imagine how that might be reduced, far less removed, from the process.

Along with most people, I find First Minister's questions lively and entertaining, and it is interesting to observe who emerges as the quickest on his or her feet, or with the most telling riposte. In January 2000, questions was separated into two distinct parts, the latter dedicated to the First Minister. This had the desired effect of providing added interest by focussing on the party leaders. Donald Dewar is a master of the art and I cannot recall ever seeing him bested on the Mound; on the other hand, I was genuinely surprised that Alex Salmond, with more than a decade's experience in the House of Commons, did not make a better job of it.

> **10 May 2000:** *A good two days for the partnership. Yesterday the SNP's tactical blunder of choosing a debate on the future of independence was compounded when Wallace got the better of Salmond and he did it again today on his FMQs debut. He was cheered by Labour members – what a difference a year has made to the partnership.*

One of the concerns of Labour members when Donald Dewar entered hospital in May 2000 was that he had dominated FMQs (as it has become known), and the partnership could lose that advantage when Jim Wallace stepped into the breach. This might hand the SNP good publicity which they would not otherwise have had, nor deserved. Such fears proved unfounded as Wallace showed a sureness of touch which few had anticipated.

Certainly Alex Salmond had not, nor was he alone in his party. 'Wallace is not as daft as he looks,' commented the shadow Finance Minister Andrew Wilson, a little unkindly. 'His performance at First Minister's Questions was better than anyone in the SNP expected. Wallace was very confident and had mastered his (arguably Labour Party) brief,' (interview, June 2000). Wilson's Parliamentary colleague, Tricia Marwick, echoed that view, although with an interesting qualification. 'In Dewar's absence, Wallace has performed better than I think anybody expected. Having said that, he doesn't answer the questions, which is frustrating; at least Dewar addresses the questions,' (interview, June 2000).

Thus, question time often succeeds as good theatre, but in holding the Executive to account it does not, because the First Minister has the ability to use discretion in both the tone and content of his response. The same is true to a lesser extent with questions to ministers. That said, all ministers must remain aware that what they say is taken as a statement of the partnership position on that issue. Given that question time is not the appropriate occasion on which to announce new or changed policy, ministers have to be alert and avoid making a commitment which could prove difficult to 'undo'.

It would be intriguing, to say the least, if the Presiding Officer, following a minister's response to a question, was empowered to interject along the lines of 'Very interesting, minister, but will you now answer the question?' Such a move would be eternally popular with the opposition of the day, but rather less so with the governing parties.

The other kind of parliamentary questions – the written variety – also play a part in the process of scrutinising the Executive. The Parliamentary clerks reported that a total of 8,764 were tabled up to July 2000, a large majority emanating from the opposition parties, as would be expected. With the average cost per question for civil servants and Parliament staff to prepare answers said to be £100, the process is expensive. Written questions have also become the focus of some controversy within the Parliament because of Executive complaints that not all questions are submitted with the aim of scrutinising the Executive; rather, a fair proportion are designed either to score political points or to provide ammunition with which to do so.

Such allegations tend to be aimed at the SNP, but the Nationalists countered by asking yet another question, seeking to establish the frequency with which the Executive asks its own backbench MSPs to table questions, to enable it to make an announcement. The opposition like to describe these as 'planted questions' while the Executive terms them 'inspired questions'. In fairness, this system does provide an effective mechanism for bringing matters which do not merit a ministerial statement or a debate to the attention of the Parliament. Without it, some of the wide range of the Executive's activities would not be made known to the Parliament at all. And, given that the Executive already knows the answers, they add little to the overall cost of parliamentary questions.

This system is similar to that operated at Westminster and might be thought to be non-controversial. But that is not, in fact, the case. Such was the concern among MSPs at the delay in receiving responses, and among the Executive at the number of questions which it deemed inappropriate, that the Parliament's Procedures committee undertook an inquiry into these matters. It produced a forty-page report, the main recommendation of which was to establish an agreement between the Parliament and the Executive 'to assist all those responsible for parliamentary questions to match resources to demand in answering questions lodged; to seek demonstrable improvements in the turn-round time for answering questions; and to monitor the number of questions asked'. Tellingly, although some tabloid newspapers reacted with horror to the revelation that parliamentary questions were costing almost £1 million of public money annually, they did not regard the steps taken by one of the Parliament's committees to regulate this as worth reporting.

Although the system of questioning the Executive parties is similar to that at the House of Commons, the extent to which the Scottish public is able to access information about their Parliament is considerably more advanced. The Scottish Parliament was established with communications as a priority and there are various means by which the institution and its elected members are accessible. For example, every MSP has her or his own e-mail address, and we are finding that more and more this is the preferred means of contact by a wide range of individuals, community groups and other organisations.

A desktop and a laptop computer are provided to all members, and many MSPs have also established their personal web sites, which have links to the Parliament's own. That provides a comprehensive guide to all of the Parliament's activities, with reports of proceedings in the committees and the chamber, as well as the daily business bulletin, making information easily accessible to those with computers. Crucially, that includes thousands of school pupils but it does exclude many people, and the Parliament has attempted to minimise those who are not able to connect with it electronically. In January 2000, an initiative involving the Parliament, British Telecom and the Scottish Council of Voluntary Organisations was launched to provide 200 computer terminals in community facilities in both urban and rural areas that give internet access to the Parliament. In addition, the Parliament has established a partner library in each of the seventy-three constituencies as a further means of facilitating access.

Access is the key word in and around the Scottish Parliament and that itself is key in setting it apart from its Westminster counterpart, which remains remote in every meaning of the word. Access to elected members and access to the business of the parliament is an essential part of the ethos and one which, in my experience, both MSPs and the Parliament's staff embrace with enthusiasm.

4 Hard pressed

2 July 1999: The papers were fulsome in their tributes to the opening day's proceedings and I bought six! With the coverage of those events still fresh in my mind, I wondered at the contrast with the attacks the Parliament and MSPs have had to suffer over the past month.

The road leading to the formation of the Scottish parliament was both slow and tortuous, starting from the devolutionary awakening of the Labour Party, caused by the surge in support for the SNP in 1974; and passing through the dashed hopes of the referendum five years later; the redefining of the institution from assembly to parliament during the 1980s; the false dawn of the 1992 general election to the brilliant sunshine of its successor; and finally to the referendum and the eventual embodiment of the Scottish people's will in May 1999.

As these events and others unfolded, the perception of, and warmth towards, the concept of a Scottish Parliament developed to the point where most of Scotland's media became fully paid-up members of the devolution fan club. With none of the country's newspapers, television channels or radio stations having ever advocated the cause of an independent Scotland, devolution was seen as being, generally, a good thing, acting as a break on demands for separatism. On the basis of 'this far and no further', the Scottish media have generally been willing to promote the concept of Scotland having its own parliament, with limited legislative powers.

That support did not traditionally extend to tax-raising powers, although by the time of the 1997 referendum, even that hurdle had been cleared, with most newspapers advocating a YES/YES vote. Among those doing so most forcibly were the *Daily Record* and *The Scotsman* and this positive agenda was maintained during the election campaign itself. Yet, since the Parliament met for the first time on 12 May 1999, these newspapers have led an onslaught against the Parliament itself, its elected members and the Scottish Executive.

Newspapers in Scotland today are different from their counterparts in England. In general, the Scottish regional broadsheets carry more political news and analysis and less UK and world coverage. *The Press and Journal* (Aberdeen) and *The Courier and Advertiser* (Dundee) both serve areas well beyond the cities in which they are based and have a greater depth of reporting on political events concerning those parts of Scotland than would, say, the *Birmingham Daily Mail* or the *Yorkshire Post* about their regions of England. To a lesser extent, the same holds true in respect of the tabloids. A comparison between the *Daily Record* and the *Daily Mirror*, its sister paper south of the border, will reveal noticeably more political stories in the former, while Scottish versions of the *Daily Star* or *The Sun* would be similarly distinguishable from their English editions.

The reason for that is the existence of the Scottish Parliament, which excites greater interest and leads to far greater coverage in Scotland's newspapers than events at Westminster do in either the regional broadsheets or nationwide tabloids in England. Broadcasters are required to be more balanced than other branches of the media, but even they felt little restriction on entering the fray in the two major constitutional events which followed Labour's 1997 general election victory. Such was the coverage throughout the media in Scotland in the run-up to both the 1997 referendum (almost universally positive) and the 1999 Scottish Parliament elections (universally anti-SNP), that a voter claiming to be unfamiliar with the issues could be labelled as someone who simply did not read a newspaper, watch television or listen to radio.

When, and why, did the enthusiasm evaporate? Why was there no 'honeymoon period' similar to that enjoyed by the Blair government? Douglas Fraser of the *Sunday Herald* believes the print media was slow to adapt. 'The press is poor at self-analysis. Devolution has altered everything, yet initially the media mindset stayed much the same, despite the extra resources they provided. Scotland's institutions have begun to change, civic Scotland is changing and even the culture of the civil service is being opened up to new ideas. Yet two of the most influential titles were adopting more and more of the London media culture when it should have been less and less. Andrew Neil at *The Scotsman* and Martin Clarke at the *Daily Record* had both worked in London and that heavily influenced their approach,' (interview, September 2000).

Two of Fraser's fellow-journalists saw it differently. BBC political editor Brian Taylor said: 'The honeymoon was used up in the twenty years of preparation for the Parliament, when most of the media campaigned for it. Then the press psyche meant it needed to revert to type by being oppositional,' (interview, September 2000). Dave King of the *Daily Record* believes, 'Blair got his honeymoon because he hit the ground running; throughout the first 100 days there was always something happening, new policy initiatives being launched. Dewar had no plan of action and you can't have a bunch of hacks gathered at the door then tell them nothing. We had to fill our papers,' (interview, September 2000).

As the Parliament was taking shape, political journalists in Scotland had combined to ensure that their collective interests would be better served in the new legislature than was the case at Westminster. They formed the Scottish Parliamentary Press Association (SPPA) and that this was done with a purpose is demonstrated by the fact that it occurred more than a year before the Parliament came into being. The organisation was led by print journalists anxious to avoid a replica of the press lobby system which operates in the House of Commons. Their colleagues in broadcasting shared that agenda to an extent, but had additional concerns relating to improvements on Westminster. They wanted access to MSPs in areas immediately outside the chamber for interviews, as well as avoiding some of the restrictions which are applied in the House of Commons with regard to broadcasting events in the chamber itself.

By the time the journalists had got themselves organised, the Consultative Steering Group (CSG) was well advanced in developing its recommendations on various aspects of the Parliament's operations. The fact that media coverage was not a part of it led the SPPA to seek special treatment, with some success. The CSG established an Expert Panel on Media Issues which reported in April 1999 yet, according to Philip Schlesinger, director of Stirling University's Media Research Institute, 'by the Parliament's first session, the in-house broadcasting infrastructure was largely in place and the media's rules of engagement [were] broadly set,' (Hassan and Warhurst, p. 165).

It seems that Scotland's political journalists obtained from the Expert Panel's report very much what they had set out to achieve. Schlesinger explains: 'Scotland's style of parliamentary television is quite distinct (from the House of Commons) and maybe this modest achievement has been rather overlooked. For newspaper political correspondents . . . a Westminster-style lobby system has been formally rejected, but accreditation to the Mound has been restricted only to *bona fide* reporters,' (Hassan and Warhurst, p. 166).

If they are satisfied with their own working arrangements in and around the Parliament, many journalists have demonstrated something less than satisfaction with happenings there. Critical reporting of the Executive and the Parliament is a legitimate part of the democratic process; however, it is not unreasonable to expect that it should demonstrate balance.

In attempting to put into perspective the kind of coverage given to much of what has occurred in or around the Scottish Parliament since its inception, a distinction should be made between the print and broadcast media. The latter has largely reported events factually, albeit highlighting events which may not have been particularly flattering to those caught up in them. For many newspaper editors, however, it has been open season on the Parliament and those within it, almost from day one.

Having given the election campaign saturation coverage and generally welcoming the dawn of a new political era in Scotland, it was reasonable to expect that Scotland's print media might have carried their enthusiasm for the project and highlighting of political issues into the post-election phase. In fact, there was a lack of willingness to allow the Parliament and MSPs a settling-in period, with any *faux pas* (and there were certainly a few) pounced on as 'evidence' that the institution, its leaders and its members were simply not up to the job.

The SNP's Kenny Gibson was no political novice, but this took him by surprise: 'I thought we'd get the benefit of the doubt in the first year, but the coverage was scandalous initially and has only improved marginally since. It's basically the product of lazy, malicious journalism. We don't want the media to say we're great, just to report what we're actually doing,' (interview, August 2000).

Tory MSP Brian Montieth placed the blame closer to home. 'The negative media coverage was the responsibility of the Labour administration, aided by the Liberal Democrats. Journalists need stories with controversy and division and the first mistake was that the Parliament opened too soon. It should not have done so until it had its full powers; instead there was a 'phoney war', with debates of no purpose on housekeeping issues. The appearance of this was not good and we got the coverage we deserved,' (interview, July 2000).

The limits of the Parliament's powers in its first eight weeks and the restrictions which that placed upon them has been examined in Chapter 2. However, the issue of differential allowances between constituency and list MSPs and decisions as to when the Parliament would be in recess were blown out of all proportion. In doing so, some newspapers deliberately disregarded the facts, the most basic being that such decisions had to be taken at *some* stage by the Parliament, because they could not have been taken by anyone else.

Ignoring the facts

> **10 June 1999:** *Tempers boiled over today as Paul Martin and I challenged the* Daily Record's *Dave King about their coverage of the Parliamentary allowances debate. 'Well, give us something serious to write about,' was the best he could do in defence of all the distortions.*

In the initial phase, the *Daily Record* seemed particularly eager to fabricate stories which showed the Parliament and its members in a bad light. Unfortunately, this included outright lies in relation to pay and allowances for MSPs, with a suggestion that each received £86,000 a year. On 9 June 1999, under the headline 'MSPs cash in on perks', it claimed we had voted ourselves 'massive expense accounts' of £46,000. This figure comprised a staff allowance of £36,000 and an office costs allowance of £10,000. With the addition of a salary of £40,000 (£6,000 less than that of an MP and around 25 per cent of that of the editor of the *Daily Record*) the total was indeed £86,000, of which the salary alone is paid to members. The remainder can be drawn only against actual expenditure, and the rules for receipting are considerably more demanding than those for members of the House of Commons.

Much the same was true in respect of decisions on the periods during which the Parliament would not sit. Because this was to total seventeen weeks of the year, it was represented as the length of MSPs' 'holidays'. The fact that this was two weeks less than the House of Commons was again not worthy of comment, because it would have deflected criticism from the main target. Even the broadsheets are still not above the occasional reference to recesses as 'holidays' and wilful misrepresentations such as this are probably the most annoying aspect of press coverage for elected members. The implication that we spend every day when the Parliament is not in session with our feet up ignores the important work done both in the committees and in the constituencies.

Unfortunately, the opposition parties have been willing to add their voices on occasion to this anti-Parliament barrage. The *Daily Record* boomed on 10 June 1999, 'MSPs yesterday gave themselves an eight-week summer holiday' quoting the SNP's Dorothy Grace Elder as branding this a 'chancer's charter' and claiming the SNP had tried to have the recess shortened. In fact, the SNP are usually most insistent that Scottish school holidays should coincide with the Parliament's recess, but while Dotty is not usually regarded as her party's mouthpiece, there was no SNP denial of her blethering on this occasion. And Tory leader David McLetchie is never slow to don the holier-than-thou mantle. He lambasted the Scottish Executive for having 'holidays on the brain' (*Daily Record*, 24 June 1999),without explaining what *they* had to do with it, and after the Parliament's first recess he felt moved to pontificate, 'I don't see why we shouldn't spend more time . . . in full sessions of the Parliament during the summer,' despite admitting that, apart from two weeks away, 'the rest of my time was spent working,' (*Daily Record*, 31 August 1999).

Not content with quoting hapless politicians, there must have been a bonus on offer for the *Daily Record* journalist who could conjure up the most outlandish claims, and the competition was fierce. Under the headline 'Who drives the gravy train?', the intriguingly-named Carlos Alba's entry railed against 'the MSPs' decision to hand themselves a nine-week [sic] summer recess,' (25 June 1999). Dave King effortlessly trumped that the same day ('From Holyrood to holidays') by revealing that 'MSPs are rushing to thumb through the travel brochures' to make the most of their 'holiday bonanza' and 'extended absences'. Political editor Ron McKenna saw that as a challenge, but bided his time before scattering all opposition to scoop the pool: 'During the seventeen weeks when the Parliament shuts down, there is no legal way to ensure MSPs are working in their constituencies. With many constituency MSPs expected to have very light workloads, it's feared some will take advantage and put their feet up,' (31 August 1999).

Demonstrating the distinction between fact and fiction makes little difference. I had personal experience of the futility of this during a live interview on BBC Radio 4's *PM* programme in September 1999. The subject was the allegation that MSPs were looking after our own interests rather more assiduously than those of the electorate. Making the case forcefully for the prosecution was Martin Clarke, then editor of the *Daily Record* and no fan of the Parliament. His newspaper had recently repeated the 'seventeen weeks holidays and £86,000 in perks' for MSPs nonsense and when he refused to set the record straight, I called him a liar on air. I made the point that he could just as plausibly have argued that we were paid £17,000 and had eighty-six weeks holiday a year, but the use of the word 'liar' appeared to touch a raw nerve. He demanded that I desist, to which I replied, 'Well, stop lying'.

The 'holidays' issue is one which has not yet died, and it has to be said that the Parliamentary Bureau hardly helped bury it by pandering to the press's obsession. The Parliament's family-friendly philosophy meant that the February 2000 schools week was scheduled as a recess, but it was announced in November 1999 that this would instead be a business week. The explanation offered by the Parliamentary Bureau was the demands of the legislative programme and few MSPs would have argued against this on principle. However, there was no disguising that the real reason was to meet some of the criticism of the amount of time which the Parliament spent in recess. Needless to say, the media took advantage, claiming that the Parliament had bowed to public pressure to 'work harder'. The basic lesson is not to attempt to buy off criticism; it cannot be done and simply encourages your critics to say 'I told you so'.

Man of Steel

> ***2 September 1999:*** *Any hopes I had that the summer recess would allow the press to rethink their reporting of events in the Parliament were soon shattered. The medals were an own goal, but judging by the media reaction you'd think we'd been given a Rolls Royce each.*

The facts of another issue failed to derail the press express as it gained speed. On the Parliament's return in September 1999, it was announced that a medal had been struck, commemorating its official opening on 1 July. Each MSP was to receive one, and in addition, in a nice gesture and a positive example of the Parliament connecting with the people, one was to be presented to the parents of every child born in Scotland on 1 July.

This matter was opportunistically raised in the Parliament on the first day of the new session by the SNP's business manager, Mike

1 September 1999: SNP business manager Mike Russell shows his 'medal'.
(source: *Scotland on Sunday*)

Russell. In a kneejerk reaction which he later came to regret because of the damage which it did to the Parliament, Russell criticised MSPs having 'medals awarded' (*Daily Record*, 2 September 1999). In the same issue, Tory John Young went further, describing it as 'awarding ourselves medals'. This was nonsense, because the decision to strike and issue the medals had actually been made, on the recommendation of civil servants, by the Scottish Office team under Donald Dewar some six months earlier. It is unfortunate that the decision was not announced at that time or on 1 July, when it would have seemed perfectly natural and would have attracted little publicity amid the coverage of events on that great occasion.

By September, the gloss had started to fade and the *Daily Record*, reminding its readers that medals should be awarded for distinguished service, suggested that 'the service for which the Scottish Parliament is distinguished is self-service' (2 September 1999). MSPs were urged either not to collect them or to donate them to charity. I had already given mine to my niece, Beth, who was born in the week of the referendum in 1997 and seemed to me the personification of the new Scotland and of the generation which would fully experience the benefits of our Parliament.

Nobody, least of all those of us involved in it, would suggest that politics is for the sensitive. But the anger generated among MSPs at press coverage of the commemorative medals was so great that it quickly reached the ears of the Parliament's Presiding Officer. Normally mild-mannered and tolerant, Sir David Steel responded in blistering fashion, choosing as his vehicle a speech to the Church of Scotland's Church and Nation Committee on 6 September 1999. He used language which was justifiably uncompromising, although the part subsequently most quoted might have been more judiciously worded. In it, he criticised the tabloid press for 'the recent trend of bitch journalism, where character assassination of a reckless and cruel kind is employed'. He went on to say that, 'Several MSPs of all parties have fallen prey to this, mainly in the tabloid press and notably the *Daily Record*', the title which was clearly his main target. Nor was that speech the only shot in his locker, because he announced his intention to refer the matter to the Press Complaints Commission (PCC), 'in the hope that those who run the paper may be persuaded to return to the standards of decent journalism'.

This was an astonishing outburst which took MSPs by surprise.

Not all were in full agreement with either content or tone and both David McLetchie and Alex Salmond asked Sir David to clarify that he was speaking personally and not on behalf of the Parliament. The Presiding Officer confirmed that his speech, which he had written himself, represented his own assessment, but it was clear that it resonated with the overwhelming majority of MSPs, who were heartily sick of the relentlessly negative coverage. The only hope was that, as the new session got underway and the legislative programme began to roll out, hitherto idle press hands would have some real work to occupy them.

Sir David's complaint did indeed go to the PCC, but was not upheld. Comments by the *Daily Record* were held to have been merely 'partisan opinion, robustly expressed', and not in breach of the PCC's Code of Practice.

In general, in the months which have followed Sir David's attack, press coverage has been better balanced and more factual, perhaps illustrating the validity of Iain Macwhirter's assertion that 'If you don't feed the bears, they feed on you,' (*Sunday Herald*, 30 June 1999). But, their hunger overcome, the press did become prone to the odd bout of indigestion, on some occasions seriously so.

'Lobbygate'

> *27 September 1999: It had to happen, but I didn't imagine it would be quite so soon. Clear echoes of the Draper case last year, which will damage our hopes of portraying the Parliament as a fresh start with nothing to hide.*

The most glaring examples of the press reinstating its negative stance – the proposal to repeal clause 2a of the Local Government Act 1986 and the Holyrood Project – are dealt with elsewhere, but there have been others of note. One of these occurred in September 1999 and was generated by the media itself through an act of subterfuge. It has become immortalised as the 'Lobbygate' affair and was broken by the *Observer*, one of whose journalists posed as a potential client of a public affairs and public relations company seeking access to Scottish Executive ministers. The journalist, Dean Nelson, secretly recorded the meeting with two employees of the company, the Lanarkshire-based Beattie Media. The two, unwisely and, it subsequently emerged, untruthfully, suggested that they had the ability to arrange meetings with Finance Minister Jack McConnell, who had himself briefly held a post with Beattie in 1998.

Despite the fact that most people believe adopting a false persona and recording someone without their knowledge or consent is sleazy at best, the story appeared to confirm both journalists' and many politicians' impression of the way in which lobbyists operate and made it a major media issue. As if that were not enough, one of the Beattie employees involved happened to be Kevin Reid, son of the Secretary of State for Scotland, John Reid. To make matters even worse, John Reid himself entered the fray on his son's behalf, attacking the underhand tactics of the *Observer*, which in turn led to a public exchange between himself and Donald Dewar (at the Labour Party conference in Bournemouth) as to who should be speaking on the matter.

It was the kind of combination which makes the media feel Santa Claus has arrived on their doorstep and it was not a story they considered underselling. The immediate decision by the Standards committee to instigate an inquiry demonstrated the Parliament's new system of transparency and decisiveness.

However, this was not fully illustrated until the committee had established how it would proceed, and this produced evidence of the extent to which the whole process represented a journey in uncharted waters. The committee decided to consider in private session how it would undertake the inquiry, prompting *The Scotsman* to challenge the decision's constitutional basis at the Court of Session. This was based on a misunderstanding that the inquiry itself would be held in private, a situation which could not have been sustained and, in any case, was never suggested. Once the process had been clarified, *The Scotsman* ended its action.

Jack McConnell was the main focus of that inquiry and, although he was subsequently exonerated, it was a period which left its mark on the Finance Minister. 'It was like a steamroller that I didn't see coming and couldn't stop. When it did come, it was clear it was going to take about six weeks for the story to reach its conclusion and there wasn't anything I could do about that except be open and upfront and get on with my job.' Despite his long experience in prominent political posts, it had a particular effect on him. 'I am much more cautious in my dealings with the media and that's

*November 1999: Finance minister Jack McConnell gives evidence on
'Lobbygate' to the Standards committee
(source: Parliament Broadcasting Unit)*

probably been a good lesson to learn.' That said, he accepts that what he encountered in the 'Lobbygate' affair was part of the rough and tumble of politics: 'People do their jobs and make their own judgements. I don't have any complaints about the way I was treated,' (all quotes from *Sunday Herald*, 13 March 2000).

The disappointment in some sections of the media at the committee's findings was palpable and there were some suggestions that its members had not pursued the issue with sufficient vigour. But as Iain Macwhirter put it, 'the final verdict . . . in true Scottish tradition, was not proven. This was not a court of law, even though . . . the questioning could have been a little more robust. Examination of serious matters like these should not be conducted on first-name terms, but the press attacks on the competence of committee members were not justified,' (*Sunday Herald*, 31 October 1999).

Thus, some of the media coverage of 'Lobbygate' failed to focus on the big picture, but other commentators did manage to spot the wood through the trees. Professor Alice Brown, part of the Consultative Steering Group and now a member of the Neill committee which established the code of conduct for MPs at the House of Commons, is one. 'In spite of the adverse publicity over "Lobbygate", the Parliament and its procedures survived the experience and gained respect in the way in which the affair was handled,' (Hassan and Warhurst, p. 56).

Journalist Douglas Fraser agreed that some of the Standards committee questioning could have been more penetrating 'but they got a fair account of what had happened and at the end of the day the case didn't stack up. I think the test was more about the committee – on behalf of the Parliament – carrying out a thorough investigation than it was about whether Jack McConnell had or hadn't transgressed,' (interview, September 2000).

Within the broader context of media reporting of the Parliament, Iain Macwhirter used the example of Lobbygate to make a point. 'You can only conclude that Scottish journalists and editors do not really understand the nature of the institution they are reporting. In fact many of the so-called "parliamentary crises" are actually indications of its success, such as the "Lobbygate" hearings,' (Hassan and Warhurst, p. 21).

The Lobbygate affair was a legitimate subject of media interest and one which merited the depth of coverage that it generated. In the end, it was of service to the Parliament as a whole, because it flagged up the danger areas for MSPs, lobbyists and journalists in terms of what is, and what is not, acceptable behaviour. Firm codes of practice already cover the first category and will shortly be issued in respect of the second. The third category – the fourth estate – are quick to lecture others, but are equally swift in calling 'foul' when any demands or restrictions are placed on them in terms of ethical behaviour. It is to be hoped the Parliamentary press pack absorb the lessons of the affair, and that the failure of Dean Nelson to acknowledge that he acted dishonourably represents an individual, not a collective, stand.

Hunting with dogs

1 September 1999: Media interest today in the Bill was out of all proportion to the significance of the event. The first day back after the recess and this is what even hardened hacks want to talk about above all else.

Another issue which has created considerable media interest is one with which I have had direct contact, the Protection of Wild Mammals (Scotland) Bill. One of six member's bills introduced during the parliament's first year, it is designed to end the cruel and barbaric practice of killing foxes, hares and mink with dogs. I have been genuinely taken aback at the strength of opposition and the media attention which this has provoked, given that the activities the bill is designed to bring to an end are practised by a small proportion of the population, in few areas of the country and for only five months of the year.

I first announced my intention to introduce the bill at a press conference in Edinburgh on 4 August 1999. Despite the fact that the Parliament was in recess and it was still the holiday season in Scotland, a time when interest in political events is traditionally at a low ebb, the entire Scottish press corps appeared, including both television channels and a collection of radio stations, many of which I had never previously encountered and some I had never even heard of. In addition, both ITN and BBC UK news programmes recorded interviews, with the BBC's new worldwide digital channel, News 24, thrown in for good measure. All of this activity was inspired by a press release issued on my behalf by the Scottish Campaign Against Hunting with Dogs (SCAHD), just the previous day.

Throughout the following year, coverage has scarcely slackened, with every nuance, every twist and turn of the bill's progress reported in detail. This has been accentuated by the attempts of the Countryside Alliance to derail it, claiming the support given to me by SCAHD was *ultra vires* the Scotland Act. They sought an interdict, which led to two Court of Session hearings. To the fury of the Alliance, my costs were met by the Parliament, and the Presiding Officer explained the rationale for this: 'I consider it very important that MSPs have an unfettered right to introduce legislation to the Parliament. Although this interdict has been taken out against Mike Watson, its intention is to block the progress of a bill. That gives me great cause for concern as it has implications for all members of the Parliament,' (*Scottish Daily Mail*, 18 November 1999).

April 2000: 'Snash' by Andy Bain
(source: The Scotsman)

Although the judges rejected their case on each occasion, the Countryside Alliance subsequently reported me to the police, alleging contravention of the Scotland Act, again to no avail. In October 1999, Tory MSP Ben Wallace had also reported me to the Parliament's Standards committee, with a similar lack of success. In August 2000, as the Rural Affairs committee prepared to begin the bill's stage one hearings, the Alliance announced it was to mount a £250,000 billboard advertising campaign, drawn up by the ubiquitous Jack Irvine of the PR firm Media House, fresh from his failure to 'Keep the Clause'.

By and large, media reporting has been measured, although the majority of opinion has come down against the bill, seeking to justify this with a number of arguments which simply do not stand up: it will set urban communities against rural ones; it will put thousands of people out of work; it will upset the biodiversity of the countryside; it is not an issue that should be added to an already over-burdened parliamentary timetable; it is not a measure that an urban MSP should be promoting; it is not the sort of measure that the member's bill procedure was designed to promote; it is my attempt to wage my own personal battle in the class war; and so on.

Attacks on the Parliament or the Executive have often been characterised by comments to the effect that MSPs have lost contact with their electors or are obsessed with issues of what are termed 'political correctness' (should we aim to be politically incorrect?), with clause 2a, fox hunting and proportional representation cited as examples. Those who argue that these and other items should not be pursued 'as priorities' are usually struck dumb when you enquire as to when they *should* be pursued, or even discussed. I introduced my bill to end the cruel and anachronistic practice of killing animals for sport. At no time have I suggested it is the most pressing issue facing Scotland today, but that is not to say it is without merit or not worth pursuing.

Equally, certain journalists have been following a particular agenda in seeking to denigrate the bill at every turn, frequently demonstrating that they have not read it closely enough, if at all.

Perhaps not surprisingly, it has been noticeable that the traditional Tory-supporting newspapers, the *Daily Mail* and the *Daily Telegraph*, have been most tenacious in pursuing the line that the bill will spell disaster for many of their typical readers and therefore must be rubbished at every opportunity. I am normally courteous with the media and generally return their calls, but with these two publications I have been misquoted or had my words so distorted that no purpose is now served by my responding to them. I draw no satisfaction from this, just disappointment that it should be necessary.

Unfortunately, the saturation coverage of the bill and issues stemming from it have obscured my other activities as an MSP, both in the Parliament and in my constituency in Cathcart. Regular news releases and speeches in the Parliament rarely seem to be regarded as worthy of reporting, perhaps because of the regularity with which my bill is covered. This can be frustrating and was certainly so when two major reports with which I was directly involved happened to be published on the same day. On 26 June 2000, both the Finance committee's report on stage one of the Budget Bill and the report of the inquiry commissioned by the Rural Affairs minister, Ross Finnie, into the economic impact of my member's bill appeared within an hour of each other. Press releases had been issued in my name in respect of both but in terms of importance to Scotland and its parliament, the first ever report on the new, transparent and inclusive form of the budget proposals clearly carried much more weight. But during that day I received twelve pager messages from journalists relating to the reports and only two of these concerned the Finance committee. This was naturally reflected in the following day's media coverage.

I do not expect sympathy from colleagues who themselves are often irritated when a speech, a campaign or the achievement of some notable success on behalf of a constituent passes unreported. That is just something which a backbench MSP has to accept and, indeed, I have had more than my share of media coverage in the Parliament's first year. But the lack of balance in terms of the local issues which I pursue is not helpful in convincing doubters that promoting the interests of my constituents – and not banning foxhunting – is my main priority as an MSP.

A lack of balance

An aspect of the media which is often underplayed is the extent to which MSPs have weekly columns in major newspapers. The SNP has done particularly well in this regard, with Roseanna Cunningham (*Scottish Daily Mail*), Margo MacDonald (*Edinburgh Evening News*), Duncan Hamilton (*Glasgow Evening Times*) and Andrew Wilson (*Sunday Mail*) all using their high-profile platforms to attack the Executive in general and the Labour Party in particular at every opportunity (which means once a week). The independent MSP Dennis Canavan has a column in *The Herald*, for which the Tory Brian Monteith writes a diary, while Scottish Socialist Tommy Sheridan appears in both the *Daily Record* and the *Evening Times*. Although some do have columns in local publications (the value of which is not to be underestimated), not one Labour (or LibDem) MSP has a column in a national Scottish newspaper. The suggestion that this reflects editors' preference for copy which is critical of the governing parties fails to acknowledge that two Labour MPs at Westminster, Douglas Alexander (*The Herald*) and George Galloway (*Mail on Sunday*), are given their say.

Youthful exuberance has seen both Hamilton and Wilson land in hot water as a result of their scribblings. In April 2000, five Labour MPs referred Wilson to the Press Complaints Commission (PCC) for what they regarded as a complete distortion of their voting records in the House of Commons. The five were furious at being named under the heading 'Labour's loafers', particularly as the attack was based on ignorance of Westminster procedures. The PCC referred the matter back to the *Sunday Mail*, which allowed the Labour side of the argument to be aired.

> **16 June 1999:** *Women members raised the issue of media abuse at today's meeting of the SPLP. I had not seen yesterday's 'Evening Times' and couldn't believe they would print such an outrageous attack. The Glasgow MSPs resolved to tackle it head on with the editor.*

More serious was the disgraceful denigration of Labour women MSPs by Duncan Hamilton in his column in June 1999. Hamilton is the Parliament's youngest member, and it shows, never more so than when he described them as 'overweight, inarticulate and an embarrassment to their party and the Parliament'. His intemperate rant caused widespread anger and earned him an internal rebuke from his own party, although one of his victims, Johann Lamont, believes the SNP response was inadequate. 'If a Labour male MSP had written what Hamilton did, the opposition parties wouldn't have got the opportunity to condemn him – Labour women would have done it immediately and publicly. SNP women failed to do that and so did Alex Salmond,' (interview, August 2000).

He was also forced to apologise in a later *Evening Times* column and the incident has proved to have long-term effects from which Hamilton is still suffering. He has been virtually anonymous in the year which followed, chastened by the reaction to an outburst which was interpreted as an attack on the Parliament as a whole. Needless to say, his column has been more carefully considered since then, and it is rumoured to be subject to vetting by his party before being submitted for publication.

I asserted earlier in this chapter that media coverage of the Scottish Parliament had been better balanced and more factual since September 1999. That is not a view which is shared by Tony Blair's press secretary, Alistair Campbell, who launched a withering attack on the Scottish media and what he called the 'dishonest' manner in which it reported the work of the Parliament and the Executive. He aimed his most biting criticism at the *Daily Record*, which he accused of printing 'complete fiction' (*The Herald*, 14 March 2000) in relation to its opposition to the repeal of clause 2a. He then widened his attack to all Scottish newspapers, claiming that, in the first ten weeks of 2000, clause 2a and 'sleaze' accounted for a total of forty-seven front page stories, while education scored four, and the economy just two.

Campbell's use of *The Herald* for his attack was interesting and seemed to suggest the rehabilitation of that publication in the eyes of the Labour leadership. During the Scottish Parliament election campaign, it was alleged – and *The Herald*'s Murray Ritchie restates this in his book *Scotland Reclaimed* (pp. 91, 104–5) – that, following Donald Dewar's assertion that the paper was 'out-and-out nationalist', the Labour Party withheld election advertising in 1999 reckoned to be worth as much as £100,000.

Campbell's attack came just four days after Tony Blair, addressing Labour's Scottish conference on 10 March, waded into the fray on clause 2a. In this speech, he attacked the 'Keep the Clause' campaign much more forcefully than any of the Scottish Executive ministers had done, although his main target was the Scottish media, sections of which he accused of 'corrosive cynicism'. Campbell clearly decided that, rather than allow Number 10's quarry time to recover, he would hit them hard again, saying, 'Journalists are very good at giving criticism but not very good at taking it. Many are not interested in scoops of fact so much as scoops of interpretation,' (*The Herald*, 14 March 2000). This provoked a 'glass houses' response from Scotland's political scribes which, given Campbell's own *modus operandi*, was not easily shrugged off.

As a spin-off, this spat produced some evidence of the rivalry which exists among Scottish newspapers. In a comment piece on Campbell's intervention on 15 March, *The Scotsman*'s Alison Hardie pointedly belittled both *The Herald* and the *Daily Record*. Perhaps miffed that her paper's Glasgow rival had secured the exclusive interview, she accused it of cosying up to the Labour Party, labelling it 'a sympathetic Scottish broadsheet', despite Murray Ritchie's evidence to the contrary. In turn, the *Daily Record* was accused of having 'vied with *The Sun* and the *Daily Mail* in the struggle to dig ever more dirt on the [Dewar] administration', with Hardie claiming that the paper, despite its unquestioning support for Labour in the elections of 1997 and 1999, 'has never warmed to Mr Blair'.

Such cameos bring a wry smile to most politicians because they suggest that the competitiveness (some might say combativeness) taken as inevitable for elected political life often extends to those who comment on our efforts. And why not? The press pack based in the Lawnmarket have a job to do and success can often take the form of denying a rival a story.

The Herald and *The Scotsman* constantly jostle for position as the leading broadsheet and the sands shift perceptibly depending on who is in charge. Despite the efforts of both to shake off their east/west tag, neither has succeeded in being 'national' in terms of their coverage as a whole. Prior to the arrival of Andrew Neil as managing editor, *The Scotsman* was generally regarded as the more pro-devolution and to my mind also carried the more perceptive journalists. Not now, on either score.

Neil's agenda is quite unsophisticated and it has meant that a newspaper which, for the quarter century prior to his arrival was an unashamed champion of home rule, has become at best the modern epitome of Burns' character in *Tam O'Shanter* 'nursing her wrath to keep it warm'. The presence in its city of the institution for which it argued forcefully is given grudging acceptance, with every opportunity to disparage it enthusiastically embraced. Harsh? Then how else should we interpret his labelling of the new legislature as a 'nursery of numpties which passes for a Parliament on the Mound,' (*The Herald*, 13 December 1999)?

On 22 February 2000, *The Scotsman* published the headline I get the impression it had had lying in a drawer since the Parliament came into being. 'Devolution achieving nothing say voters', it claimed, as the lead-in to coverage of a poll which it had commissioned, asking Scots how they rated their Parliament after its first eight months. Closer inspection revealed that the poll actually said something quite different. Five per cent thought the Parliament had achieved 'a lot', while no less than 69 per cent thought it had achieved 'a little'. So, even at that early stage in the Parliament's life, more than two in three people living in Scotland had begun to feel it making some difference to their lives – not by any means the gloomy message permeating the pages of *The Scotsman*. In Neil's own weekly column in the paper three days later, he claimed that, despite the poll, the Parliament had 'proved to be (let's put this mildly) something of a disappointment', then went on to admit with more than a whiff of hypocrisy, 'Of course it is far too early to assess the work of the Parliament'.

The regular downplaying of the early development of an institution which Neil did not want and the worth of which he is never likely to acknowledge fully, made *The Scotsman* the target of a waspish advert for *The Herald* which appeared soon after, stating, 'We don't pan Scotland. We are Pan-Scotland.'

Neil's arrival did not simply shift the title's axis towards a much more questioning approach to the whole concept of devolution, it has been followed by the departure of some of the paper's best writers, and the odd good editor, too. Since the Parliament came into being, *The Scotsman* has not recovered from the departure of two experienced and respected political writers in Peter MacMahon and Robert Tait, while *The Herald* has been able to build solid coverage and analysis on the back of the experienced Robbie Dinwoodie and Murray Ritchie, ably bolstered by Iain Macwhirter's weekly column.

Macwhirter appears to have an uncanny (make that unprecedented) knack for a journalist of being able to read political events as a politician would. That is not to say that his conclusions are by any means always kind to Labour, but they nevertheless tend to be ones which strike a chord with many Labour MSPs. A straw poll within the SPLP revealed that *The Herald* is the more widely read of the two broadsheets, although most feel the need to compare coverage of the major issues.

The arrival of the *Sunday Herald* last year was well timed and it seemed to pick up on the mood of the moment in the run-up to the elections. It has since developed along with the Parliament to the point where it has now, in my opinion, overtaken the established *Scotland on Sunday*. That title tends to be regarded as pro-nationalist by most Labour MSPs, a view to which I cannot wholeheartedly subscribe. But it does give free reign to the most unashamedly right-wing views outside the British National party in Gerald Warner, a man whose outrage knows no bounds; I find his indignant response to everything that the Parliament or Executive does hilarious. I frequently react similarly to *Scotland on Sunday*'s mischievous diary of a fictional Labour MSP, some of whose antics seem remarkably close to actual events, which has on occasion caused some discomfort within the SPLP.

> **17 December 1999:** *Surely Tom Brown's homophobic tirade yesterday has put the 'Record' beyond the pale. It might have been right to give it the benefit of the doubt when we were arguing over allowances but this was beneath any definition of a decent standard of newspaper reporting.*

Of course, the one paper no Labour MP or MSP can afford to ignore is the *Daily Record*. Labour loyalist up to its armpits, it is read by the vast majority of Labour voters, which explains why so many of us in the SPLP groaned with dismay as Martin Clarke turned the paper into a battering-ram against the door of the Executive (and by extension the Scottish Labour Party) over clause 2a. This came on top of attacks on the issues already mentioned, such as MSPs' allowances and the commemorative medals. Catherine Macleod, *The Herald*'s political editor, got it right when she proclaimed, 'Scottish Labour has been stunned, like rabbits in the headlights, as the *Record* has in turn poured ridicule, contempt and condemnation on the party's performance,' while the party leadership 'still abjectly pander to the *Record*'s agenda,' (*Herald*, 14 March 2000). No less so most Labour MPs and MSPs, which makes it all the more commendable that the Executive's determination to repeal clause 2a held firm (well, relatively so).

Will the fact that the *Daily Record*'s uncompromising message in that campaign was ultimately ignored by the Executive have a bearing on where the paper directs its efforts (and its readers) at the 2001 or 2003 elections? I cannot envisage it and not just because of the view expressed by its political editor, Ron McKenna, on the clause 2a stand-off – 'just a falling out between old allies and I don't think it's terminal,' (*The Scotsman*, 15 March 2000). Where else would the *Record* go on election day? The prospect of it urging its two million readers to cast their votes for any other party is not so much slim as anorexic. And the appearance of the words 'Make up your own mind,' as the conclusion to a *Record* editorial would bemuse even its newest reader.

Much as I have been disappointed by the *Daily Record*'s discordant tone in its reporting of the Parliament, its members and the Executive, I don't think it's terminal, to echo McKenna. I believe most of the blame can be laid squarely at the door of its then editor, Martin Clarke. His abrupt departure in August 2000 and his replacement by Peter Cox was enthusiastically welcomed by Labour MSPs and Scottish Executive ministers alike, and I am not alone in anticipating that the paper will in future adopt a more measured approach to the institution which it played a major part in bringing about.

For most MSPs, media reportage in general, and newspaper coverage in particular, has been at best disappointing, at worst infuriating. I have not come across anyone who feels it has been fair or balanced or has reflected the real priorities and achievements of the Parliament's first year.

John Home Robertson, deputy Rural Affairs minister (and still an MP as well), was typical in his surprise at the press reaction. 'For them to go full pelt in the first month was a disgrace. The running-down and attacks on the institution right from the start caused damage which has not yet been repaired. Though improved, their coverage since is often quite inappropriate, usually preferring style over substance,' (interview, July 2000).

Glasgow Kelvin MSP Pauline McNeill drew attention to the fact that there are no shortage of journalists to cover what the Parliament does, but a real shortage in the spread of that coverage. 'Even since we got over the initial period, coverage has been disappointing. At times in the press gallery, there are up to forty journalists; they are close to the Parliament, yet they hardly cover the real issues, especially what goes on in the committees,' (interview, June 2000). This is a recurring complaint among members and the SNP's Tricia Marwick agreed: 'The committees have spent hours scrutinising bills and taking evidence. There is no comparison with Westminster, yet there is virtually no recogntion of this from the media in Scotland and that naturally affects the public perception of what we are doing,' (interview, June 2000).

However, not all Labour members are as disapproving. Malcolm Chisholm said, 'I don't generally criticise the media for their coverage. It's part of their job to hold the Scottish Executive to account and it's fair enough that the newspapers give them a hard time. The *Daily Record* is really the only example of outrageous and unfair behaviour,' (interview, September 2000).

Labour assistant whip Duncan McNeil detected some irony in the quality of much of the reporting: 'The press accuse the Executive, the Parliament and MSPs of underperforming, but they should look to themselves. Since the Parliament started they haven't improved the standard of their reporting – they seem to be reporting a council, not a parliament,' (interview, June 2000).

That is an assessment with which I concur. It seems to me that, whereas before the Parliament the Scottish media had political reporters, they did not (other than at Westminster) have parliamentary correspondents. Although some based in the Lawnmarket media centre have now adopted that description, they have largely failed to make the leap from being political reporters. To a great extent, it is the personalities or the political issues themselves which constitute 'the story' for them, rather than what the Parliament is doing in terms of scrutinising important legislation or what the Executive is doing in developing policy initiatives.

The *Sunday Herald*'s Douglas Fraser accepted that criticism and took it a step further. 'The print and broadcast media made a big commitment to the Parliament in advance of it starting. Prior to that there had been at most a dozen full-time political journalists in Scotland. Now there are around forty, very few of whom had worked at Westminster, so they're still political journalists,' (interview, September 2000).

Switching off from Westminster

Fraser's comment connects to a further irony, in that much of the work done by the Scottish media's parliamentary correspondents at the House of Commons prior to May 1999 has been reduced or, in some cases, discontinued. For instance, following the establishment of the Scottish Parliament, it was noticeable that *The Herald*'s coverage of Westminster affairs virtually dried up and this was said to have been the major reason for their parliamentary correspondent, Ben Brogan, leaving to join the *Daily Telegraph*. His replacement, Catherine Macleod, presumably secured some agreement with her editor over the level of coverage, because it increased noticeably after her arrival. A further instance of Westminster being shunned was the withdrawal by Scottish Media Group (SMG) of their correspondent, Michael Crow, who had hitherto reported for both Scottish and Grampian. It still happens, because more recently the *Glasgow Evening Times* dispensed with the services of freelance journalist Ian Hernon, who for many years had supplied their House of Commons coverage.

Although these events may be driven primarily by the relative newsworthiness of political events in and around the two legislatures, there are other considerations, in respect of the broadcast media at least. Alastair Moffat, editor of *New Statesman Scotland*, believes 'the simple facts of geography' play a significant role. 'MSPs and Scottish Executive ministers are now far more accessible than Westminster MPs ever were, or could be. Parliamentary television in Edinburgh is not only easier to make, it is better to watch. In addition, Westminster used to be covered for Scottish bulletins by one or, at most, two correspondents based in London. Now all of the specialists in a newsroom, from sports to the arts, have ready access to MSPs,' (*New Statesman Scotland*, 13 December 1999).

Labour MPs have certainly noticed a diminution in the coverage given to their efforts since the advent of the Scottish Parliament, although there is a feeling that the worst is now behind them. According to MP Maria Fyfe, 'It was only right that the Scottish Parliament should get a lot of attention, but some of the media have become "switched off" from what's happening at Westminster. To some extent, that's a reflection of the issues which MPs now cover, but even where I have some success with a constituency case, it does not get covered now in the way it would have done in the past,' (interview, August 2000).

Brian Donohoe feels the corner has been turned. 'For a period of seven or eight months, there was virtually no Westminster coverage at all. It was a real concern and several Scottish MPs raised the matter with journalists; some were as frustrated as we were. *The Herald* is certainly better now, although I still feel the press in general are under-reporting what goes on in the Commons,' (interview, July 2000). Donohoe, who himself had a high local profile prior to May 1999 in terms of constituency issues, recognised the need to ensure that it stayed that way and has perceived no reduction as a result. But, as he put it, 'I'm having to run hard just to stand still.'

Maria Fyfe used the Mike Tyson controversy of May 2000 to highlight the shift in media focus. 'I raised the issue with Tony Blair (during Prime Minister's questions) when the debate was at its height, yet no Scottish newspaper reported this – in the past they would have done. And I submitted an early-day motion urging Jack Straw not to admit Tyson; it attracted the support of over 100 MPs (well above the average) but again it was ignored. Unless Scottish journalists were literally fed a story they would not pick it up,' (interview, August 2000).

The Parliament's arrival blew a chill wind in the direction of Frank Doran. 'Initially, there was a huge switch in attention away from Westminster. In terms of my local papers, *The Press and Journal* and *Aberdeen Evening Express* retained their correspondents, but they found it much harder to get their stories carried. As far as television was concerned, there had been a major investment by SMG in Holyrood from which they had to get a payback, so naturally that became their focus in the Parliament's first year. But I now detect a bit of a shift back and I believe it is difficult to see Holyrood sustaining the level of coverage it has been getting as the general election approaches and the issues highlighted tend to be more those related to Westminster, such as pensions and social security,' (interview, July 2000).

Doran himself was instrumental in achieving greater coverage of the work done by him and his colleagues. Frustrated at SMG giving Scottish matters in the House of Commons a wide berth, he lodged a formal complaint with the Independent Television Commission (ITC) relating to their franchise obligations on regional programming. The ITC largely upheld his complaint and one of the effects was SMG's decision in June 2000 to restore a Westminster correspondent for both channels.

Douglas Fraser believes the scaling-down in importance of Westminster is already having an effect. 'The news agenda between London and Scotland has diverged and there's minimal coverage of Westminster. That means people in Scotland don't get a lot of news from London in general and that will become the norm, shifting back only temporarily in the run-up to general elections,' (interview, September 2000).

So as the first year of the Scottish Parliament draws to a close, it seems that neither Scottish MSPs nor MPs are satisfied with the coverage of their respective legislatures. In the former case, the issue is quality, in the latter quantity, but it is to be hoped that both are no more than symptoms of the settling-in process. That said, better communications between political journalists and elected members may be capable of dealing with discontent, which is also felt to some extent by the fourth estate over the quality of information which is made available to them.

Ultimately, editorial decisions are what make the difference and a generally more positive approach to the reporting of the Scottish Parliament would make a major contribution towards providing a more comprehensive service to the people of Scotland. This would enable them to see what their parliamentarians (of both varieties) are *really* doing to help the new politics take shape.

5 The people speak

25 September 1999: Four months into the Parliament and already we're being blamed for almost losing a Westminster seat. It would be funny if it wasn't being said seriously. No mention of the fact that voters resent avoidable by-elections.

Events of the Parliament's first year undoubtedly influenced the fortunes of the respective political parties. Opinion polls during that period reflected this, with no established pattern emerging. What is interesting is the extent to which events at Holyrood or Westminster have affected – or have the potential to affect – the parties' electoral performance.

A cliché it may be, but it is true nevertheless that the only opinion polls that matter are those involving the ballot box. Since May 1999 there have been two such tests, by-elections in the Westminster seat of Hamilton South and the Scottish Parliament constituency of Ayr. Both produced campaigns in which the performance of the new Scottish Parliament was judged, one fairly, the other unfairly.

I have little time for the notion that, in general, the Scottish electorate are unable to distinguish between their two legislatures. Such a view is at best patronising, and more importantly it ignores the monthly opinion polls where levels of support for the political parties are shown to differ, often to a substantial extent, between the two parliaments. Political awareness reaches its height at election times, including by-elections, and for that reason I believe that voters in Hamilton and Ayr knew precisely what they were doing when they marked their ballot papers. They were well aware of the occasion, but used it to deliver their comment on the political parties across the levels of representation, from local authority through the Scottish Parliament to the House of Commons.

The Hamilton South by-election, caused by the appointment of George Robertson as Secretary-General of NATO, took place in September 1999. The Scottish Parliament had been in existence for just twenty weeks (and had been in session for a mere twelve days since the transfer of its legislative powers) yet commentators, as well as some Scottish Labour MPs, claimed it was a judgement on the fledgling institution. It is certainly true that the attacks by sections of the press had led some Scots to question priorities at Holyrood, but only the harshest of critics would seriously suggest that a meaningful evaluation could be based on such a snapshot.

My experience of canvassing in Hamilton was that the main source of disaffection with the Labour Party was South Lanarkshire council. Complaints were largely based on a perceived failure to deliver services effectively; this could have been the result of the resources available to the council, which by extension would have been a criticism of government at Westminster, or it could have been a direct criticism of the council's priorities or its ability to deliver on promises. Despite introducing myself as an MSP, on no occasion did I encounter criticism of the Scottish Parliament, and this experience was mirrored by that of colleagues.

Labour's candidate, Bill Tynan, was a well-known local figure and, given that he retained the seat by a mere 556 votes (Robertson's 1997 majority had been almost 16,000), this factor might have made the difference between success and failure. Certainly, such a narrow margin took everyone in Labour's campaign by surprise, but the same must have been the case at SNP HQ, because their last-lap campaigning did not suggest they scented victory.

A subplot in the latter stages of the campaign was the battle for fourth place between the Scottish Liberal Democrats and the Scottish Socialist Party (SSP). This turned out to be a mismatch, because the SSP finished third, and the LibDems, to their embarrassment, sixth, behind the candidate campaigning for a new ground for Hamilton

Accies football club (my Labour colleague Scott Barrie suggested this left the LibDems as the Albion Rovers of Scottish politics, which seemed a bit harsh on the Coatbridge club).

There were, however, serious implications from that contest within a contest. First, it suggested that the LibDems (albeit in a seat where they have always had a very low level of support) may have suffered as a result of their identity being submerged within the partnership at Holyrood. Secondly, the SSP achieved 9 per cent of the vote in their first real showing outwith Glasgow, suggesting that party may be capable of profiting from discontent among core Labour voters who might otherwise have stayed at home. Neither thesis could be argued convincingly on the basis of such flimsy evidence but, within six months, more was to become available.

> **20 December 1999:** *I was leaving an MSPs' meeting with the Glasgow Alliance with Janis Hughes when her phone rang and we learned that Ian Welsh had resigned his seat. 'Self-indulgence,' was the kindest reaction we could muster.*

If the Scottish Labour Party had been offered the opportunity of ranking in order of preference the seventy-three Holyrood constituencies which might host the Parliament's first by-election, Ayr would have been their seventy-third choice. The party had won the seat on 6 May 1999 with the slenderest of all majorities recorded that day: just twenty-five votes. It had seen a hard-fought contest between the Tory, Phil Gallie, who held the seat (before boundary revisions) as an MP until 1997, and Ian Welsh, Labour leader of South Ayrshire council. When it was announced in December that Welsh had resigned his seat, I was not alone among Labour MSPs in anticipating that we could not win the by-election.

Ian Welsh had been a high-achiever since his youth. He played first-team football for Kilmarnock while still at school, went on to gain an honours degree in English at Glasgow University, and then became a teacher, rising to the post of deputy head. He later became head of human resources at Prestwick Airport, a position he had to give up when he was elected leader of South Ayrshire council, although he did manage to combine the leadership with another full-time post, that of chief executive at Kilmarnock FC.

Like most Labour Party activists, Welsh had been a vigorous

campaigner for a Scottish Parliament since the mid-1980s, and it was natural that he should seek selection as a candidate for the first election. Having taken his seat at Holyrood, the reality of life as an MSP soon hit home. Contrary to media reports, Welsh insists he did not resign because of family commitments or the daily grind of travelling two hours each way, three days a week. His family commitments did mean that he could not stay overnight in Edinburgh, but both they and his daily travel routine were as he had anticipated prior to his election. What he had not anticipated was the extent to which he would be marginalised from the political process at Holyrood.

'I never expected to be given a ministerial post, although I did have hopes. I recognised that, by and large, the younger generation were preferred and I accepted the reasons for that. What I had not anticipated was being so ideologically remote from the decision-making process. This doesn't mean actually *making* the decisions, but having an *input* to the process which results in decisions on policy. I would hear on my car radio of major policy announcements by ministers ahead of a Labour group meeting later that day. There was a gulf between backbenchers and the Executive; there were a number of senior Labour members who were former council leaders and current or former MPs, with expertise which should have been tapped. I know I wasn't by any means the only Labour MSP who felt that way.'

That was certainly the case, although it has to be said that while the weekly SPLP meetings provided the opportunity for such issues to be raised – and they were – I cannot recall Welsh contributing to that debate. As a former council leader, he had been accustomed to being at the heart of decision-making, but the same could be said in respect of Labour colleagues such as Cathy Craigie, Hugh Henry and Kate Maclean. Each of them, as well as many others, made their feelings known, and changes have resulted in the style of operation and the relationship between the Executive and backbenchers.

By October, Welsh was considering standing down. 'I talked it through with my wife and decided to tough it out, but by early November I became dispirited at the antics of the opposition parties in the chamber. The Tories and SNP were willing to see absolutely nothing of merit in what the Executive were doing, and I could see the whole thing slipping into the old Westminster ways.'

In mid-November, he decided to go and e-mailed Tom McCabe to discuss how it might be made 'as painless as possible'. Although the two had a discussion soon after, it was a month later before Donald Dewar spoke to him. According to Welsh: 'Donald offered to "make things easier" for me. But he had failed to grasp what my dilemma was. I couldn't stand the inertia; I wanted more to do, not less!' Ironically, after he had decided to resign (but before he had announced it), he was approached to contribute some ideas to Wendy Alexander's Communities team; but by then his decision was made.

Ian Welsh was under no illusions as to the consequences of his resignation. 'I accepted that Labour could not win the by-election and that it was likely to go to the Tories, although I knew this would not significantly affect the balance in the Parliament. Had that balance been a delicate one, I would have had to thole it and would have done so,' (all quotes: interview, August 2000).

The scene was thus set for the Scottish Parliament's first by-election, on 16 March. The expectation was that Phil Gallie, having run Welsh so close, would again take up the challenge. Not so. As a list member, Gallie would have been required by the Scotland Act to resign his seat before seeking nomination as the by-election candidate. This is surely an area where an amendment is called for. With list vacancies being filled simply by the next name on that party's list, there is no reason why a list member who would prefer to represent an individual constituency should not have the right to contest a by-election, resigning his or her list seat only if successful. However, this was not what dissuaded Gallie from seeking his party's nomination: it seems he is an MSP only on sufferance, aiming to return to Westminster, where he represented Ayr for ten years.

Gallie's colleague Ben Wallace, a list MSP for North East Scotland, is of the same mind, energetically seeking a nomination for the next UK general election. Their stance seriously undermines the Tories' claim to be committed to making the Parliament work and enabling it to become established. If MSPs are seen to treat the Scottish Parliament merely as a staging post to what they presumably regard as 'greater things', this sends a clear message to the people of Scotland. It seems to be uniquely a Tory problem, because it is difficult to envisage an MSP from any of the other parties pursuing such an opportunistic course of action.

February 2000: Candidates get campaigning underway in the Ayr by-election: left to right Rita Miller (Lab); John Scott (Con); Jim Mather (SNP); Stuart Ritchie (SLD)
(source: The Herald)

The by-election campaign got underway with Labour on the back foot from the start. According to *The Scotsman*, 'party sources' had said that 'the Labour vote was in meltdown and indicated it would come third in the poll,' (25 February 2000). This seemed unduly pessimistic, although the party had come through a messy candidate selection process, which had left some local party members disillusioned. On the day the party's campaign was launched, the clause 2a issue was top of the news agenda, following the insertion of the phrase 'stable family life' into the Ethical Standards in Public Life Bill, forcing Donald Dewar to deny that this represented a 'U-turn'.

Before long, things began to look bleak for Labour's candidate, Rita Miller, who was damaged by the decision of South Ayrshire Council to announce, during the campaign, the closure of a popular senior citizens' day centre in Ayr. Not only was Miller a councillor, she chaired the committee which decided on the closure. During campaigning, I was confronted by an SNP canvasser who could not believe the Labour Party had not ensured that such a decision had at least been postponed until after the by-election.

Nor could I. Nor could Labour's campaign manager, Andy Kerr, who did not attempt to disguise his frustration at the lack of assistance from Labour-controlled South Ayrshire Council: 'Even minor comments in support of our candidate were difficult to achieve, despite

Rita Miller being a member of the Labour group. It's a problem you don't expect to have in a by-election. And this was at a time when Ayr resembled an ad-trailer convention [containing Brian Souter's clause 2a message], which was making it difficult to get our message across,' (interview, June 2000).

The campaign was not going well, yet the seasoned election pundit Professor John Curtice of Strathclyde University believed the position in which Labour found itself was nothing out of the ordinary: 'Governments are meant to lose midterm by-elections. With the Labour-dominated Executive under fire from its friends and the Westminster government losing some of its shine, there seems little reason why that rule should not operate now,' (*Scotland on Sunday*, 5 March 2000).

The reference to 'its friends' concerned criticism aimed the previous week at the First Minister and his MSPs by Labour MPs Michael Connarty and Ian Davidson. Davidson, the MP for Glasgow Pollok, had claimed Dewar's leadership 'was reminiscent of the worst days of John Major's', and the mantle was taken up by his colleague in Kelvin, George Galloway, who called for Dewar to be replaced. 'Maybe there's a need for someone younger, hungrier, leaner and fitter. He's a parliamentary operator of great experience, but he seems to have lost the plot,' (BBC *Holyrood*, 5 March 2000).

Such candour, wholly inappropriate during a by-election campaign, was naturally seized upon by opponents, occurring as it did at the time when suggestions were being made that the Labour Party had effectively thrown in the towel. A morale-boosting visit to the constituency by Tony Blair was anticipated by party workers, especially as the Prime Minister was visiting Scotland to address Labour's Scottish conference on 10 March. The announcement that he would not be making an appearance at Ayr was portrayed, understandably, as an attempt to avoid being tainted with failure, but Andy Kerr made it clear that prospects of a Blair visit were invented by journalists. 'In fact, the decision that the Prime Minister would *not* play a part in the campaign was made early on. We had a programme of key campaign visits, including UK cabinet ministers, and it was never suggested that would include Tony Blair,' (interview, June 2000).

6 March 2000: *It's a long time since I recall committee room morale in a by-election being so low. I was canvassing with Sandra Osborne MP who was* *fearful that a bad result for Labour next week would seriously damage her chances of holding the seat at the general election.*

Labour's downbeat approach continued right up to the eve of poll, with Donald Dewar unwilling to predict victory for Rita Miller, saying only 'we are travelling hopefully,' (*The Scotsman*, 16 March). At least Dewar was not raising false hopes – when it came, the result was a bad one for Labour, but no worse than had been anticipated over the closing days of the campaign. Third place, more than 2,000 votes behind the SNP, was evidence of the swing away from the Labour Party, but more telling was that the Conservatives had won over 5,500 votes more than Labour.

Polling analyst Malcolm Dickson was blunt in his assessment: 'For Labour, the result is deeply worrying. [Their] share of the vote was 22 per cent, a historic low. Less than three years ago, Labour won Ayr on the back of a 48 per cent share of the vote. Over that short period of time their vote has almost halved,' (*The Herald*, 18 March 2000). Of further concern was the fact that the SNP attracted more of the lost Labour votes than did the Conservatives, which Dickson described as 'just the type of shift the SNP needs to threaten Labour'. In similar vein, Angus Macleod, political editor of the *Scottish Daily Express*, suggested that following the result Donald Dewar 'would have been relieved, because an SNP victory... would have been perilous indeed for Labour,' (18 March 2000).

Clause 2a had been predicted as the issue which would dominate the by-election, but this proved not to be the case. Not that the 'Keep the Clause' campaign could be blamed for that. Millionaire Brian Souter had funded the campaign's intervention, enabling it to buy up every billboard site in Ayr, as well as flooding local newspapers with adverts urging voters to support parties committed to keeping clause 2a. With only the Tories having such a policy, that message was not exactly subtle. Given the persistent scaremongering of the 'Keep the Clause' campaign's publicity, the appearance in the constituency of (unsigned) posters claiming, 'A vote for Labour is a vote for sodomy' carried a certain inevitability.

Nonetheless, the involvement of 'Keep the Clause' in the by-election raised fundamental questions of democracy. Candidates are limited by law in terms of what they are permitted to spend on their campaigns. No such restrictions apply to non-party organisations, which are not officially part of the by-election at all. Yet the message being peddled on clause 2a – and its obvious association with one particular candidate – left serious issues to be resolved. Not least of these is the denial to political parties of access to billboards, which are an established part of by-election campaigns. Some means of preventing the distortion of by-elections must be found before this kind of single-issue circus grows out of hand and actually decides the outcome, without any accountability over its expenditure in doing so. Should that day ever arrive, it would constitute a danger to parliamentary democracy in Scotland.

Although clause 2a had been an issue, it was not the one on which the by-election turned. Indeed, as *The Scotsman* reported (17 March 2000), 'all parties (were) claiming that it had ranked only fourth in the voters' list of concerns'. In the experience of James Douglas Hamilton, the Tory business manager at Holyrood, it was even less prominent than that: 'It was only a background issue. I canvassed several hundred electors and only two of them said clause 2a would decide how they voted,' (interview, July 2000). All of this should have prompted Brian Souter to question whether his resources were being used in pursuit of best value. Undaunted, he seemed satisfied at the outcome claiming that 'the parties that opposed repeal of clause 2a [the Tories] won and the others lost,' (*Sunday Herald*, 19 March 2000). Applying that kind of logic might just as easily lead to the conclusion that the by-election was a defeat for Souter and his campaign because nearly 60 per cent of those voting did so for parties in favour of repeal.

More prosaically, as at Hamilton, people voted on the basis of issues decided at different levels: in the council (cuts in services and jobs), at Holyrood (the cost of the new Parliament building, clause 2a and health service waiting lists) and at Westminster (pensions and plans to privatise air traffic control services). Bread-and-butter issues are what concern people most and the only surprising thing about this is that political journalists seem to be surprised by it.

The result presented John Scott with a clutch of 'firsts': the first Scottish Parliament by-election winner, the first directly-elected Tory MSP, the first Tory by-election gain in Scotland since 1967, and the first Tory parliamentarian elected for a Scottish constituency since 1992. For some in his party, the symbolism of the result could not be overestimated. 'I believe Ayr could turn out to be as significant as Roxburgh, Selkirk and Peebles in 1965, when David Steel triumphed,' said James Douglas Hamilton. 'That sounded a warning to Tories in Scotland, which we did not heed. We were then the establishment party and from that point the pendulum swung away from us. Sometimes, by-elections can have a disproportionate influence, serving as a watershed for both the losing party and the electorate because they affect the general credibility and standing of the party. There is a possibility that we could see the same happen to Labour in Scotland this time,' (interview, July 2000). Forewarned is forearmed.

If Labour left Ayr licking its wounds, the other partnership party also performed badly. The LibDems limped home in fifth position, again behind the Scottish Socialist Party, having captured a mere 2 per cent of the vote. In fairness, the party had gained only twice that in May 1999, so they had little on which to build, but this does suggest that the partnership is less popular among LibDem voters than among LibDem members. Party profile is a key issue in elections because it impacts on voter recognition. With the partnership dominated by Labour cabinet ministers, perhaps the LibDem identity is not as visible as was previously the case in terms of media coverage; then again, it had never featured in government within living memory, so the balance of advantage could fall either way.

It would have been interesting had there been a by-election while Jim Wallace held the position of acting First Minister, or immediately thereafter. Undoubtedly his profile and that of his party increased dramatically during the period in which he was deputising for Donald Dewar and this might have provided a more useful yardstick as to the electoral effect of the partnership on the LibDems.

The mystique surrounding the way in which the LibDem group operates is often a source of frustration to Labour MSPs, accustomed as we are to the discipline of the group or the party. Margaret Smith confirms there is no such culture within her party: 'Basically, the concept of group discipline doesn't exist. Members have a right of "opt-out" but it does carry the responsibility to ensure it's not abused. This would mainly be exercised on constituency issues, for example Nora Radcliffe and Mike Rumbles who felt they had to take a stand on the local government settlement for Aberdeenshire in March. But people do their sums and would not threaten the partnership,' (interview, July 2000).

The extent of the effect on the LibDems of being the junior members of the partnership remains to be seen. It is often suggested that the price which the party has had to pay for being in government is a loss of its distinct identity, but I am not convinced that this has great validity. There is certainly an absence of a party label when Scottish Executive statements are made or a major policy development is being launched, but that affects the senior partner too. Such events or announcements cannot be Labour-branded any more than they can be LibDem-branded. Occasionally press coverage has featured the term 'the Labour-led Scottish Executive', but apart from being somewhat cumbersome, it is not a description that can be used in an Executive press release.

That said, the LibDems have shown that they are able to gain centre stage when Executive initiatives carry their stamp. A recent example concerned the Freedom of Information Bill which forms part of the Executive's legislative programme for 2000–1. The bill is long-standing Liberal Democrat policy and falls within the remit of their leader, Jim Wallace, in his role as Justice Minister. When he departed for Dublin in August 2000 for talks with his counterpart in the Dail, the visit was reported as being part of Wallace's preparation for the delivery of a major plank of LibDem policy. So, there is no good reason why both partnership parties cannot retain their own identity while simultaneously deriving credit from the electorate for legislative changes or fresh initiatives.

But it is the Tories who claim to have gained most, ironically as a result of the Scottish Parliament and the proportional voting system, both of which they opposed bitterly over many years. Their leader, David McLetchie, appears not in the least embarrassed to admit: 'The Scottish Parliament has been a lifeline for us. Every day of the week we are making news, we are quoted and our profile has been raised. Without the Parliament and the PR voting system, it would have been extraordinarily difficult to do that and we would have been heavily handicapped in a general election campaign,' (*New Statesman Scotland*, 13 March 2000).

For the Tories, the test will be the extent to which they are able to regain some of their Westminster seats in Scotland at the UK general election. They appear to have come to terms with the reshaped Scottish political scene, although McLetchie and his colleagues in the Scottish Parliament still cast a doleful shadow in the chamber and the committees, often projecting a disdainful approach which suggests they would rather be elsewhere. It does not take much imagination to deduce where that might be, and it may require a new political generation, one which has grown up in a Scottish political scene dominated by Holyrood, to articulate with sincerity the party's vision of a devolved Scotland.

Returning to Ayr, the SSP was another party that did not emerge with much, although admittedly Ayr was hardly fertile territory (it did not field a candidate there in 1999); nonetheless, at 4 per cent, its share of the vote was less than half what it had achieved at Hamilton. It is still too early to judge the SSP's likely impact in future, although opinion polls show the party has already built upon the May 1999 electoral performance. The resources and exposure which flow from having a presence in the Parliament have been used to good effect, although it seems to me the party will need to break out from its 'one-man-band' image if it is to make real electoral progress.

The SSP's main target concerns those in Scotland who are most marginalised in terms of housing, employment, consumerism, and the political process. These are people who have always been regarded as Labour's core support and it is the ability of the SSP to set up camp on that territory which has the potential to cause a division within the Scottish Labour Party in terms of its future policy priorities. It could lead to a calculation by Labour's Scottish strategists that any damage caused by the consequent loss of some of that core vote is less serious than might otherwise have been the case. The nationalists are Labour's major electoral enemy and if that loss were to be split, thus limiting any potential advance by the nationalists at Labour's expense, then it could be seen as mitigating the damage. This in turn might lead those seeking to direct Labour's strategy to conclude that, with the SNP and the SSP arm-wrestling over Scotland's dispossessed, that section of the population no longer represents a constituency to which Labour has to direct its main effort.

The social inclusion agenda being pursued by the Scottish Executive since the introduction of the Parliament does not suggest any such motivation. However, should such thinking within the party be permitted to develop – as a result of an advance by the SSP at the UK general election in 2001 or following the by-election capture by the SNP of one or more Labour seats in the Scottish Parliament – then it would create tensions leading to a serious rift within the party. Already there are strains over the extent to which Labour in Scotland has the ability to opt out of parts of the party's UK policy agenda on the basis of Scottish priorities. These strains have at their root the extent to which the need to combat poverty should dominate the Executive's political programme – and how it should be paid for – irrespective of what the UK government is doing on the same issues in England and Wales. The continued advance of the SSP would ensure that that pot, simmering gently on the back-burner at present, had its heat turned up.

The arrival of the SSP is not just of concern to the Labour Party. In aiming to capture disaffected Labour voters, it is in competition with the SNP, which would previously have expected to capitalise as of right. The election of John Swinney as party leader is likely to ensure that a mainstream social democratic agenda will be pursued, one not far removed from that shaped by Alex Salmond. Had Alex Neil and his 'route-one' path to independence prevailed, this would almost certainly have been followed by a policy thrust designed to have greater appeal to the less well-off. Such a populist approach would have enabled the party to compete head-to-head with the SSP, but would probably have frightened sections of the party's voters (and not a few of its MSPs).

It seems likely the SNP will quickly unite behind Swinney, for two reasons. First, the leadership contest was not as publicly damaging as was anticipated, and those rifts which it opened up will be quickly repaired. Secondly, the party must contest the UK general election although it is no longer its main focus. Retaining its six seats is likely to concentrate minds in what will, in any case, form a honeymoon period for Swinney.

However Swinney fares, he may yet emerge at the head of a new partnership following a future Scottish Parliament election. An SNP-SSP coalition would not require a huge leap of imagination, nor would it necessitate major policy concessions on either side, given the SSP's support for an independent (Socialist Republic of) Scotland. Such an eventuality could only emerge if the Labour Party is deserted by a core vote much wider than that which the SNP and

SSP are currently contesting, which could never happen... could it?

This is speculation of course and apologies will be demanded by Labour colleagues for even contemplating such heresy, but in the fluidity of the new Scottish political battlefield, almost anything has become a possibility.

6 Events

> **14 May 1999:** *News that the partnership agreement had been signed was less surprising than the fact that it contained an understanding on student tuition fees. This could only result in their demise and the irony of this, after we had defended them throughout the campaign, was not lost on Labour MSPs.*

'Events' are what happen to governments, and they have a habit of wreaking havoc much like a typhoon. The Scottish Parliament has not had to go looking for its own variety, sensitive or controversial issues coming thick and fast during its inaugural year. The aim of this chapter is to assess the major ones, with the exception of the clause 2a debate, which is covered in Chapter 8.

In the days immediately after the election in May 1999, attention was focussed on the discussions involving Labour and the LibDems. It is fair to say that there was never serious doubt that these would result in a partnership to enable the parties to implement a programme of legislation for the Parliament's first four years. But the terms of that agreement would be crucial, because they had to contain a basis on which the vexed question of student tuition fees could be resolved.

The Cubie report

For reasons which many had difficulty in understanding, tuition fees had become one of the dominant issues in the first Scottish Parliament election campaign. This could not have been envisaged when, within months of taking power in 1997, Tony Blair's government introduced student fees, while phasing out the remaining grants and replacing them with loans. Although the abolition of grants was potentially more of a financial burden to students, tuition fees were more controversial because they involved payment for education itself, rather than for subsistence while studying. The charging of £1,000 a year in fees struck at the central tenet of the state education system in Scotland: that access to it should be free.

Nevertheless, like all other Labour candidates in the Scottish Parliament elections, I defended party policy. Few of us were prepared for it becoming quite the issue which it did, but with the other three major parties (including, shamefully but shamelessly, the Tories) and all of the minor ones promising to abolish fees, Labour was kept on the back foot throughout the campaign. It was certainly the most difficult issue I encountered, particularly at hustings meetings, and I have no doubt that it cost Labour votes in middle-class areas the length and breadth of Scotland. No matter that most of the propaganda put around by the other parties was bogus; no matter that students from the poorest families would not be required to pay a penny; no matter that only families with an income in excess of £35,000 would pay the full fees, it was impossible to escape the accusation that Labour was breaching the fundamental principle of free education.

Although tuition fees had been introduced by the UK government, this was one of the powers devolved to the Scottish Parliament. So when the dust had settled on 7 May, the Parliament had 129 new members, fifty-six of whom were committed to retaining tuition fees, while seventy-three were determined to get rid of them. The issue was undoubtedly a timebomb and, had the partnership talks proved unsuccessful, there can be little doubt that the opposition parties would have wasted no time in uniting to inflict a damaging and highly public humiliation on Labour's minority administration. Within weeks of the Parliament's birth, tuition fees would have been abolished in Scotland; what might have replaced them would have been impossible to predict.

For that reason, it was vital from Labour's point of view that a deal was done on the issue of tuition fees at the negotiations which led to the agreement with the Liberal Democrats; and so it was. The importance of the issue was demonstrated by its inclusion as the first policy item contained in the partnership document. With what, even at this distance, seems an understatement, the document stated: 'We are agreed that the controversial issue of tuition fees is too important and too complex to be decided in the short period of time between 6 May and the formation of this Partnership Government.' And with due deference to the new legislature, it continued: 'We intend that a resolution of the Parliament should call on the Executive to establish urgently a Committee of Inquiry on the issue of tuition fees and financial support for those participating, part-time or full-time, in further and higher education.'

This the Parliament duly did on 2 July 1999, in the first example of exercising its devolved powers, when it agreed to establish the Independent Committee of Inquiry into Student Finance. The debate on tuition fees on 17 June had seen the Liberal Democrats heavily criticised by both the SNP and the Tories for failing to press for the immediate and unequivocal abolition of fees. The Tory education spokesperson, Brian Monteith, did not mince his words: 'I do not propose to revisit the debate on tuition fees. It would be too painful for Liberal Democrat members to be reminded of the treachery that they visited upon the Scottish electorate when they entered into their deal with Labour.'

The Committee of Inquiry was known by the name of its chair, Andrew Cubie, an Edinburgh lawyer who had made a powerful contribution to the workings of the Consultative Steering Group. It was a classic example of a government dealing with a troublesome issue by buying time. Cubie was asked not simply to consider the question of fees, but student hardship in the wider sense. Its consultation was also wide, both in terms of the organisations that made submissions and the fact that evidence was taken at meetings around the country.

Although Labour had cleared the first hurdle – enabling the partnership to be established – there remained a further obstacle in the form of Cubie's recommendations and whether the two parties (particularly the LibDems) would be capable of formulating a joint response, and then implementing it.

21 December 1999: Andrew Cubie launches his report on student finance
(source: *The Scotsman*)

Before the report was published, there were dire warnings from several quarters (not least certain LibDem backbench MSPs) that it would mean the end of the partnership if it did not call for the outright scrapping of fees. Iain Macwhirter, not known for indulging in hyperbole, believed, 'no-one is in any doubt that after "Cubie Tuesday", we could be saying goodbye to Britain's first mainland experiment in coalition government,' (*Sunday Herald*, 19 December 1999).

In the event, Macwhirter's gloomy prediction proved unfounded. When the report was published on 21 December 1999 (a Tuesday, hence Macwhirter's allusion), it recommended the abolition of upfront fees for Scottish students attending college or university in Scotland; Scots studying elsewhere in the UK or abroad were excluded. The report also contained an innovative proposal: the introduction of a graduate endowment fund which would assist students from the least well-off families, partly through the reintroduction of grants.

After considering the report for more than a month, the Executive responded by accepting most of the principles, although in a diluted form which reduced the threshold at which graduates would begin repayments from £25,000 to £10,000 (according to the National Union of Students Scotland, the average first-time salary for graduates in 1999 was £17,500). Additionally, grants were to be capped at the level of £2,000, rather than Cubie's recommendation of £4,000. Predictable fury emanated from the SNP and Tory benches during a lively debate in the Parliament on 27 January, at the end of which the Executive motion was endorsed by a margin of sixty-eight votes to fifty-three, with the support of all Liberal Democrats.

As one of those who believed that the LibDems 'fudged our position at the outset' (that is, when the Partnership Agreement was signed), Donald Gorrie regarded the end as justifying the means. 'The final outcome is amazingly good. Not perfect, but much better than I had imagined it would be; tuition fees are effectively dead,' (interview, July 2000).

The partnership survived and for many families across Scotland there was a collective sense of quiet satisfaction, because tuition fees were to be brought to an end for most Scottish students with effect from October 2000.

There was the additional consideration that this was a powerful example of the Parliament developing and implementing policy tailor-made for Scotland, irrespective of English political sensibilities. Cubie did indeed have an impact at Westminster level in terms of financial policy and it extended beyond mere student considerations. 'The report was widely seen as embodying a social-democratic view of government and redistribution which challenged the fiscal orthodoxies of the UK Treasury, and the UK government was reluctantly forced to find £68 million for widening access to higher education [in England and Wales],' (Gerry Hassan, *Renewal*, July 2000).

Professor Lindsay Paterson, editor of *Scottish Affairs*, offered additional reasons why the outcome of the Cubie report was of wider significance: 'It showed the effect of proportional elections: Labour could not get its own way. It inaugurated a new style of policy-making: [it] broke new ground in the thoroughness with which [it] sought evidence. It invented a new source of revenue for the Parliament: the graduate endowment payment is not a tax, and yet provides income from mostly well-off people that the government proposes to redistribute to the poor,' (Hassan and Warhurst, p. 92).

Although the issue of tuition fees must have caused some sleepless nights for Donald Dewar, Jim Wallace and their business managers, I believe it was a healthy experience for the partnership. From the start, the merchants of doom have been predicting the partnership's demise on each issue which has demonstrated the slightest difference of opinion between the parties or elicited the mildest reproach from a LibDem MSP. To counter this, a baptism of fire was required to show the partnership could sustain attacks (from within as well as without) and emerge stronger for the experience.

Cubie provided that testing ground and at an important period, during the first year of the Parliamentary session. For the partnership, it has proved to be the most demanding issue of the first year; there have been closer votes, but none was based on differences of policy between the two parties. That is not to say I could predict with certainty that the partnership will last the full four years (proportional representation in local government elections may yet prove an issue too far) but it now has the benefit of having come through a potentially fatal challenge. Not only that, but it did so through a compromise which demanded much more from the senior than the junior partner. Before Cubie, few MSPs in either Labour or the LibDems properly understood what partnership meant and involved. The experience which it provided over the first nine months was one of the most useful as we edged warily along the learning curve.

The new Parliament building

> **16 June 1999:** *The SPLP discussed our tactics in preparation for tomorrow's debate on the new Parliament building. The extent to which members from the other parties have used the new Parliament building as a political football was disappointing, forcing us to defend rather than celebrate the project.*

It is inevitable when any public building project is proposed that questions will be raised. Do we need it? Can we afford it? How else could the money be spent? These considerations alone are usually sufficient to start a serious debate in the media. When, added to that, the issue becomes the subject of political arguments, it is a recipe for lurid headlines and a story that will run and run until the project is either completed or abandoned.

In this case of a new home for the Scottish Parliament, there is the further dimension as to where it should be sited. Since the late 1970s, it had been assumed that the institution, when it was finally established, would be housed in the old Royal High School on Calton Hill. The refurbishment of the building had been commissioned by Secretary of State Bruce Millan, with the intention that it should house the Scottish Assembly, following the referendum of 1979. That aim – and the wishes of a majority of voters – having been thwarted by Westminster chicanery, the building was rarely used, although one of its regular visitors was the Scottish Grand Committee, comprising Scotland's seventy-two MPs. By the time the committee held its last meeting there in March 1999, the decision had been taken by Millan's Labour successor, Donald Dewar, that the building, and others nearby including St Andrew's House, were unsuitable for housing the Scottish Parliament.

This itself became a controversial issue, with Dewar rumoured to have decided against Calton Hill because it was regarded as a 'nationalist shibboleth'. That description, which has now entered Scottish political folklore, is widely assumed to have emanated from Brian Wilson MP, then in his initial sojourn as a Scottish Office minister and a man who cedes second place to nobody in his opposition to the SNP. Little purpose is served by rehearsing the rights and wrongs of where the Parliament should have been sited. At the time, my own preference was for Calton Hill, although I now accept that the piecemeal nature of the site and the difficulty in adding to St Andrew's House makes Holyrood the better option.

Following a competition, a design by the Catalan architect Enric Miralles was chosen in July 1998. The fact that the decision on where to base the Parliament was taken more than a year before the Parliament was elected, was later criticised, although that in itself was not an issue at the time. The LibDem MSP Donald Gorrie believes that where the building was sited should have been left to the Parliament itself to decide. 'The decision should not have been taken before the Parliament was elected. I respect Donald Dewar and believe in many ways he really is the Father of the Nation, but he went seriously astray on this issue. It is not right that one man should have decided where the new building will be; that's the kind of decision MSPs should make,' (interview, July 2000).

SNP MSP Tricia Marwick agreed: 'The decision to locate at

Holyrood and the appointment of the architect should have been taken by the whole Parliament; if so, none of the other problems associated with the project would have occurred,' (interview, June 2000).

Gorrie and Marwick have a point, but Donald Dewar would no doubt have been criticised for lack of forward-thinking had he delayed a decision, because doing so would have made it impossible for the Parliament to occupy the new building during its first four-year session. Dewar believed that was important and most MSPs I have spoken to agree. The irony is that, despite the decision on the site having being made in 1998, there is still a possibility that the project will not be completed in time for it to be occupied before May 2003; the best estimate at present for an entry date is the end of 2002, which allows little room for slippage.

As soon as the Parliament came into being, the Holyrood project emerged as a major issue, and its future was the subject of the Parliament's first debate of real significance, on 17 June 1999. In opening, Donald Dewar launched an acerbic attack on the SNP, which had whipped its members to oppose the continuation of the project. 'I have no doubt that we would carry this vote comfortably on a free vote. Given the subject matter, it is absolutely disgraceful that the chamber will not get that chance. If I sound angry, it is because I am angry.' This was so atypical of the First Minister that it induced Mike Russell of the SNP to comment in his contribution: 'I commend the First Minister on the passion of his speech. I have seldom, if ever, seen him so passionate.' This was indeed an indication of the extent to which Dewar felt himself embodied in the project and he finished with a strong personal plea for support, saying: 'Today, the Parliament has the chance to stand by a radical vision; I hope it will take that chance.'

It did, but only after a close shave. Donald Gorrie had moved an amendment seeking a three-month delay in making a decision while a special committee examined the options in detail. This was defeated by only sixty-four votes to sixty-one, following which the Executive motion was carried by a margin of sixty-six to fifty-seven. Only eleven of the sixteen LibDems supported the Executive position, but the partnership had passed its first test.

Thereafter, responsibility for overseeing the project was placed in the hands of the Parliamentary Corporate Body, which is chaired by

Donald Gorrie and Margo MacDonald have been unrelenting in their stand against the new Holyrood building
(source: *Donald Gorrie picture – Sunday Herald;*
source: *Margo MacDonald picture – Parliamentary Broadcasting Unit)*

the Presiding Officer, and the opposition parties reluctantly accepted that Holyrood was the settled site. However, the issue continued to simmer, largely because two tenacious and vociferous MSPs simply refused to accept the verdict. Although unhappy at the escalation of the price from the £50 million (which covered building costs only) originally quoted by Donald Dewar in 1998 to the then figure of £109 million, their opposition was essentially based on the fact that neither believed Holyrood was a suitable site. The zealotry of Donald Gorrie and Margo MacDonald ensured that the issue was never far from the public eye.

By the beginning of 2000, reports began to appear suggesting that the costs had taken a further dramatic leap. Given that the original budget of £50 million had been for a building of 17,000 square metres and that the required area was now up to 29,000 square metres, it was hardly surprising that projected costs had also risen. The increase in size was largely due to the demands of the main parties for additional office space for support staff, but it was claimed that projected costs were now in excess of £200 million and that building work was behind schedule and 'in chaos'. This culminated in the Presiding Officer, Sir David Steel, taking the unprecedented step of addressing the Parliament on 24 February.

In his statement, Steel did little to quell the growing fears among MSPs, not least those in the Labour ranks, by saying, 'Unfortunately, the information on costs and timescales which are currently available do not allow for the Corporate Body to provide the Parliament with sufficiently robust information. In that context, we have commissioned an assessment of the current position of the project, which will be undertaken by independent experts.' This may have bought some time for the Corporate Body, but by then it was clear that they were not in control of the situation; they could hardly claim to be, once their chair had admitted that they were unable to report to the Parliament.

By this time, despite the fact that the Executive had relinquished control over the project following the debate in June 1999, the opposition parties used every opportunity to make political capital out of the latest revelations. Certainly they were serious, and the future of the project at that time did appear to be in some doubt, but what could not be ignored was the fact that the decision eight months earlier had been made by the Parliament as a whole. Simply being on the minority side in the vote could not absolve the nationalists and Tories of their share of any blame, particularly as each had a member on the Corporate Body and thus could not claim to have been entirely unaware of the project's progress. This they were unwilling to acknowledge, sensing that the whole argument was back in the melting pot and that there was likely to be another opportunity to debate and vote on the continuation of the project.

Unsurprisingly, Margo MacDonald seized on this, saying with more than a hint of wishful thinking, 'I think the project may be doomed. There seems no sense in pouring good money after bad to try to accommodate the project which has been so drastically changed from the original design concepts,' (*The Scotsman*, 25 February 2000). The Presiding Officer hardly helped to douse these flames when, asked about the possibility of scrapping the Holyrood site, he replied, 'That cannot be ruled out,' (*The Herald*, 28 February 2000).

As the review of the project got underway, headed by John Spencely, a former president of the Royal Incorporation of Architects in Scotland, two of the Parliament's committees also decided to instigate inquiries. The Audit committee invited Robert Black, the Auditor General for Scotland, to examine its 'economy, efficiency and effectiveness'. Black, the first holder of the post when it was established in April 2000, is regarded as the Parliament's watchdog for ensuring propriety and value for money in the use of public funds. His report was due to be received by the Audit committee in September 2000. Meanwhile the Finance committee had decided to look ahead, appointing one of its members, Ken Macintosh, as a reporter with a view to establishing the possible impact on future Scottish Executive spending, should the increasing costs of the project need to be met from existing budgets.

Prior to the Spencely report being published, the SNP attempted to maximise the pressure on the Executive, and Alex Salmond was the first to refer to the project as 'Donald's Dome'. Nonetheless, Labour MSPs were surprised when the First Minister's press spokesperson, David Whitton, conceded that, since the term had become common currency beyond political circles, 'That makes it our business,' (*The Herald*, 3 March 2000). This ran counter to the position being stated to SPLP members, who were encouraged to stress – correctly – that the project was not the responsibility of the Executive, but of the Corporate Body. What might happen as a result of the Spencely report remained to be seen, but it was not the Executive's problem. Yet.

Salmond made strenuous attempts to accuse Dewar of a cover-up over the costs of the project in respect of the period prior to the Parliament's inauguration. These failed to stick, and Dewar showed his exasperation at the developing political opportunism, saying, 'There is a danger that what should be a rational and sensible debate about how to get this great project on track . . . has been turned into some kind of witch-hunt. I fear there is a great deal of politics in this and it isn't the way to approach it,' (*The Herald*, 29 March 2000). The following day, writing in the same newspaper, Murray Ritchie confirmed this view: 'The issue is now less to do with the Scottish Parliament's future home than with a naked party political fight.'

That was the day the Spencely report was published and a briefing was held for MSPs. I was not alone in being struck by Spencely's reluctance to embellish, or even explain, aspects of his report, his responses being curt to the point of rudeness. Even those of us who had little sympathy with Margo MacDonald's tunnel vision on Holyrood appreciated her attempt, having failed to elicit information by conventional means, to do so in a light-hearted manner. Not so the stone-faced Mr Spencely, who retorted: 'You may think this is an issue for levity, Mrs MacDonald; I do not.'

Spencely's principal conclusion was that, 'Should the Parliament decide to proceed with the Holyrood project, it can be completed to latest design . . . and delivered within a total budget of £195 million. The design and construction teams have advised that the building can be completed, fitted and commissioned by the end of 2002.' The bad news was that this meant savings, which confirmed that the rumoured figure of £230 million had been correct, but the good news was that the commitment made was better than had been anticipated in terms of both cost and timing, making it at least a possibility that the complex could be occupied during the present parliamentary session.

As MSPs prepared to debate the report and decide on Holyrood's future, the SNP and the Tories re-doubled their efforts to taint the First Minister with having misled the Parliament about the actual costs. But the wind was taken out of their sails when the Presiding Officer accepted that, as head of the five-member Corporate Body in charge of the project, he bore full responsibility for the rising costs. 'The buck stops with the corporate body. We are the clients who are elected to carry out this task on behalf of the Parliament,' he told the BBC's *Holyrood* programme on 2 April.

Nor did Sir David attempt to duck his responsibilities when the issue was debated in the chamber on 5 April, leaving his seat in order to speak for the motion which, for the first time, was in his name. It advocated accepting the Spencely report and continuing with the project, although two amendments to it were also on the agenda.

The first had been submitted by that indefatigable duo Gorrie and MacDonald, and urged that the project should be subject to a moratorium, allowing for full costings to be carried out on other possible sites. In moving his amendment, Gorrie said, 'MSPs' loyalty is to this Parliament on this issue, not to any party.' He was both right and wrong. That should have been the case, but the politicisation of the issue had long since decreed otherwise, and this was illustrated as much by those who supported Gorrie as those who did not. In the event, the amendment was defeated by sixty-seven votes to fifty-eight, with all SNP and Tory members in support and all Labour members opposed. Only two of Gorrie's LibDem colleagues, Euan Robson and Mike Rumbles, supported him, which represented a less even split than had been in evidence in the LibDem group when the issue was debated in June 1999. As with Labour members, the LibDems had been left in no doubt as to the necessity of supporting the First Minister, the Executive, and the partnership. This was stressed at our group meeting immediately prior to the debate, which we left with the words of Tom McCabe ringing in our ears: 'It's too close to call. . .'

In fact, this was not an issue on which a whip was necessary for the SPLP. There was obvious concern as to the possible political damage which could be caused both to the First Minister and to the partnership. That apart, the overwhelming view was that Holyrood must go ahead, largely because calling a halt then re-starting elsewhere could end up costing at least as much, as well as delaying the project for a further two or three years. That would do little for the public perception of an issue which had produced more critical media coverage than anything apart from clause 2a. The time had come to end the doubt and drive the project through to conclusion, which is what I stated in my contribution to the debate, in support of the second amendment. That appeared in the name of my parliamentary neighbour, Gordon Jackson, and effectively represented the Executive position. It called for the establishment of what was termed a 'control group' to monitor progress and ensure completion by 2002 and within the budget of £195 million.

After the Gorrie/MacDonald amendment had been lost, Jackson's amendment was accepted by the same margin, with the final vote on Steel's motion, as amended, carried by sixty-eight votes to fifty-six, a more comfortable margin than anyone would have predicted prior to the debate.

On the day of the debate but after it had taken place, it was announced that the Holyrood architect, Enric Miralles, had undergone brain surgery. He never returned to work and died three months later, leaving completion of the project to the remaining three members of the design team, one of whom is his widow,

5 April 2000: Donald Dewar voting during the stormy debate about the Holyrood parliament building (source: The Scotsman)

Benedetta Tagliabuie. Although some questioned whether they could turn Miralles' dream into reality, Andrew MacMillan, *emeritus* professor of history at Glasgow University and a member of the panel that selected the winning design, had no doubts. Together with the other design team members, Michael Duncan and Brian Stewart of Edinburgh firm RMJM, MacMillan believes Tagliabuie will 'finish the job', saying, 'The drawings are 95 per cent complete; it's just the final tweaking to be done,' (*Sunday Times Ecosse*, 9 July 2000).

Whether that proves to be the case, only time will tell, although the Holyrood Progress Group will doubtless do its best to ensure that it is. This was the name given to the 'control group' referred to in Gordon Jackson's amendment, but its formation was delayed amid some controversy and not a little political point-scoring. George Reid, one of the Parliament's Deputy Presiding Officers, comes as close as it is possible to get to that virtually unheard-of political animal: someone liked and respected by MSPs of all parties. He was suggested as the ideal person to chair the group, but in early May the SNP blocked his appointment. Iain Macwhirter called this 'mindless party political sectarianism', explaining his judgement thus: 'Reid had the skill, authority, determination and experience to make a go of the Miralles building. But Alex Salmond said no. The reason? It's Dewar's hole, so why should a Nationalist MSP dig him out of it? Better a failure under Labour than a success under a Nat,' (*Sunday Herald*, 28 May 2000).

At least the Nationalists were prepared to nominate a member of the group, something which the Tories, exhibiting all the political maturity of a primary school playground, have resolutely refused to do. When eventually established, the group comprised three MSPs (Labour's Lewis Macdonald, as convener, LibDem Tavish Scott and Linda Fabiani of the SNP), two senior civil servants (Robert Gordon and John Gibbons from the Scottish Executive) and two professionals (quantity surveyor David Manson and architect Andrew Wright). The group, whose remit includes the rather lofty aim of being 'a source of political liaison on technical, professional and administrative issues relating to the project' met for the first time on 4 July.

Two of the lessons which might be drawn from the Holyrood project experience were suggested by contributors to Hassan and Warhurst's book *The New Scottish Politics*. Political columnist Iain Macwhirter's suggestion was positive: 'If the experience of the project has brought a new fiscal realism into the debate north of the border, and impressed upon Scots the importance of living within your means, then this . . . is surely a good lesson for an infant Parliament to learn,' (p. 22). Design consultant Janice Kirkpatrick's reaction was less so: 'We bickered over the cost of the project rather than understanding its true value. We embarrassingly revealed our amateurism and parochialism by expecting to build our Parliament for less than the price of a shopping mall then rudely berating the architect for not being Scottish, whatever that means in our multi-cultural society,' (p. 31).

I share Kirkpatrick's despair. Why is it that we Scots seem to feel obliged to don a collective hair shirt at times like this? The greetin' and bleatin' which has accompanied each and every phase of the Parliament building is not worthy of the institution. Of course, cost is important and profligacy must be avoided, but no such feelings of guilt or recrimination engulfed the people of Germany over the re-building of the Reichstag in preparation for the return of government to Berlin after an absence of just fifty-five years. Had the same meanness of spirit existed in Edinburgh 200 years ago, it would certainly not have earned the title of 'Athens of the North'. Equally, we should be thankful that Glasgow's municipal representatives had the self-assurance to commission and construct the city chambers a century ago, because it would never even reach the drawing-board today.

Vision, emanating from a feeling of self-worth, is a vital aspect in building a nation's confidence and the Holyrood project has that. But we are not allowed to acknowledge it, for fear of being labelled 'wasteful', or accused of possessing a warped sense of priorities – never mind the jobs or the tourism potential; never mind the national prestige which might put Scotland on the world map; never mind the quality, feel the width.

Special advisers

> *9 November 1999: 'Just what do the special advisers do?' Angus Macleod of the 'Express' asked me today. 'Counter the influence of civil servants, I suppose,' was my response. But only they themselves really know, or care.*

One of the most controversial aspects of modern government is the use of special advisers. Generally attached to cabinet ministers, their role is to provide political advice in a manner which civil servants cannot. Outside the civil service (and often paid more than the civil servants with whom they share the minister's office), they give the appearance of being popular with no-one other than the minister who appointed them. Ministers at Westminster who have moved from one department to another often take their special advisers with them, suggesting they are Jacks and Jills of all trades, who inevitably master none. Special advisers were not a Labour invention, although Tony Blair's government has attracted criticism for appointing a total of seventy-two, an increase of 50 per cent on his predecessor, John Major.

For that reason – allied to the high-profile departures of some special advisers from Whitehall amid suggestions that they were being used to promote their own minister's interests at the expense of others' – First Minister Donald Dewar decided to make his appointments on a different basis. With the exception of his own special advisers, he announced his intention of appointing a centralised team of advisers, known as the Executive Policy Unit, with none attached to a specific cabinet minister. If the intention was to avoid some of the controversy engendered in London, it misfired right from the start.

John Rafferty, a close friend of Dewar's, had played a key role in Labour's Scottish Parliament election campaign, following which he was offered the job of head of the Executive Policy Unit. While considering whether to accept, he had continued to assist Dewar in an unpaid capacity and was still doing so when the first cabinet meeting took place at Bute House, the First Minister's official residence in Edinburgh, on 20 May. As he explains: 'I was in Donald's office and he said, "Right, let's go to cabinet". I went along but it hadn't been confirmed that I was going to take the job. Word got out that I had been there and there was a huge rumpus. My appointment was instantly confirmed and my mind was then made up,' (*Sunday Times Ecosse*, 26 March 2000).

The 'rumpus' occurred because journalists waiting inside Bute House for the press briefing spotted Rafferty – who at the time held no position either in the party or the Executive – leaving the meeting. The announcement later that day that Rafferty was now Dewar's chief of staff could not disguise the fact that the appointment had been handled badly.

John Rafferty, special adviser to Donald Dewar May to December 1999
(source: *Scotland on Sunday*)

John Rafferty had been visible to SPLP members from the day we arrived at Parliament and had been in attendance at our early group meetings. None of us expected other than that he would take up a post within the Policy Unit, although some colleagues questioned his presence at group meetings even when his role had been confirmed. I had known Rafferty for many years, both through our membership of the MSF union and as a leading member of my campaign team during the Glasgow Central by-election in 1989. Cerebral and a constant source of ideas, I respected his opinions, which I had sought on political issues in the past. I regarded his appointment as good news for both the Executive and for the First Minister. He was also held in high regard by many Labour MSPs, particularly following his efforts in the election campaign, a status they would not necessarily confer on every member of the Policy Unit.

If I had been asked to rate the chances of Rafferty providing a safe pair of hands and seeing the four-year Parliamentary term through to its conclusion, I would have advised the questioner to put his or her mortgage on it. That said, the incident which led to his downfall seems to have been the result of the breakdown of the relationship which he was attempting to establish with political journalists. He was unable to disown allegations that he had wrongly briefed journalists that Health Minister Susan Deacon had received death threats as a result of announcing a development of the family-planning programme for girls and young women. Briefing the press was not within his job remit, although his proximity to the First Minister meant he was regarded as an impeccably informed source for a journalist, whether the hack or Rafferty himself initiated the contact. His dealings with the media were said to be a matter of concern to Donald Dewar's press spokesperson David Whitton, although like most members of the SPLP I saw no evidence of it.

Nonetheless, Iain Macwhirter expressed the predominant view among political journalists when he said, 'Rafferty was the agent of his own downfall. He attempted to use the spin techniques of Westminster, such as inviting journalists to speculate about something without the spinner actually uttering the words. [But] there is no Holyrood lobby elite and Rafferty came to grief trying to establish one,' (*Sunday Herald*, 12 December 1999).

Journalists were not alone in resenting some of Rafferty's interventions. Committee conveners were incensed at comments widely believed to have emanated from him following the leaking of the Arbuthnott committee's recommendations in December 1999. The committee – whose report was not welcomed by the Scottish Executive – had the description 'Mickey Mouse' attached to it in a manner which was seen to be a catch-all criticism of the manner in which the committees were operating. The Conveners' Liaison Group discussed this and were inclined to regard it as a back-handed compliment, but there was considerable anger, and Labour conveners, myself included, made our feelings known to ministers.

That did not prevent my personal sadness at John Rafferty's departure, regarding it as a serious loss both to Dewar and the Executive, who might well have drawn on his measured approach and ability to think strategically when the clause 2a debate spiralled out of control in the weeks immediately following his departure. I do not believe self-serving tabloid claims that they secured his head as a result of their largely synthetic outrage at the Deacon episode. It is simply not in Donald Dewar's character to bow to such pressure and the same applies to suggestions that a tough, although thoughtful and well-argued, speech which Rafferty made shortly before his departure about modernising the role of civil servants led to a delegation of mandarins informing the First Minister that this had made his position untenable.

I am more inclined to believe that underlying strains in both the personal and working relationships between Dewar and Rafferty led to the parting of the ways, although the death threats incident may well have constituted a final straw. Rafferty summed it up thus: 'I became the story and when that happens politicians, quite understandably, get very sensitive. Donald and I sat down and appraised the facts and I said that it was apparent that I was becoming increasingly unable to do my job. We reached an agreement that I would go,' (*Sunday Times Ecosse*, 26 March 2000).

Agreement or not, Dewar had clearly decided no other option was available and those who accuse the First Minister of being indecisive cannot cite the Rafferty departure as evidence, his chief of staff and friend of more than twenty years clearing his desk just forty-eight hours after the incident grabbed the headlines.

Rafferty's departure on 9 December, and the manner of it, had a knock-on effect on the Policy Unit, which has never been allowed to develop as originally intended. The aim was to include up to a dozen people in the unit, including secondees, but only four have been appointed (a total of ten special advisers were employed by the Executive in July 2000 at a gross annual cost of around £600,000). Seven weeks after Rafferty's departure, Philip Chalmers resigned as head of strategic communications amid circumstances which were never convincingly explained. Coming at a time when Brian Souter was launching his 'Keep the Clause' campaign, Chalmers' way-going attracted a further round of bad publicity to the Executive and (unfairly) the First Minister. Within the SPLP there was a feeling that it had been brought on the party quite unnecessarily, with some anger expressed at the fact that Chalmers' reported behaviour suggested he had learned nothing from previous events and in failing to do so had paid scant regard to the public perception of the Parliament, far less the Executive.

Neither Rafferty nor Chalmers (who were not part of the Policy Unit) has been replaced and, although Brian Fitzpatrick is regarded as being the unit's most senior member, his *de facto* leading role has never been formalised by Dewar, leaving both men more exposed politically than might otherwise have been the case. The First Minister seems to be in no mood to replenish the unit and may be wary of attracting unwelcome media attention by doing so. In the meantime, the Executive has been getting on with business rather effectively and with no obvious disadvantage as a result.

The Census Bill

> **16 February 2000:** *Lobbied by Kate Maclean today on my views on the Census Bill. It was clear she was in no mood to let the issue drop and will push it to a vote in the SPLP if necessary.*

Two events in the first year illustrate the extent to which, unlike the government at Westminster, the Scottish Executive cannot always guarantee to have its own way on legislative matters. This is not simply because Tony Blair has a majority of 179 in the House of Commons, whereas the partnership has, at most, fifteen at Holyrood. It is also a reflection of the different approach in the Scottish Parliament and within the partnership, one which allows space for differing, perhaps even dissenting, views not just to be expressed but to be considered and, in some cases, taken on board. The Parliament's first year has produced two high-profile examples.

Events

In February 2000 the Census (Scotland) Amendment Bill was introduced by the Justice Minister, Jim Wallace. It was designed to update the legislation providing for censuses, and it was assumed that amendments introduced for England and Wales would apply in Scotland also. However, Wallace announced there would be no question on religion in the Scottish bill; he maintained there were other means of obtaining this information for Scotland and claimed his position had the support of the head of the General Register Office, which has responsibility for undertaking the census in Scotland.

This immediately provoked a clamour for religion to be added so that Scotland could be compared with the other parts of Britain. Labour backbencher Karen Whitefield was energetic in arguing the case, stressing that, as one of the functions of a census is to monitor trends, if such a question was not asked in 2001, then no comparisons could be made with the 2011 figures, should the question be added for that year. The matter was taken up by the Parliament's Equal Opportunities committee, which invited Wallace to justify his decision. Attending the committee meeting on 16 February, the Justice Minister made a spirited attempt to do so, but he was given a torrid time by the committee members who left him in no doubt that they would submit amendments to the Bill if he did not relent. Convener Kate Maclean emphasised her committee's view: 'There is a groundswell of opinion from across the country that we should be doing this. If we are serious about mainstreaming equality that's the kind of information we need on a detailed area-by-area basis,' (*Scotland on Sunday*, 13 February 2000).

Feeling was no less strong within the SPLP, where Angus MacKay unsuccessfully attempted to convince us that the Executive position should be supported. It was made clear that Labour members were minded to support the committee's amendments and that this represented a cross-party view which would carry the day if the matter was put to the vote in the Parliament. Happily, and in recognition of the willingness of the Executive not only to listen but to act on what they are hearing, Wallace finally acknowledged the concerns and the bill was suitably amended in a manner which brought Scotland into line with England and Wales.

If that provided an example of one of the Parliament's committees directing the Executive down a path it had not intended to tread, the second could claim to be a victory for the committee system in its wider sense. More, it was a victory that produced arguably the most enervating two days the Parliament had seen, culminating in a debate which was pure theatre – a real 'whodunnit', right down to the final twist in the tail.

The Warrant Sales Bill

29 June 1999: Asked Gordon Jackson for a QC's opinion on a Member's Bill to ban warrant sales. He thought it should be done but warned that it could become complicated because of its knock-on effects on other legislation.

The Abolition of Poindings and Warrant Sales Bill was the first Member's Bill to be submitted to the Scottish Parliament. It was introduced in September 1999 by the Scottish Socialist Party's sole member, Tommy Sheridan, and initially attracted the signatures of five Labour MSPs, myself among them.

I had originally intended to submit a bill on this subject myself, but was advised that it could prove problematic; the alternative of a ban on fox-hunting was supposed to be more straightforward!

The Scottish Labour Party first adopted a policy of abolishing warrant sales in 1893, the era of Keir Hardie (presumably there were fewer lawyers in the party in those days). Even if the inclination were there, ridding Scotland of this centuries-old system of debt collection through the forced sale of personal property was the kind of legislation for which the House of Commons would never have found the time. Out of place in modern society it may have been, but out of use it was not: in 1998 there had been 23,000 poindings, where sheriff's officers enter homes to identify household goods that can be auctioned off to recover debts. More tellingly, the same year saw 251 warrant sales carried out, not one of which raised enough to cover the debt and 82 per cent of which did not even cover the cost of the action itself.

Sheridan's bill had begun its progress through stage one of the parliamentary bill procedure in November 1999, with Justice and Home Affairs designated as the lead committee. It subsequently went to two other committees, Local Government and Social Inclusion, Housing and the Voluntary Sector. They heard evidence from a wide range of organisations, both for and against the bill. At the end of the process, all three committees endorsed the general principles of the bill, although each also stipulated that some alternative form of ensuring debt collection would be required. The bill then completed its stage one progress on 27 April 2000 with a debate on the report of the committees' considerations. Four days prior to that, the fun started.

Not that the word 'fun' immediately occurred to me when I read in the Sunday newspapers on 23 April that the Executive intended to block the bill, because there were fears it could pave the way for debt repayment becoming optional. This came out of the blue, because there had hitherto been no indication of any such opposition by the Executive and scarcely a mention of the bill at SPLP meetings. The reaction of East Kilbride's Andy Kerr was typical of many Labour members. When we met in the Parliament on 25 April, he was unequivocal. 'Party members won't wear it. I've been telling them in the constituency for months I'm supporting the bill, there's no way I can stand on my head now.'

There was talk of little else throughout the day and into the Wednesday, with a showdown at the weekly SPLP meeting inevitable. Ninety tense minutes of discussion failed to resolve anything, which may have been to some extent a reflection of Donald Dewar's absence (he was having heart tests in hospital). Jackie Baillie spoke for the Executive and urged support for their amendment which would kill the bill stone dead. I happened to be sitting next to ministers Jack McConnell and Henry McLeish. Jack revealed that Jim Wallace was so opposed to the idea of submitting an Executive amendment that he had had to be browbeaten into it at the cabinet meeting the previous day. Henry endorsed this, saying he felt Wallace was opposed to the whole concept of scrapping warrant sales. 'It's the lawyer mentality,' he added disdainfully.

In the exchanges which followed, the point was repeatedly made that Labour members had endorsed the principle of the bill in committee and could not ignore either what they had heard, or how they had voted. I was by no means the only one to warn of the damaging effect of headlines announcing 'Labour defends warrant sales', which would inevitably follow such an outcome. Also, as one of those who had signed the bill on day one, I could not possibly have jumped ship at that stage, even had I wanted to. But I did not want to and there were few contributions in favour of doing so.

The mood of the meeting was one of tension and anger, the latter largely because we had been given no notice of the Executive's intention. Indeed, the decision had been taken by the cabinet just the previous day, which prompted several members to ask why such a possibility had not been flagged up when the bill was going through the committees. There was a clear feeling we were being taken for granted. With several group members more known for their loyalty to the leadership speaking forcibly against voting the bill down, it was quite evident that, had the matter been put to the vote at that meeting, the Executive position would have been lost.

Tom McCabe announced that, for the first time ever, the meeting would be adjourned and reconvened later that afternoon. On our return at 4.00 pm, the air was electric. Still involved in meetings with senior LibDems on the issue, McCabe was unable to be present and Jackie Baillie outlined the plan developed over the intervening two hours in response to the great unease within the group. To cheers, she announced that the Executive would not now submit an amendment, but would support the Sheridan Bill, albeit with the proviso that an amendment would be put forward at stage two, introducing an alternative system of debt recovery. The new system would be complete not less than six months prior to the next election – by November 2002.

26 April 2000, 4.30 pm We waited thirty minutes for Tom McCabe to appear; he confirmed the new position and was roundly congratulated for his efforts. He looked drawn – it had obviously been tough going. I told him 'It's a triumph for practical politics,' and he merely shrugged; but on reflection it was more the result of pressure politics by ordinary SPLP members.

McCabe made it clear the LibDems had been extremely reluctant to go along with the altered position, which explained the protracted negotiations. Ultimately, they had been convinced of the necessity of doing so in order to avoid a damaging defeat for the Executive and the partnership. Although unspoken, the prospect of handing Sheridan a propaganda coup also weighed heavily.

Arriving back at the Parliament chamber just before decision time, I met Brian Taylor, BBC Scotland's political editor. Aware of the SPLP meeting, he asked me what had happened to make the Labour members so animated and when I told him he replied,

'Good God, they've backed off, then.' He asked for some details and then said, 'Can I run with this?', his intention being to use it on that evening's *Reporting Scotland* programme. I assured him he could, as it now constituted the SPLP position.

Back in the Labour members' offices in the Parliament HQ building, the talk was of nothing but the dramatic about-turn during the afternoon and the fact that it had been brought about by the strong will of Labour members. By 5.45 pm, most had either left for home or were about to do so, but a group of four or five of us were still chewing over the day's events when our pagers rang, as they always do, simultaneously. It was a message asking us to contact Tom McCabe's office. Before any of us could do so, Trish Godman rushed into the main office to gasp, 'The deal's fallen through; the LibDems won't wear it.' Everyone was stunned, but when the news was confirmed I realised I would need to contact Brian Taylor to prevent him broadcasting the information which I gave him. I was unsuccessful: with the programme due to begin in less than half an hour, he could not be reached.

The news from Tom McCabe's office was simply that a majority of the LibDem group had rejected the McCabe/Wallace agreement, so the amendment had to be submitted before the deadline of 5.30 pm that day. When I arrived home, there were several calls from Labour colleagues, anxious to talk about what had happened. One was from Janis Hughes who, along with Kate Maclean and Scott Barrie, was ensconced in an Edinburgh restaurant, doing calculations as to how many votes from the Labour group might go against the Executive amendment. Bearing in mind not even a clairvoyant could have any idea how the LibDems would go, I said it would require at least twenty-three Labour votes to save the bill. Janis replied that that many were already assured.

She also told me that she had watched *Reporting Scotland* and Brian Taylor had used the story of the Executive climbdown. I felt rather guilty, because Brian is a man whom I like and respect and he used information from me which was out-of-date by the time it was broadcast. But it was an accurate description of the situation when I gave it to him, and it is a classic example of how quickly things move in and around the Parliament.

The following morning, I was surprised that Taylor did not relate the full story of turn and counter-turn in the *Good Morning Scotland* radio programme. *The Scotsman* also failed to do so, with only *The Herald* carrying it. However, in doing so their Scottish political correspondent, Robbie Dinwoodie, inaccurately characterised it as an Old Labour-New Labour struggle, saying it was being seen as a 'class issue', with the Labour group being 'happy to rebel'. This was a serious mis-reading of the situation, the uniqueness of the anti-Executive stance of the group being that it involved many who were what might be termed 'first-time rebels'. It was certainly a class issue up to a point, but the consistency – and hence credibility – of Labour members was also an important factor.

During the morning, we learned that the SPLP office-bearers were being asked by Tom McCabe and Henry McLeish to try to win support within the group for the revised Executive position. Convener Marilyn Livingstone and her deputies, Scott Barrie and Pauline McNeill, all relayed the message that group members were resolutely holding to the views expressed at the previous day's meetings.

I later spoke with Margaret Curran, one of the deputy Labour whips, who was about to meet with McCabe, McLeish and Duncan McNeil, the other deputy whip, on the same issue. Margaret is not easily fazed, but she was clearly on edge. She asked me how I felt and when I said nothing had changed, she acknowledged that was her position also (we had both heard evidence on the bill in the Social Inclusion committee). As a result, she said she would have to resign from her position as deputy whip. I told her forcibly that she should not; it was not a resigning matter because she was simply supporting the position agreed by the group less than twenty-four hours earlier. If Tom McCabe thought she should go because she could not support the new Executive position, then he would tell her. My estimation was that, given the circumstances, Tom McCabe would not push her; but she should certainly not jump. Although Margaret was told she was expected not just to support the Executive, but to convince others to do so, she made it clear she could not on this occasion and the matter was taken no further.

At the special SPLP meeting Donald Dewar made the case for supporting the Executive position, which included the revelation that the bill could not be amended at stage two because to introduce an alternative system of debt recovery would be outwith its scope. The First Minister is widely respected and usually his contributions at SPLP meetings are heard in silence. On this occasion, and despite his return from hospital, there was audible disbelief at what we were being told. Why had none of this been foreseen? What were the civil servants doing while the bill was being discussed, in considerable detail, in three committees?

> **27 April 2000:** *There was anger in the SPLP, and as Parliament assembled we were told there was to be a special group meeting at lunch-time, the third on the issue in two days. Rumours that Wallace and the LibDems would not agree to vote for the bill fuelled the concerns of those who doubt his ability to fill in during Donald's hospitalisation.*

My own concern reached new heights when Transport and Environment minister Sarah Boyack, who was sitting next to me, asked what the Executive amendment said. 'Don't you know?' I asked incredulously. She clearly did not and I turned round to ask her cabinet colleagues Wendy Alexander and Susan Deacon if they had seen it; they too were in the dark and it transpired that the Executive had not discussed the issue of the amendment at all.

The situation was now verging on the chaotic and the debate on the bill was due to start in just two hours. With one exception, all contributions from backbench SPLP members were opposed to altering the position of the previous day. There was a clear view that the LibDems had to be faced down and the bill supported, whatever that might mean in terms of personal embarrassment for Jim Wallace; 'Hell mend him,' was probably the kindest remark sent in his direction.

No vote was taken at the meeting, because none was necessary. I have never seen such concerted anger at a meeting of the SPLP, nor such determination that those opposing the Executive position were absolutely in the right. Tom McCabe is a pragmatist and he read the signs, saying that Labour's Executive members would use the next hour to 'consider the position'. Nobody leaving the meeting was in any doubt as to what that would mean, although there was no rejoicing. The following day's headlines were already forming in our minds and we were only too aware that they would not make pleasant reading. The overwhelming opinion was that this need not have happened, and would not have happened had proper consultation within the SPLP taken place.

Pauline McNeill echoed the predominant view within the SPLP: '[Executive] people should have anticipated that Labour members were going to vote for the Bill; it would have been illogical for us to do anything else,' (interview, June 2000). A suggestion as to why this did not happen was offered by Duncan McNeil: 'Donald Dewar's illness was a factor in this – he was not at group meetings where he would have seen what was happening. Donald would have sensed the mood of the group,' (interview, June 2000). This view is supported by the fact that the Executive position changed following Dewar's presence at the meeting on 27 April.

In the chamber, the debate had an element of surrealism about it. Jim Wallace opened for the Executive, moving the amendment which had caused such turmoil. Contrary to press reports, Wallace *was* aware before getting to his feet that a decision had been made that it would not be put to the vote at the end of the debate. He had not been aware of this for long, however. Nevertheless, he had to speak for the amendment in order to outline the Executive's concerns over the need for an alternative means of debt collection. There was the further practical consideration that, had he announced the about-turn at the start, the opposition parties would have had a field day, dancing on his – and the Executive's – grave for the remainder of the debate.

As it was, things went from bad to worse, although the debate had started well from Labour's point of view with Johann Lamont presenting a compelling case for ending the existing system. But the Nationalists and Tories were successful in making capital out of the fact that the decision to withdraw the amendment leaked out during the debate. This left Jackie Baillie, closing for the Executive, the unenviable task of 'announcing' a decision of which every member in the chamber was already fully aware. This brought cheers from both the chamber and the gallery and drew the curtain on an episode which had a single redeeming feature: it kept the clause 2a issue off the front pages for a couple of days.

Speaking in the debate, Labour backbencher John McAllion, a co-sponsor of Sheridan's bill, had summed up the view of many of his colleagues: 'Warrant sales and poindings will be rightly, justly and finally abandoned. It is for days like this that I came into Scottish politics. We will have a wiser, more experienced Executive as a result. It was the first big test of the sovereignty of the Scottish Parliament and it has passed resoundingly.'

The bill's stage one was also passed resoundingly, its general principles being backed by seventy-nine votes to fifteen; Executive ministers and most of the LibDem group abstained. Ian Macwhirter called it 'a great parliamentary occasion', which was 'a victory for minority parties; a reaffirmation of Labour's radicalism; and a vindication of the committee system'. But, he added portentously, 'It didn't do a lot for relations between the coalition partners,' (*Sunday Herald*, 30 April 2000).

Macwhirter was correct in his analysis, with both Labour and LibDem MSPs blaming each other's Executive members for the indecision which caused the fiasco. My view was that the episode should act as a salutary lesson to those who believed there should have been no partnership, with Labour instead operating as a minority administration. The Abolition of Poindings and Warrants Sales Bill provided a graphic example of what life would be like under such conditions, with no natural majority and each issue being assessed by the other parties on its merits, and on the political capital to be made out of it. The scope for protracted and very public wrangling would be unlimited.

An hour after the debate, as the heat began to subside, I and some colleagues were attending a Parliamentary reception held by the British Council. We were earnestly attempting to avoid discussing the issue with MSPs of other parties but eventually I was cornered by Tricia Marwick of the SNP. She asked just one question: 'How did you allow yourselves to get into such a mess?' My response was an honest one, 'If I knew, I'd tell you.'

Thankfully, the rift between the partnership parties had no time to develop. In fact, it was remarkably quickly bridged, thanks in no small measure to the earlier than anticipated entry of Donald Dewar to hospital in May. Jim Wallace's gutsy performances in the chamber as acting First Minister inspired a sense of solidarity among many Labour members who might otherwise have harboured resentment at the Justice Minister's ultra-cautious approach on the ending of poindings and warrant sales.

The snappily-titled Cross-Party Parliamentary Working Group on a Replacement Diligence to Poinding and Warrant Sales met for the first time in July 2000. As it settled down to business, the events of late April were already beginning to fade from the picture. That is inevitable but, in terms of the effects which ultimately they will have on Scotland's poorer communities, they should not be underestimated. That aside, the salutary effect on the Executive's relations with its backbench members is among the most significant events of the Parliament's first year.

The Parliament heads west

> **16 May 2000:** *The fifteen-minute walk from home to the Parliament forced me to question my judgement in believing that the new legislature had to be based in the capital. It also reminded me of the European Parliament's monthly decampment from Brussels to Strasbourg, and to wonder how that wasteful farce avoids the sort of criticism we attract.*

Two weeks after the excitement of the Warrant Sales Bill, the Parliament decamped to Glasgow for three weeks. The Church of Scotland, which had found an alternative venue in the capital for its General Assembly in 1999, exercised its right to return for the following year's assembly, so the Parliament was temporarily rendered homeless.

It was a situation which could surely have been avoided, either by convincing the Church that it had an opportunity to take its annual gathering to other parts of Scotland or, if that failed, the Parliament could have concentrated on committee work for the three weeks. The latter solution would have illustrated to sceptics in the media that MSPs did not suffer from idle hands when the chamber was not in session and would have forced them to report the work of the committees. Certainly, such was their workload at the time, the committees would have had no difficulty in filling the additional sessions. And the Parliament would have saved around £500,000 in moving west.

Nevertheless, the appearance of the Parliament in Glasgow did serve two important functions. First, it allowed us to meet outwith Edinburgh, which was good for the Parliament's image. Secondly, it benefitted the local economy of Scotland's biggest city, which responded with excellent civic support and hospitality and an enthusiastic public interest in our business.

It was during our sojourn in the west that one of the most heated, and controversial, debates of the first year took place. The controversy was not simply the issue itself, which concerned whether the US boxer Mike Tyson should have been allowed to come to Scotland for a bout in Glasgow; what provided an added dimension was the fact that the Parliament discussing the matter made it a constitutional issue.

Immigration matters being clearly a reserved issue, the decision as to whether or not Tyson should be granted an entry visa was one for the Home Secretary, Jack Straw. This he did, giving Tyson the green light the day after the acting First Minister, Jim Wallace, had telephoned Straw's deputy minister, Barbara Roche, to inform her that such a decision would be unwelcome both in the Parliament and beyond. There was some embarrassment among Executive ministers that Straw had ignored Wallace's entreaties, but it is possible that the very fact that he made them ruled out Straw taking into account Scottish sensitivities. As a man known to have been at best lukewarm about devolution, Straw probably resented any encroachment by the Scottish Parliament on Westminster responsibilities.

Some, although not all, Scottish Labour MPs resented the Parliament discussing the issue at all. 'Some colleagues said it was "no business of theirs" and "they claim not to have enough time to do their own work, so why try to do ours?" but I believed what the Scottish Parliament did complemented what was being done by myself and others in the House of Commons. The Parliament did not act outwith its powers, it merely expressed its views on an issue of wide concern, which is their right,' said Maria Fyfe MP (interview, August 2000).

Given my belief that devolved and reserved areas should not become blurred, I was initially uneasy about the Parliament becoming embroiled in the issue of whether Tyson should be allowed to enter the UK. But there was a further dimension which clearly did concern our Parliament: it concerned violence against women and our reaction to it. Tyson's jail sentence for rape would have been sufficient to have anyone less prominent denied access, but his total lack of contrition made him even less acceptable. And in a city like Glasgow, where many Asian Scots experience great difficulty in achieving visitors' visas for family members, the decision smacked of double standards at the very least. So, while the decision on admitting Tyson was undeniably Straw's, he failed lamentably in exercising it. If my ability to express such an opinion as an MSP can be questioned, my right to do so as a Scot and a British citizen cannot.

I questioned the visa decision on the grounds of the message which it sent to men who commit violence against women in Scotland; that is why it was appropriate for the matter to be debated in the Scottish Parliament. The motion, on 24 May, was initiated by the SNP who were more than willing to use the issue to draw attention to the limits of the Parliament's powers. That was patently obvious in the debate, despite two of their members, Dorothy Grace Elder and Shona Robison, departing from the script to deliver contributions which drew applause from many Labour members.

But the most powerful and convincing (were it required) contribution came from Labour's Margaret Curran, who said in conclusion: 'I appeal to the Parliament and beyond: do not get lost in constitutional politics. This is not about the powers of the Scottish Parliament; this is about solidarity with women in England and Wales. That is where that argument properly is. We should never believe that we have dealt with the crime of rape. We have begun to tackle violence against women in our society; do not let Mike Tyson deter or undermine that.'

Maureen MacMillan and Jackie Baillie also made powerful speeches from the Labour benches as the agenda was dragged back to the major issue, rather than the matter of a Holyrood-Westminster power struggle. There was never much doubt that, sooner or later, a constitutional tug-of-war would arise, although like most people I imagined it would involve an issue such as the Barnett formula, Trident or broadcasting. A sporting event would have been so far down the list of possibilities as to have been out of sight, yet that was what gave birth to the first such confrontation.

The SNP motion attempted to get the Parliament to challenge Jack Straw's decision through a judicial review. In doing so, they were doomed to fail because any other outcome would have provoked a genuine heavyweight contest of the constitutional variety. Fail they did, but not so the Parliament's women who, across the parties, were the driving force in ensuring the issue was not allowed to pass just because it was one on which the Scottish Parliament could not take a decision. Ian Macwhirter drew this out effectively, saying, 'We all wondered what difference the 40 per cent [sic] female representation in the Scottish Parliament would make. Well, now we know. This issue has been driven not by SNP opportunism, leftist radicalism or discontent at the constitutional settlement but by the sheer revulsion felt by women MSPs at the prospect of a convicted rapist being given privileged access to this country,' (*Sunday Herald*, 21 May 2000).

The Parliament may have lost the war, but it won the battle. The fact that it was a minor victory should not be allowed to detract from the fact that the people of Scotland witnessed their parliamentarians discussing an issue with great passion *because it mattered*. It may seem ironic to highlight the Tyson issue as one which advertises the Parliament and its ability to deal with issues of substance. All of the issues examined in this chapter can lay claim to that description and, with the exception of the last, all have produced or will produce lasting legacies of the Parliament's decisions.

Much of the legislative programme of the first year also comes into that category, with the Adults with Incapacity Act, the Ethical Standards in Public Life Act and the Abolition of Feudal Tenure Act all introducing aspects of law which are distinctively Scottish. Had the newspapers not rushed to judgement, suggesting to their readers that MSPs were more interested in our own expenses, 'awarding' ourselves medals and maximising our 'holidays', then the people of Scotland might have had a rather more positive view of their Parliament in its first year.

However, now that legislation of real substance and importance to the daily lives of Scots are beginning to flow, it is becoming apparent that the overused cliché that devolution is a process not an event may be true. But the success or otherwise of devolution, in the public perception at least, will be measured not as an event, but as a sequence of events.

7 Turf wars

6 October 1999: A discussion over coffee with colleagues Cathie Craigie and Alan Wilson revealed how strong their feelings were against their SNP list opponents. I said that the situation in Glasgow was more relaxed, but Cathie countered, 'Just wait until one of them decides to camp in your constituency.' She was not joking.

Politics has long been characterised by the cult of the personality and clashes of egos. Despite, or perhaps because of, the new electoral system and the much heralded new politics, the early days of Scotland's Parliament illustrated few signs of breaking that mould. Previously, political rivalries tended to occur between parties; since May 1999, they are just as likely to occur within a political party, particularly Labour.

Constituency and list MSPs

The additional member system (AMS) used to elect the Scottish Parliament introduced an entirely new concept into British politics. Previously, life was simple: only the winning candidate got elected. On 6 May 1999, there were no less than thirty-five instances of two of the candidates who contested the same constituency seat securing a place in the Scottish Parliament; there were five cases where three of them did so. This was possible because of the additional members' seats, which account for fifty-six of the total of 129. These were allocated from party lists on the basis of each party's share of the vote within each of the seven regions into which the country had been divided. It was not a system specifically devised for Scotland, having been tried and tested in several countries, most notably Germany and Spain. But it was new, unfamiliar and, particularly for many in the Labour Party, unwelcome.

Initially, it proved at best disconcerting, at worst infuriating, for some candidates who had won their constituency seat, having seen off a vigorous challenge from a particular opponent, to arrive at the Parliament the following week and see them sitting across the chamber. Under the old system, a defeated opponent disappeared until the next election campaign. Now, not only were they still very much 'in your face', they had the status and resources to begin the next election campaign straight away. Or so it seemed.

As I outlined in Chapter 2, that was the main reason for the row during the debate on allowances on 8 June. Despite the fact that the partnership won the vote that day, the issues causing the divide remained unresolved and it was clear to Sir David Steel, the Presiding Officer, that some form of regulation of the relationship between constituency and list MSPs was necessary. The debate had been reported in terms which were damaging, not just for MSPs, but for the Parliament as a whole. With that in mind, Sir David established a small, informal working party to circumscribe relationships not just between the two types of MSP, but between MSPs and MPs, where some tension was also beginning to emerge.

It was known as the Ad Hoc Liaison Group, making it sound like some shadowy organisation set up by MI6. I was one of those invited to participate, largely because of my experience of Westminster. The other members were Deputy Presiding Officer and former MP George Reid, Conservative Party Deputy Leader Annabel Goldie, and the LibDem MP Archy Kirkwood. The Presiding Officer did not himself participate, but nominated Reid to be convener. The group met for the first time on 30 August 1999, assisted by the Clerk of the Parliament, Paul Grice.

Before attending, I had spoken to Tom McCabe and, on the basis that the group would do no more than make recommendations to the Bureau, he was relaxed about my taking part. Although the group contained a member from each of the four main parties, there was no question of any of us representing their views. In my case, that was not difficult as no view had been arrived at; indeed, following the debate on 8 June the matter had not even been raised at the weekly SPLP meeting, although several colleagues had voiced concern about certain activities in their area during the summer recess. But it was clear this was not an issue which would simply fade away and I was pleased to have been invited to assist in resolving it.

The reason for Kirkwood's involvement was to contribute on the Holyrood/Westminster level, but it was decided this should be shelved until our more pressing internal problems had been dealt with. None of us, meeting in the first week following the 1999 summer recess, could have foreseen that the Parliament would not agree a protocol on such relationships until the week prior to the next summer recess, which is an indication of the fraught nature of the issues.

The Ad Hoc Liaison Group met only twice, the second occasion being 15 November, and by that time a storm had blown up in the SPLP. We had produced a draft report which stated, essentially, that all MSPs were to be regarded as equal in rights and status and equal in the eyes of the electorate. It further stated (although this rarely emerged in reports) that the main priority in dealing with constituents' issues was the elector who had raised the issue in the first place, and that ensuring it was dealt with was of greater importance than which MSP did so.

It had been intended that the meeting on 15 November would sign off the proposed protocol, which would then go to the four main parties for them to take forward and, hopefully, agree. However, a leaked copy of the draft had managed to find its way into the hands of *The Scotsman*, which published an extract. This caused a furious reaction among some Labour members and the matter was raised at the SPLP meeting two days later. Although I had never sought to hide it, few of my colleagues were aware, until *The Scotsman* article, of my involvement in the group. Several were less than pleased that I appeared to be contributing to an agreement, on behalf of the party, without reference to them.

This was not the case but, in retrospect, I should have discussed the matter with colleagues at a meeting of the SPLP, to ensure I was fully aware of their concerns. That would not necessarily have brought an earlier resolution of the difficulties, but it would have avoided the impression that some kind of behind-closed-doors plan was being developed. It subsequently emerged that SNP members were no more impressed with the draft and, largely as a result of this, the group was disbanded and the task handed to the Parliamentary Bureau.

As with the dispute over allowances in June 1999, when the issue emerged into the public eye it provided another rod with which the media could beat MSPs and their parties. The *Sunday Herald* provided perhaps the most rational assessment: 'Accusations are hurled of MSPs "poaching" voters and "cherry-picking" local issues. If things go on like this, the whole of Scotland will shortly resemble a primary school playground filled by fractious children scrapping with each other,' (editorial, 28 November 1999).

Nevertheless, a considerable number of SPLP members were in favour of preventing list MSPs from attending meetings called by organisations such as local authorities, health boards and Scottish Homes. Ayrshire appeared to be the place where problems were at their height, with my colleagues Irene Oldfather and Allan Wilson concerned over the activities of two of the SNP's senior list members, Mike Russell and Kay Ullrich. The example was given of Ayrshire and Arran Health Board which, prior to the creation of the Parliament, had been in the habit of inviting to its briefing meetings all four of the MPs whose constituencies formed a part of its area. Now, given that the Board's boundaries did not follow the boundaries of the Parliament's regional constituencies, they invited a total of no less than twenty-two MSPs in order to avoid offending anyone. This was patently ridiculous, but it got worse. The MPs then complained that they had been excluded – quite reasonably, since they no longer had responsibility for health care – and the situation threatened to make the Parliament and its representatives a laughing stock.

Ultimately, sanity prevailed with interim guidance being issued by Sir David Steel suggesting that, where more than one list MSP from a party represented part of a local authority or health board area, only one should be invited to briefings. The guidance also stated that list members had to be seen to be active in more than one constituency to avoid charges of cherry-picking issues in an area which might be politically advantageous for them. It was a common-sense approach, and things calmed down.

This was an example of the mutual mistrust (sometimes disguising fear) that exists on the part of many Labour and SNP members. As candidates are selected for the 2003 elections to the Parliament, it would be surprising if this did not produce a re-emergence of territorial disputes, prominent in the local media.

John Home Robertson believes the problems so far encountered will be overcome eventually. 'The additional member system has produced a blurring of responsibilities between list and constituency MSPs which has not yet been resolved. The protocol won't do it by itself, it will take time and it's as often about personalities and the local ambitions of the list members as anything else,' (interview, July 2000).

The guidance further provided for list MSPs, when taking up an issue as a result of having been approached by a member of the public, to send a courtesy note to the directly-elected MSP for that constituency, informing him or her that the case was being taken up. According to colleagues, the extent to which this is observed is patchy; in my own case, only two of the seven Glasgow list members (Robert Brown and Nicola Sturgeon) keep me informed in this way. Nicola is the only list member who holds surgeries in the Cathcart constituency and I have no difficulty with this.

Having been an MP for more than twenty years, James Douglas Hamilton, the Conservative list member for Lothians, is able to compare the two roles. 'As a list member I have more time to concentrate on specific issues and deal with them in depth. I do follow the protocol by informing the appropriate MSP or MP. Tory MSPs are in a unique position, filling the vacuum left after the 1997 general election, though it's still relatively rare for me to be asked to take up a reserved matter. But when I do, I have no difficulty contacting a Whitehall minister,' (interview, July 2000).

Where squabbles occurred, they were probably an unavoidable feature of the bedding-in process as members, many holding elected office for the first time, came to terms with being a public representative. It seems now to have passed as an issue and it is likely that a system will develop similar to that in Germany and Spain where electors seeking assistance with a problem gravitate to an MSP from the party for which they voted. Constituency MSPs need not see this in any sense as a threat, since they cannot lose votes from people who did not originally vote for them. The floating or non-voter has a wide choice and will more often approach their directly-elected constituency MSP, who is likely to have a built a local profile through general activity and holding surgeries in the constituency.

The protocol (entitled 'Relationships between MSPs: Guidance from the Presiding Officer') was issued by the Parliament's Standards committee as an addition to the Code of Conduct for Members and it was agreed by the Parliament on 6 July 2000. At the same time, it was announced that a further amendment would be published in due course on the working relationships with our Westminster counterparts. Where difficulties have arisen in this regard during the first year, they are often a result of the lack of familiarity with the new system. But it has to be said that among some MPs there is a feeling of resentment at being largely denied the level of media coverage which they enjoyed prior to May 1999.

Testing the bounds of Westminster and Holyrood

> *11 June 1999: At Labour HQ for meeting between Glasgow's MPs and MSPs. Ian Davidson reported that most of his Scottish colleagues did not intend relinquishing an interest in devolved issues if constituents raised them.*

Any rational assessment of the manner in which reportage of political events as they affect Scotland was likely to develop once the Parliament was established would have concluded that Westminster was bound to diminish in importance. Of the subject areas which, in my experience, dominate an MP's caseload, only benefits and immigration/asylum remain within the remit of an MP. An inordinate amount of my time as an MP was taken up in dealing with cases relating to the Child Support Agency or Disability Living Allowance. These issues remain, but they must account for a larger share of an MP's caseload now than previously. Equally, although macro-economic policy, foreign affairs, international development, the armed forces and employment law are all important matters, none generated a great deal of correspondence from constituents requiring action. And they are not issues that the Scottish political media has ever reported to any great extent.

Mind you, it is nonsensical to suggest (as some in the SNP do) that Scottish MPs no longer have a meaningful role in the House of Commons. In terms of the issues on which Westminster continues to legislate for Scotland, it is quite clear that they retain influence over issues which have a major impact on the day-to-day lives of everyone living in Scotland. But that is not the same as suggesting that what they do on a daily basis is always worth reporting; in most cases it is not, and it is unrealistic to expect that it should be. It is this point which, in my view, some MPs fail to grasp. The Scottish Parliament is not just the new kid on the block, it is a new block; and with the old block 400 miles away, it is understandable that most of the attention should be focussed on what is happening in Scotland.

Where difficulties have arisen between MPs and MSPs during the Parliament's first year, it can usually be traced back to a failure to accept that there are well-defined parameters within which both should operate. As a handy guide, all that is required is a glance at the Scotland Act, where devolved and reserved matters are clearly set out. I make no apology for taking a hard line on this. As an MSP, I deal only with matters which fall within the remit of the Scottish Parliament, and I expect MPs to deal only with those which are reserved.

After a year, some patterns have begun to emerge in terms of working relationships between MPs and MSPs, although there is considerable variation. MPs Brian Donohoe and Frank Doran say that their constituency postbag has remained much the same since the Scottish Parliament came into being. Maria Fyfe has experienced a decrease in the volume, although the content has not changed.

Where Doran's caseload has changed, this is mainly as a result of housing being removed from his area of responsibility, although immigration cases have expanded (largely the result of new legislation). He alternates constituents' surgeries with his Holyrood counterpart, Lewis Macdonald, and they deal with each other's responsibilities 'in order to save time. The public don't care who deals with them, they want the issue taken up and dealt with efficiently and effectively,' (interview, July 2000). Doran also writes regularly to Scottish Executive ministers, particularly on health issues, but always keeps Macdonald informed by copying correspondence (the two have separate offices). However, they do operate a strict demarcation line in one respect. 'On policy or campaigning issues, we don't get involved in each other's areas,' explains Doran. 'This means trying to get a minister to change policy over something like a hospital or school closure,' (interview, July 2000).

Donohoe initially adopted the position that anything to do with local government was strictly the responsibility of his MSP colleague, Irene Oldfather. 'But, as we don't have a joint office, I would be turning away people who came to see me and this is not something I'm comfortable with. So now I pick up issues relating to health, housing, education and so on. The constituent is paramount and I don't want them to feel let down by the Labour Party. Irene is quite happy with this arrangement,' (interview, July 2000). Needless to say, he not only corresponds regularly with Scottish Executive ministers, he has even met with them.

A much firmer arrangement operates between Maria Fyfe and Patricia Ferguson in Maryhill. Fyfe believes that her postbag and surgeries have changed little because 'many people see the MSP as yet another option and some think the best thing to do is to bring in every level of elected member! Neither Patricia nor I would send anyone away, but we mainly pass on appropriate cases to each other and our assistants are instructed to direct people when they phone. I would tend to take up, say, a health issue only if it was someone who came to me because I had dealt with them before or where a multi-agency approach was needed, such as a housing case in which housing benefit was involved,' (interview, August 2000).

Interestingly, although all three MPs do, to varying degrees, deal with issues which are no longer the responsibility of Westminster, they have not received local publicity for them in the way that they would have done prior to the establishment of the Scottish Parliament. This is because they do not issue press releases on devolved matters, which amounts to tacit acceptance that in progressing such issues they are operating outwith their own territory. It will be interesting to observe how this aspect of the MP/MSP relationship develops over the remainder of this four-year term.

Still retaining his seat at Westminster, MSP Malcolm Chisholm is not yet in a position where he has to draw a line between issues brought to him; but he is in no doubt how he will adapt when he ceases to be an MP: 'I will pass on constituency issues on reserved matters to the MP and I will expect him to reciprocate as a sensible working arrangement,' (interview, September 2000). Perhaps it has something to do with having experience as an MP, as Malcolm and I seem to have a harder position on the respective responsibilities than most MSPs.

In Cathcart, when I receive a letter from a constituent asking for assistance with a benefits matter, I pass it to John Maxton MP. When John receives one relating to housing, he refers it to me. On each occasion, the constituent receives a covering letter explaining why this is being done and the matter is then progressed appropriately. The same applies at surgeries, where we take details of each other's cases; nobody is turned away. I fully accept that the interests of constituents must always be prioritised and their cases taken up as quickly as possible, but MPs and MSPs have distinct responsibilities which are not yet widely understood, and blurring them does not help achieve this. In my experience, the majority of constituents *do* know where to direct their complaint, but if MPs and MSPs themselves affect not to know who does what, is it any surprise that some electors have doubts?

Nor do I make exceptions in the case of list MSPs. My Labour list colleagues have made it plain that they disagree on this issue and argue that, in order to maintain a high profile against the local directly elected MSPs, they are not willing to turn away cases which are directed to them, whether they involve reserved matters or not. My colleague, Maureen Macmillan, describes her position thus: 'Being a list member for the Highlands and Islands, I feel I am treated as an exotic creature. I enjoy the overview of how industries operate throughout the region without being constrained by boundaries. The downside is that I am responsible for such a vast area, which means work hours that are not family-friendly. I do have fairly close contact with other Labour list MSPs and we try to share out the work and divide issues into our areas of expertise,' (interview, June 2000).

List members are also reluctant to refer cases to an MP if that person represents a different party. Kenny Gibson, an SNP list member for Glasgow, sees his job as 'just covering a wider area than a constituency member. I inform them if I take up an issue which is constituency-wide, for instance planning or a school closure, but not if it's personal, which I treat in confidence. I deal with reserved matters, especially where – as is usually the case – the person has been to an MP first but has not got it resolved.'

Their views are shared by many list MSPs from other parties but I believe they are treading on dangerous ground here; there has to be consistency on this matter, and if we fail to build that in the

Parliament's initial session, we may subsequently find it impossible. The fact that in the Highlands and Islands (where all three Labour list members are based) there are few Labour MPs is not the point; as MSPs we were elected to deal with devolved matters and I believe we should restrict ourselves to that. If we don't, then we have no grounds to challenge an MP who decides to improve her or his political profile by taking up, say, a controversial health issue. If this is allowed to develop, it can only lead to confusion, with those suffering being the people whom we were *all* elected to represent.

There are of course some grey areas. Two examples which I encountered concerned a claim for compensation for Gulf War syndrome and the issue of asylum seekers coming to Glasgow. In the case of the former, was it a health issue or a defence issue? In fact, it was both and was dealt with accordingly. Although asylum and immigration policy is a matter for Westminster, I regard asylum-seekers or refugees as constituents while they are accommodated within Cathcart and assist them accordingly. This can involve dealing with Glasgow City Council on matters of housing, education or social services, or perhaps with the NHS. Such cross-cutting issues do arise, but they are few and far between and can be resolved with the application of common sense, providing there exists the will to do so.

Ministers in both legislatures have an important role to play in the who-does-what issue. I was amazed to learn that, in the Scottish Parliament's first year, while Executive ministers had received 6,900 letters from MSPs, they had also received around 2,500 from MPs. That such a flood had emanated from members of another legislature was in itself an eye-opener; but the fact that Executive ministers had responded was even more so. I had neither the time nor the inclination to enquire of Whitehall departments the extent to which correspondence from MSPs burdened their in-trays, but I could find no evidence, other than from my list colleagues, of significant traffic in the opposite direction.

All of this could be seen as unnecessarily heightening tension between MPs and MSPs and inviting media speculation on 'turf wars'. That need not, and should not, be the case. The political landscape of Scotland changed dramatically on 6 May 1999 and all that is required is for this to be given due recognition by elected members – and ministers – at both Holyrood and Westminster.

Characteristically, columnist Ruth Wishart got to the heart of this issue and offered MPs some home truths. 'Some of these changes carry a very heavy price for the participants. You can hide in Westminster a damn sight easier than in Holyrood. Electors and organisations are able to have much easier access to their elected representatives. The press have more time and fewer targets. Very healthy and very scary,' (*The Herald*, 10 February 2000).

What of the Januses, those two-headed monsters who hold what is termed a dual mandate at Holyrood and Westminster? (I do not include David Steel, James Douglas Hamilton or myself in this category, since membership of the House of Lords cannot be described as a 'mandate'). There are fifteen MSPs who are also MPs and they have few opportunities of attending the House of Commons other than when the Scottish Parliament is in recess.

Perhaps surprisingly, one of those who does so most often is also a Scottish Executive minister. 'I have a dual mandate which will last until the next election and I take it seriously,' says Sam Galbraith. 'I see it as important that I continue to operate as an MP and I go to Westminster when ministerial duties allow. I also speak whenever I can – although I restrict my contributions to reserved matters – and I have spoken on issues such as rural post offices and air traffic control services recently,' (interview, June 2000).

Malcolm Chisholm has no doubt which of the two mandates is the most onerous, despite having his home in Edinburgh. 'I am definitely under more pressure as an MSP. There is more committee work, backbenchers are more involved in the Parliament than at Westminster, and then there's the proximity of my constituency, which means meetings during the week. These are things which my Westminster colleagues have a hard time understanding,' (interview, September 2000).

Of the others, all yearn for an early general election, which will enable them to concentrate fully on the Scottish Parliament. Asked for comparisons between the two legislatures Donald Gorrie was the most succinct: 'Are you serious? Night and day,' (and he was not just referring to the respective hours which they keep).

Although Gorrie's comment might seem odd, comparing the job of being an MP with that of being an MSP is not easy, because the two really are quite different. The working week of an MP is certainly longer in terms of hours spent in the Parliament, although in general it is much less intensive. The Scottish Parliament only operates from Tuesday to Thursday, but on these days there is rarely a minute of free time with committees, the Parliament itself and further meetings with outside groups or constituents leaving little time even to return phone calls. On the other hand, business is over by 5.30 pm each day.

Another difference concerns the committees. Most backbench MSPs are on two, unlike in the House of Commons where being a member of one select committee is the norm, although some are not on any. Certainly, standing committees at Westminster can take up a considerable amount of an MP's time, although despite the name they are *ad hoc* in nature and typically last for four to six weeks, depending on the size and complexity of the Bill which they are considering.

One of the greatest bugbears of an MP is the amount of time in the evenings, and often late into the night, when you are required to be in the House of Commons. Even an early night at the Commons from Monday to Wednesday finishes five hours later than in the Scottish Parliament. Mind you, since making the transition from one to the another, I can better appreciate the value of those evenings, until 10.00 pm at least. They provide an opportunity to prepare for committee meetings, to draft speeches or to tackle some constituency correspondence. Time for these activities is rarely available in Edinburgh from Tuesday to Thursday, which is a major reason why many MSPs within daily travelling distance now spend at least one night a week in the capital.

The concept of a family-friendly parliament was an integral feature of making the legislature more attractive to people with school-age children. However, while the motive was admirable, the practice presents real problems for many MSPs, particularly women, who have to spend up to two hours a day (each way) in transit. Often, this is unproductive time and can lead to frustration. For obvious reasons, this is something which Scottish MPs are spared, although equally they are denied the opportunity of seeing partners and children during the week when Parliament is in session.

As is largely the case with MPs, it was the intention that Mondays and Fridays should be kept as constituency days for MSPs, when correspondence can be dealt with, surgeries held, visits made to local organisations and meetings arranged with individual constituents. Generally, that is how it works out, although there is a tendency for Parliament committees to encroach into Mondays, especially when meeting outside Edinburgh. Although understandable, it adds considerably to the workload, because it simply means that the work which would have been undertaken on the Monday is shifted to another day, usually to the weekend, which encroaches on family time ...

Of course, being in London from Monday afternoon until Thursday evening excuses MPs from constituency activities during that period. Not so MSPs, who are often expected to attend events on weekday evenings (and occasionally during the day), because groups are aware that they are available. That forms part of the greater accessibility of the Scottish Parliament but it has an obvious impact on more directly Parliament-related activities.

So, while adhering to my caveat that direct comparisons are not too meaningful, my experience is that being an MSP is both more demanding in terms of time and energy than being an MP, and more rewarding. There is a much greater sense of achievement, partly because legislation moves so much more swiftly through the Scottish Parliament, and there is the feeling that in terms of the committee input, individual members can and do exert influence in shaping a bill. Also, access to ministers is simple and often effective in terms of outcomes. I was an MP only in opposition, but when I wanted a meeting with a cabinet minister, it was not uncommon to be shunted on to his or her junior. As an MSP, getting a cabinet minister to meet, officially as well as on an *ad hoc* basis, is much more straightforward and often successful in terms of the outcome. The civil servants hate informal meetings because they occur outside their territory but, depending on the minister, these can often be an extremely effective use of time.

> **8 September 1999:** *Interesting and illuminating discussion over lunch with the Minister of Finance from the South African province of KwaZulu-Natal. The Parliament has to develop links with sister parliaments, but such contacts could be used by the SNP to argue for the Parliament to debate reserved issues.*

Unsurprisingly, the SNP do not miss opportunities to highlight the limitations of the Scottish Parliament's powers and to call for them to be extended. The classic example is their long-running demand that broadcasting be included in the devolved powers. That battle was fought and lost when the legislation was going through the Houses of Parliament, but the subject is regularly revisited by the nationalists. The issue of the so-called *Scottish Six*, an entirely separate BBC Scotland early evening news programme, has become the canvas on which the wider issue of broadcasting is painted.

This issue excites much less interest among MSPs than is the case with our Westminster counterparts. The latter are said to fear that a teatime news programme without any London input could move Westminster yet further from the minds of Scots at a time when levels of coverage are already much diminished. This seems to me to ignore the point of an opt-out production, which would be to incorporate news, events and sport from outwith Scotland, including London and events in the House of Commons. Newsworthy political events from Westminster would be reported from a Scottish perspective, rather than from that of London. BBC Radio Scotland successfully performs that role on a daily basis with its flagship news and current affairs programme *Good Morning Scotland*. That has done no damage to relations with the rest of the UK or Scotland's place within it, so why should an evening equivalent on TV? This issue has been greatly over-hyped; I hope common sense prevails and we get a *Scottish Six* soon. It would not require an amendment to the Scotland Act, and broadcasting powers could quite safely remain at Westminster.

The issues which the SNP utilise in attempting to widen the Parliament's remit can be large or small. The furore over the entry visa granted to the boxer Mike Tyson was a major one, while SNP Transport spokesman, Kenny Macaskill, railed against the Executive when he was denied the right to ask a written question on vehicle registration plates. Appearing – not by accident, I am sure – to miss the whole point of devolution, Macaskill claimed the Executive was 'trying to stop MSPs asking awkward questions on the grounds they might involve Westminster responsibility. This is an attempt to reduce the authority of the Parliament and turn it into a regional council,' (*The Herald*, 7 April 2000).

Another method of attempting to broaden the Parliament's horizons concerns discussion in the chamber on reserved issues.

This is marshy ground for Labour MSPs, committed as we are to making the present devolution settlement work. Nevertheless, the Parliament does have the right to discuss and debate any matter, devolved or not. This means that whether the UK should join the euro or what form a revised housing benefit system might take are legitimate subjects for discussion – but not legislation – by the Parliament, even though both impact greatly on areas for which we do have legislative responsibility.

That begs the question: if the Parliament is already over-burdened with work in the chamber and the committees (which is certainly the case), how can it be justifiable to devote scarce time to matters which we cannot affect? The simple answer is that it cannot be justified, but things are rarely that simple. Subjects do not always fit neatly under 'devolved' or 'reserved' headings. For example, in November 1999 the Parliament debated a motion under the title 'Working Together in Europe'; foreign affairs is, of course, reserved but individual issues arising from them are devolved, such as agriculture and fisheries.

In fact, in the year from 1 July 1999, there were fifteen debates in the main chamber on matters outwith the devolved agenda. Of these, nine were initiated by the Scottish Executive and six by the SNP (Scottish Parliament Information Centre, August 2000). They involved subjects as varied as the millennium date change, the plight of pensioners, the British-Irish Council and the role of post offices. The Tyson issue was the most prominent, but there was also a high-quality debate on ending the religious discrimination of the Act of Settlement. This included one of the most impassioned speeches of the first year, improbably from the urbane Lord James Douglas Hamilton, the former Tory Scottish Office minister. During the same period, a total of eighteen debates on reserved matters took place under Members' Business, the equivalent of an adjournment debate in the House of Commons.

The SNP's Kenny Gibson draws an analogy with local government. 'When I was a member of Glasgow City Council, I recall discussing issues like tuition fees, Chechyna, and nuclear weapons, none of which we had any ability to influence. If councils can discuss these things, it would look odd if the Scottish Parliament couldn't,' (interview, August 2000).

We do have the right to discuss any topic under the sun and it would be wrong were we to avoid doing so. It will be on the extent to which consideration of such subjects is exercised that the Parliament's stature will be judged. But the main focus has to be those subject areas which we can influence. I am not advocating that discussion should be closed down, but the Parliament must not be seen just as a debating chamber; wherever possible there must be a political outcome to its deliberations.

Scots, both by nature and practice, are outward-looking and indeed internationalist. The Parliament has affiliated to the Commonwealth Parliamentary Association and I have participated in welcoming groups from KwaZulu-Natal, New South Wales and Quebec. At the same time, cross-party groups have been established covering areas such as refugees and asylum seekers, Cuba and international development.

I myself was a founder-member of the last-named, the inaugural meeting of which was addressed by the Department for International Development Minister George Foulkes. On that occasion, MSPs were outnumbered by representatives of a wide range of aid and charity organisations based in Scotland, and this kind of event forms a valuable additional means of the people of Scotland linking with their Parliament. I would not, however, expect time to be made available in the Parliament chamber for a debate – a Member's debate excepted – on, say, humanitarian relief for those suffering the effects of earthquake, floods or civil war. But it is unrealistic to expect MSPs not to have a view on such issues and not to want to discuss them in the presence of experts; that is the function of cross-party groups.

If we in the Scottish Parliament are to act appropriately, then we have a right to expect that it should be a two-way process. The resurrection of the Scottish Grand Committee in March 2000 by the Secretary of State for Scotland, John Reid, was not a positive move in this direction. I had the misfortune to attend many meetings of that toothless tiger during my time at Westminster. It may have had some legitimacy when it was established in 1894 to debate, and vote on, exclusively Scottish bills, but that role had long since been stripped from a body which was universally derided during my time at Westminster (although that did not stop the Scottish whip from making it clear we were expected to attend).

When Michael Forsyth was Scottish Secretary, he opportunistically took the committee on tour round the country, stopping off at places well off the beaten track, such as Montrose and Selkirk, all in a vain attempt to convince Scotland the Tories cared about it. It was something of a surprise that it continued after he was succeeded by Donald Dewar in 1997, but when the committee met in March 1999, symbolically in New Parliament House in Edinburgh, the clear implication from Dewar was that we had witnessed its swan-song.

Scotland's MPs have a perfect right to meet whenever they see fit to discuss reserved issues and, if they believe the Scottish Grand Committee is an appropriate vehicle, then that is a matter for them. But these meetings should be seen as part of the Westminster Parliament and as such should be held there. For the committee to meet in Scotland, as it did in July 2000 (not by coincidence, I suspect, in the first week of the Scottish Parliament's recess), is to my mind an error of judgement and a matter of concern.

Many Labour MSPs were unhappy, feeling this played into the hands of the SNP in two ways. First, it left John Reid open to attack on the 'turf war' front, which both he and Donald Dewar had worked assiduously to defuse. Second, it seemed to highlight the fact that Labour MPs were anxious to be seen to be doing something, anything, having been out of the limelight for too long. On both counts, the SNP were wrong, but the view among some of the SPLP was that the nationalists were well able to manufacture their own bullets, without the Labour Party handing them any extra ones.

The media in Scotland are obsessed with the perceived conflict between Donald Dewar and John Reid. This sub-divides into whether Downing Street seeks to maintain a hand on the First Minister's shoulder on 'difficult' issues and whether the Scottish Executive attempts to keep Whitehall in general and Dover House (the Scotland Office's London base) in particular at arm's length.

I have to say this is not an issue which greatly exercises Labour MSPs, although it does our counterparts in the SNP and, to a lesser extent the Tories and some Liberal Democrats. In my view, the evidence is that, while Whitehall ministers have on occasion been concerned about the knock-on effect in England and Wales of certain legislative proposals from the Scottish Parliament, this has not resulted in attempts to impose the will of the UK government. If it did, it did not succeed, as examination of the two most prominent examples reveals.

The Cubie report proposed a solution to the tuition fees issue (see Chapter 6) which meant that students from low-income families in England and Wales would be denied the support given to their equivalents in Scotland. Education Minister David Blunkett's concern was not disguised, but ultimately his response was to find additional funds for a safety-net for those south of the border. Catherine Macleod, *The Herald*'s political editor who is based at Westminster, believes the issue was a defining one in the relationship between London and Edinburgh and illustrated the UK government's understanding of the political realities. 'The Cubie proposals . . . had the potential to generate real division between Westminster and Scotland as they spelt the end of a uniform system of funding throughout the UK. At the end of the day, the well-being of the settled government of Scotland took precedence over the political will of the policy's critics,' (Hassan and Warhurst, p. 118).

Macleod sees this pragmatism as being symbolic of Tony Blair's approach to the Scottish Parliament. 'For the Prime Minister, devolution is a box ticked – Westminster has delivered it – the Scottish politicians have to get on and make it work. It is almost as simple as that,' (Hassan and Warhurst, p. 119).

On the planned repeal of clause 2a, it seems this caused little concern in Whitehall when Wendy Alexander made the announcement, although the situation changed once it became clear that it was mushrooming into a major issue in Scotland. It was reported that the Prime Minister himself had spoken to Alexander and asked her to pull back; whether or not he did, she patently did not. On the other hand, there can be no doubt that the guidelines issued by David Blunkett associated with the repeal of similar legislation in England and Wales, containing explicit references to marriage, had an effect on the eventual form of the guidance which was added to the Scottish version.

One occasion when friction occurred between Westminster and Holyrood did not involve allegations of control being exerted; in fact, quite the opposite. On 25 May 2000, during the Parliament's sojourn in Glasgow, it emerged that the Rural Affairs Minister, Ross Finnie, had been kept in the dark over genetically-modified contaminated seed being sold to farmers. The Ministry of Agriculture,

Fisheries and Food (MAFF) told Finnie on 15 May that the seed had been supplied to farmers, yet MAFF themselves had learned of this on 17 April. Finnie, who has impressed many Labour MSPs with a confident grasp of his brief, forestalled any criticism from the opposition parties, telling the Parliament he was 'annoyed that there was a total lack of communication between MAFF and ourselves' as a result of which he would be 'writing to them to make it clear that this is unacceptable'. His no-nonsense stance was rewarded shortly afterwards when he received a fulsome public apology from the Agriculture Minister, Nick Brown.

There was some suggestion that Brown's (or at least his department's) failure to keep Finnie informed had something to do with the fact that both the Rural Affairs minister and the acting First Minister were LibDems. BBC political editor Brian Taylor believed the reason was more basic: 'I think it's more a case of Westminster snubbing the Parliament rather than the party,' (BBC *Holyrood*, 28 May 2000).

London calling

14 March 2000: *Evidence at the Finance committee today from Gill Noble of the Treasury. It provided an insight we could not have got any other way and seemed to fit well with the ethos of joint ministerial committees recently established between Holyrood and Westminster.*

Despite criticism from MSPs, including some Labour members, the system of joint ministerial committees does not signify to me attempts at 'control' from London. This has been argued by certain journalists, although few have seen the ghosts which appear in front of Murray Ritchie: 'Quite apart from [Gordon] Brown's own interest in keeping a firm grip on his power base in Scotland, this represents an anxiety in Westminster that Scotland must not be allowed to slip further, possibly beyond recall, from the grip of central government,' (*Scotland Reclaimed*, p. 217). This does tend to ignore the accepted fact that Gordon Brown has been, over many years, one of the staunchest advocates of devolution and is as determined as any Scot that it should succeed.

Provision for the establishment of joint ministerial committees was included in the memorandum of understanding between the

UK government and the executives of the Scottish Parliament and the Northern Irish and Welsh assemblies; five had been set up by the summer of 2000. Ritchie's Westminster-based colleague Catherine Macleod welcomed the innovation as it related to Scotland, describing it as 'fostering familiarity and an element of trust between ministers in every department in Edinburgh and London [which] will encourage co-operation, diminishing the need for problem-solving,' (Hassan and Warhurst, p. 117).

SNP opposition has been voiced, but this was tempered by Andrew Wilson: 'I am not against the idea in principle, but all the power seems to lie on the Westminster side. The emphasis so far has tended to be on the short-term PR benefits, an excuse for UK ministers to visit Scotland. The real test of the value of the committees would come either when there was a disagreement between the two administrations or – even more so – if there were different parties in power in Edinburgh and London,' (interview, September 2000).

Labour assistant whip Duncan McNeil does see value in the committees. 'Co-operation is important; the success of the devolution process depends on joint working on major issues like drugs,' (interview, June 2000). There are indeed a number of areas where joined-up government is necessary to ensure that the best possible outcomes are achieved on issues such as poverty, health and unemployment which span the two legislatures. This has been recognised by some Scottish Parliament committees calling for UK ministers and civil servants to come before them to give evidence. When these requests have been declined, the fiercest criticism has, paradoxically, come from the SNP.

Of course, these committees run wider than Westminster and Holyrood. There have been occasions on which ministers from the Northern Irish and Welsh Assemblies, as well as the Scottish Parliament, have met with UK ministers. One of these famously took place in June 2000 at 10 Downing Street when Tony Blair invited the health ministers from all three to meet with him and the Secretary of State for Health, Alan Milburn. What made the news that day was not the fact that the meeting took place but that the Northern Irish Assembly's representative was Sinn Fein's Barbre de Bruin. This was the clearest possible sign that devolution was about the future and not the past, and that 'can do' had to be its maxim.

Where now for the Scottish Secretary?

One of the major questions concerning Holyrood/Westminster relations is the future of the post of Secretary of State for Scotland. Since the Scottish Parliament came into being, it has been generally acknowledged – inside as well as outside the country – that Scotland's claim to its own seat at the cabinet table was barely sustainable, certainly in the long term. Following John Reid's appointment as the new Secretary of State, less than two weeks after the elections for the Scottish Parliament, he made it clear why the post should continue: 'I want to dispel any notion that the Scottish Office will not deal with significant issues. Things like education are extremely important but so is taxation, so are pensions, so are benefits – bread and butter issues to be dealt with at UK level. We now have the opportunity not only to decide our affairs locally, distinctly Scottish things, but also at British level,' (*Daily Record*, 20 May 1999).

> *27 September 1999: The* Observer's *'cash for access' allegations broke on the first day of the annual conference. It was bizarre to see Dewar and Reid toe-to-toe in an argument after the Scottish reception.*

Throughout the first year there have been occasions when the role of the Secretary of State and that of the First Minister have been placed in conflict. The most obvious was during the so-called 'Lobbygate' affair in September/October 1999, in which Reid's son, Kevin, was embroiled. Donald Dewar made it clear, without ever stating explicitly, that whether or not the issue was referred to the Standards committee was a matter for the committee itself and thus one on which he, as First Minister, should be commenting. The implication was that, despite his obvious concern over the affair, it did not fall within John Reid's remit.

That was the only occasion on which there has been any manifestation of a 'turf war' between the two men, who despite being like chalk and cheese, clearly have a good working relationship. This was at its clearest during the campaign to save the Kvaerner shipyard in Govan in autumn 1999. Although inward investment is a Scottish Parliament responsibility, the need to smooth the path to BAe Systems' takeover required a UK government input. Donald Dewar and Enterprise minister Henry McLeish played important roles, but once the takeover was completed, John Reid had the *gravitas* (not to mention his experience as a former junior Defence minister) to stress the importance of UK government military orders to the yard's future and to ensure that the necessity of retaining shipbuilding on the Clyde was driven home.

Although there was the potential for conflict, the importance of the issue meant that neither the SNP (who in different circumstances might well have sought to gain political advantage) nor the Scottish media attempted to bring it out, and both Reid and Dewar emphasised the need for the holders of Scotland's two major political offices to complement each other on the crucial questions of protecting manufacturing jobs.

So what future has the post of Secretary of State for Scotland? It has been widely suggested that, with devolution now in place in Northern Ireland, London and Wales as well as Scotland, there is a need for a minister of cabinet rank with the power to oversee all four administrations. Given that the three assemblies have little in common with each other, far less with the Scottish Parliament, I am not convinced that such a role has a great deal of relevance. However, if, as I hope will be the case, English devolution in the form of regional assemblies is to follow London, then it would require someone with a seat at the cabinet table to drive it. On the other hand, it could be argued that this would be an English responsibility and would not have much relevance (with the possible exception of London) to developments elsewhere in the UK.

In any case, there are few signs that Tony Blair or his senior cabinet colleagues yet share an enthusiasm for extending devolution and they may prefer that the constitutional developments of the past year are allowed time to settle down. In that context, a Minister for Decentralised Government might have a clearer role, although it would be interesting to witness reaction in Scotland should the appointee not be a Scot.

No doubt the existing Secretaries of State for Northern Ireland, Scotland and Wales would each possess the credentials required for an expanded post, although not all would want it. Indeed, the current Welsh Secretary, Paul Murphy, does not want to lose his job, believing there is 'merit in having a special Welsh or a special Scottish voice in the cabinet,' (*The Herald*, 26 May 2000). At present, as with John Reid, his remit includes assisting in the transitional phase between centralised government and devolved power; Murphy does not envisage the need for that role diminishing. In the same article in *The Herald*, speaking of all three secretaries of state, he said (perhaps wistfully), 'If our role is to make the transition smooth, and if our role is to bring the three nations together, and if our role is to represent the partnership between the UK and the devolved administrations, then I hope that will never go away.'

John Reid has been more circumspect on the matter but there is little doubt that he would relish the opportunity of having a lead role in ensuring that the devolution settlement across the UK was a success. It would be surprising if the post which he now occupies is still in existence following the next UK general election, although there will be a clear requirement for a Whitehall minister with direct responsibility for liaising with the Scottish Parliament and its First Minister. The benefits of such a link could be extended were that person's responsibility to include speaking on behalf of the UK Parliament at committees of the Scottish Parliament, perhaps in the company of a senior official from the relevant Whitehall department.

Brief fling or lasting relationship

> **16 December 1999:** *When the partnership was announced, nobody said we had to dance with the LibDems! But last night we went clubbing together, all in the spirit not just of Christmas but of parliamentary solidarity. A bit stiff at first, but drink is a great socialiser.*

One of the many 'firsts' in the Parliament's opening year has been the operation of coalition, or partnership, government. This has meant that Labour MSPs have been working in (relative) harmony with our LibDem counterparts in order to guarantee the majority needed to progress government business.

With the exception of the occasions on which we had encountered them as election opponents, few Labour MSPs had much first-hand knowledge of individual LibDem members. At the Scottish Parliament elections, Labour's Duncan McNeil, in Greenock and Inverclyde, had a LibDem as his main opponent, but he was the only one in that situation (although three LibDems had Labour candidates as their closest rivals). It is neither unfair nor unkind to generalise that, traditionally, Labour Party members have not taken the LibDems too seriously in political terms. That was certainly the prevailing view within the SPLP in the period immediately after the election when, as I outlined in Chapter 1, several group members questioned whether we should be entering into partnership with them at all.

That view was not based on hostility, but on a belief that we should be forming an administration on our own, to some extent because LibDems had no experience of running anything and could therefore cause us problems by nit-picking over issues on a day-to-day basis. In fact, the relationship has worked out remarkably well. Individual Labour members have no difficulty operating in partnership, although the only joint meetings involve the group office-bearers. The SPLP convener, Marilyn Livingstone, suggested inviting the LibDems to our Christmas party and this proved a successful event, allowing us to get to know each other better. It paid dividends in the months which followed in terms of co-operation in the chamber and, on occasion, in our committee work.

However, the event which played the most important part in bringing the two groups together was undoubtedly the unfortunate absence of Donald Dewar for his heart-valve operation. This caused him to miss the last two months of the session prior to the 2000 summer recess and, initially, the thought of Jim Wallace filling in for that length of time caused serious concerns to be raised by some SPLP colleagues. Indeed, there were suggestions that we should insist on Henry McLeish, as Dewar's *de facto* number two, taking his place. That argument carried the basic flaw that the First Minister does not have a number two, *de facto* or otherwise. It was simply that McLeish, having been Devolution Minister and the most senior cabinet member (in terms of experience) after the First Minister, had become established in many people's minds as the party's deputy leader in Scotland.

In any case, Donald Dewar informed the SPLP on the day prior to his entry to hospital in May, 'In my absence, the Deputy First Minister will take over, because that's what deputies do.' And he said it with a finality which precluded any further discussion of the matter.

Acceptance of Jim Wallace's role did not mean that initially he commanded the support of the majority of the SPLP in the chamber. When he stood in at First Minister's questions for the first time on 11 May, we were relieved that he dealt confidently and competently with Alex Salmond; he received tentative vocal and

11 May 2000: Jim Wallace fields First Minister's questions for the first time
(source: *The Scotsman*)

manual backing, although some in the Labour group put it down to a combination of beginner's luck and a lacklustre effort on Salmond's part. The following week the performance was repeated and there were thunderous cheers as Salmond was despatched again. It is remarkable to record that, in total, Jim Wallace fronted FMQs on nine occasions, and came out on top every time.

Most Labour members were genuinely impressed, adopting the Deputy First Minister as one of our own, something which had certainly seemed improbable at the time of Dewar's departure. For me, this confirmed the maturing of the partnership, a point which was emphasised at the second social occasion involving the groups, a joint end-of-term party in July 2000. It has been a remarkable development, and one which exemplifies the adoption of the new political agenda of the Parliament by a majority of both groups. Of course, it also reflects the extent to which each party needs the other in terms of getting our legislative programme implemented.

The fact that in many policy areas it would be difficult to place a piece of tissue paper between the two parties has been helpful, but the love affair will be put to the test in much the same way as wartime liaisons test the strength of a marriage. The analogy is not strictly accurate, because in terms of Labour/LibDem relations it will be the outbreak of war in the form of the UK general election which will test the new relationship. Constituencies will be contested independently as they always have been, although in Scotland very few head-to-head contests are likely to result. Although the SNP and the Tories will doubtless attempt to use the relationship to damage both parties, I do not envisage a great deal of confusion resulting. The electorate is considerably more sophisticated than we politicians generally give it credit for and when going to the polls in Scotland on general election day, most will be clear in their own minds that they are casting votes for the House of Commons, as distinct from the Scottish Parliament.

8 Scotland under the microscope

2 July 1999, 2.00 am: What a day, what an occasion. It was not as good as I had hoped it would be – it was much better. I campaigned for twenty-three years for this day and all the effort was more than justified. I feel prouder than ever before to be a Scot.

When the people of Scotland voted decisively in September 1997 for the re-establishment of the Scottish Parliament they did so in the hope that it would signify a break with the past. A past which meant – for most of recent memory at any rate – government which was inflexible and insensitive, incapable of recognising the distinctiveness of Scotland.

Anecdotal evidence suggests that by the time elections for the Parliament took place, some people at least had also started to hope that the Parliament would act as a potent symbol for modern Scotland, a sign of our developing confidence as a nation. The openness and inclusiveness on which the legislature was to be based should reflect the maturity of its people as they entered the third millennium. Scotland, as a window to the world, would project a bright, welcoming message. Thus far, that hope remains unfulfilled.

Yet it all started so well. For many Scots at home and abroad, 1 July 1999 will remain one of those days etched in the memory:

Scotland under the microscope

1 July 1999: Sheena Wellington sings 'A Man's a Man'
(source: *Parliamentary Broadcasting Unit*)

'Where were you the day the Scottish Parliament was opened?' It was a day when everything came together, with the parade from Parliament Hall, where the original Scottish Parliament sat 292 years earlier, to the Assembly Hall on the Mound where its successor had taken up temporary residence. Thousands lined the streets of the capital, waving saltires and actually cheering politicians (the most surreal part of a surreal day). The Queen presented the new Parliament with a silver mace bearing the timeless values of 'wisdom, justice, compassion, integrity'.

First Minister Donald Dewar's speech embraced the nation and won genuine applause from those of all parties. It could have been distilled to a single sentence, one which captured the mood and the purpose of the occasion: 'Today there is a new voice in the land, the voice of a democratic parliament.' Moving though his oration was, the most poignant moment was reserved for Sheena Wellington, who sang *A Man's a Man*, a song of humanity. Refuse to believe anyone, inside or outside the Assembly Hall, who claims they had dry eyes as her voice ebbed for the last time.

Bathed in brilliant sunshine from start to finish, culminating in a fireworks spectacular, it was a truly momentous day; my own abiding memory is of wishing it would never end. Beamed round the world, it projected a powerful vision of Scotland, as its re-born legislature took its first steps in the warm glow of national pride.

Scotland that day offered such a confident beginning. Perhaps the heights of 1 July meant there was only one direction to travel thereafter.

23 October 1999: In the constituency office dealing with a huge correspondence backlog, I am struck by the number of letters which begin 'Congratulations . . .' But people are not yet clear who does what – I sent several cases on to MP John Maxton.

The furore surrounding the Scottish Executive's plan to repeal clause 2a of the Local Government Act 1986 was *the* major political issue in the Parliament's first year. My diary entry for the day which followed Communities Minister Wendy Alexander's announcement of the Executive's intention to repeal that pernicious piece of legislation did not mention the issue, even though I had read about it in that day's newspapers. Having long campaigned on gay rights as an equality issue, I naturally welcomed the announcement, but did so also on a secondary level, in anticipation of a clear example of the Scottish Parliament taking legislative action before the House of Commons was able to do so. Never in my wildest dreams – or, more accurately, my darkest nightmares – did I foresee how big that issue would become and the dramatic impact which it would have on political life in Scotland.

In 1988, the Thatcher government introduced the Local Government Act, section 28 of which prohibited 'the promotion of homosexuality' in schools. There was little evidence that such behaviour had been occurring south of the border, and absolutely none north of it. Nevertheless, exhibiting the kind of insensitivity towards Scotland for which they were soundly punished at the following two general elections, the Tories introduced an amendment to the Local Government (Scotland) Act 1986, with clause 2a being added

Scotland under the microscope

to include the same wording. This led to many local authorities erring on the side of caution and deciding to curtail their provision of funding and facilities for gay, lesbian and bisexual groups, none of whose activities were aimed at school children. Indeed, many of these groups were primarily involved in giving advice or assistance on AIDS-related issues, and in some cases local authorities took such a defensive line after the introduction of the legislation that much valuable activity had to be stopped altogether.

Despite protests when the legislation was going through its various stages at Westminster, the measure rarely hit the headlines in the years which followed. Although repeal was clearly-established Labour Party policy, and appeared in the Party's manifesto for the general election in 1997, it was excluded from that for the Scottish Parliament elections two years later.

This is the kind of major issue on which Scotland's Parliament will be judged, because it sends out messages not just to the people of Scotland but further afield. The Parliament will have the effect of putting Scotland under the microscope in a manner which was not possible when legislation was looked after by Westminster. Indeed, Scotland will be judged on a number of issues, and on the basis of those judgements its reputation will be enhanced or diminished.

The first test was passed – though hardly with flying colours.

During the Parliament's early days, one of the issues making the political headlines had been the Bank of Scotland's proposed link-up with the rightwing US evangelist and failed presidential hopeful, Pat Robertson. The link would have involved a company owned by Robertson being used as a vehicle for the bank to offer financial services to millions of potential customers, thus gaining a foothold in the US. However, Robertson's homophobic and sexist views had been well documented and repeated far beyond his own backyard. The result of the bank's proposals was to arouse immediate protests, not just from the lesbian and gay community and political activists, but from many Scots, particularly customers of the Bank of Scotland, who were outraged at the connection with someone espousing such extreme and offensive views.

Initially, the bank's senior management not only refused to countenance that they had blundered, but seemed unable to comprehend what all the fuss was about. This changed when customers began closing accounts but their position showed no signs of shifting before Robertson, reacting to the widespread criticism, announced on 18 May that Scotland was 'a dark land' where homosexuals have 'incredibly strong influence'. Such a gratuitous insult, aimed at Scotland as a nation, provoked widespread media fury. Columnist Tom Brown fulminated: 'Until now, Robertson has only offended gays, feminists, Moslems and Hindus. This time he has consigned the whole of Scotland to hellfire,' (*Daily Record*, 1 June 1999). He went on to brand Robertson 'the biggest-mouthed bigot in broadcasting' and called on the Bank of Scotland to 'break their links with this arch-zealot'.

That newspaper's editorial of the same day, criticising the Bank for 'stalling' on ending the link with Robertson, said it could now be 'described as the Bank AGAINST Scotland'. With pressure mounting among MSPs for the Scottish Parliament to move its account elsewhere and similar threats emanating from various quarters, the welter of bad publicity proved too much even for the bank's hitherto intransigent board. The relationship with Robertson was brought to an end, although reportedly more than £2 million in compensation had to be paid to him.

This did not prevent the *Daily Record* using another editorial to berate the bank, saying, 'They should have seen the ethical argument against getting into bed with a bigot and they should not have been so arrogant when it was pointed out to them. The Bank of Scotland are finally doing the right thing, but for the wrong reason,' (3 June 1999). The last comment related to the fact that the bank were less than contrite when the deal was aborted, their press statement admitting only to 'changed external circumstances' which had made it 'unfeasible'.

Nonetheless, people such as myself, who had spoken out against the proposed link-up, were gratified that opposition had been so swift and decisive on the part of people across Scotland, the letters pages of *The Herald* and *The Scotsman* demonstrating that outrage had spread well beyond the traditional voices of opposition. It was in that spirit that, on 7 June, I submitted a motion (my first) to the Scottish Parliament, welcoming the bank's decision and congratulating 'all those who, by speaking out against the proposed deal, made a major contribution to its demise and reinforced the reputation of Scotland as a diverse nation with equality of treatment for all.'

Thus, when Wendy Alexander announced the repeal of clause 2a, in a speech to students at Glasgow University, she seemed to be in touch with the mood of modern Scotland, a small country gaining in self-confidence as it came to terms with having greater control over its own affairs. How wrong is it possible to be?

Although her announcement was reported the next day, it did not make the front pages and there were no immediate signs that it would become a major issue. Initially, opposition was restricted to commentators and columnists, many of them questioning why valuable Parliamentary time was being devoted to such an issue. This tactic (deriding a proposal as 'a waste of time') may become a common one at Holyrood; it has also been used by opponents of my Member's Bill to ban hunting with dogs.

Fanning the flames of intolerance

But on 8 November, the *Daily Record* carried the headline 'Cardinal warns of gay threat to school pupils' and before long the trickle of criticism had turned into a flood. The paper reported Cardinal Thomas Winning's fears that the proposal to repeal clause 2a was a threat to 'our children' which could 'expose them to predatory and abusive relationships'. Tory MSP Phil Gallie fanned the flames of intolerance, saying (in the same article) that the Cardinal was 'bang on'. However, even within his own church, the Cardinal was questioned, with Fr John Breslin of St Bride's Church in Cambuslang disagreeing: 'If you exclude the whole issue of homosexuality in schools then you are not teaching children the whole truth,' (same article). This was not a view which was to be repeated from such sources.

By 13 December an embryonic campaign was in motion, with senior figures in the Church of Scotland, the Free Church of Scotland and the Scottish Episcopal Church joining Winning in issuing an open letter to the Scottish Executive urging it not to scrap the clause. This was the excuse for the *Daily Record* to jump aboard, with columnist Tom Brown – the same Tom Brown who, just six months earlier, had labelled Pat Robertson 'the biggest-mouthed bigot in broadcasting' – showing himself to have a remarkably short memory. In tones which would have done Robertson himself proud, Brown asked how homosexuals got 'priority' treatment by the Scottish

Executive, adding, 'When did Scotland vote for pink politics? How come an insidious minority with a perverse agenda commands the attention of a new minister?' (16 December 1999).

From that point, open season on tolerance was declared. Adapting Brown's 'agenda', on January 13 Cardinal Winning described homosexuality as 'a perversion'. This outraged people across Scotland, including many Roman Catholics, but the ante was soon to be upped still further. It was announced that the millionaire bus magnate Brian Souter was to fund a campaign aimed at retaining clause 2a on the statute book, as a means of protecting children and promoting family values. Uncompromisingly titled 'Keep the Clause', the campaign was to be a joint one with the Scottish School Boards Association (SSBA), and it was stated that up to £1 million was to be made available to the SSBA to front it.

This was fraught with difficulties as some senior SSBA office-bearers were making contradictory statements on repeal, without having consulted their members. Ultimately, the SSBA used only about £1,000 of Souter's money in order to carry out a survey of their members, from which it emerged that a majority were not

March 2000: Communities minister Wendy Alexander shows her view of the 'Keep the Clause' campaign
(source: *The Scotsman*)

actually opposed at all. They had also been involved at an ill-starred launch of the campaign, which took place on 19 January. This turned into a fiasco when David Macauley, of public relations company Media House, grabbed the leading role from a faltering SSBA official. Macaulay then swam into deep water himself when it was revealed by journalists that the names of several personalities – such as rock star Jim Kerr and car dealer Ian Skelly – had been listed as supporters of the campaign, when in fact they had never even been approached.

> **10 February 2000:** *It was heartening to receive the unanimous backing of the Cathcart Constituency Labour Party members for my stand on clause 2a. Out of thirty present at the meeting, only one questioned the Executive's decision to introduce the repeal, which is not the case at all other CLPs.*

At about this time, MSPs began to receive a growing postbag on the issue from constituents, most of whom were opposed to the repeal. I seemed to be fairly typical in that the ratio ran at about three to two against, although that was not unusual; no matter the issue, people are always more likely to write asking you *not* to do something than the opposite.

Nevertheless, this does pose a dilemma: how does an elected representative effectively represent her or his constituents on controversial issues? Attempting to please everyone does not work. Apart from the fact that it is self-evidently an impossibility, anyone attempting it will probably end up pleasing nobody at all. MPs or MSPs usually rely on party policy or a government bill to provide refuge, but occasionally issues like clause 2a will arise which are deemed 'matters of conscience' and we have to decide for ourselves.

I approached the Executive's repeal of clause 2a from the standpoint that I believed it to be the correct course of action because the legislation was discriminatory and did not fit with the new Scotland, which should be about ending intolerance, not encouraging it. I explained this in detail to every constituent who wrote to me, together with my belief that when parents send their children to school, they entrust them to teachers, confident that they will be taught appropriately in all aspects of their education. For that trust to embrace every facet of school life except sex education is just illogical: even if an individual teacher somehow failed that test, it is inconceivable that her or his colleagues and the headteacher would also fail. My message was, basically, 'I trust teachers, and I think I am justified in asking you to do the same.'

In doing so, I am convinced I was reflecting the view of the majority of voters in Cathcart, although that majority did not feel sufficiently exercised by the matter to write to me. I would have adopted precisely the same position had the ratio of letters to me been reversed.

As the letters pages of newspapers filled up with the issue and an inordinate amount of time was devoted to it, there seemed little doubt it would play a major part in the Ayr by-election, set for 16 March. This had been anticipated with some trepidation by Labour since the resignation of the sitting MSP, Ian Welsh, in December; two months ahead of polling day, Labour's expectations were realistically limited to securing second place. But the Tories were the only one of the major parties contesting the by-election with a stance against repeal of clause 2a, so it appeared that the SNP could inflict little damage on Labour on the issue.

The issue was also the subject of heated discussion within the SPLP. At weekly meetings several members reported pressure on them mounting, and these included a number who were not minded to give way on the issue on ideological grounds. There was a call from opponents of the repeal to provide statutory guidelines, to ensure that 'protection' was given, in much the same way as those issued by Education Secretary David Blunkett for England and Wales.

The campaign against repeal was mounting. The *Daily Record* was at the forefront, but the attack was a three-pronged one, also encompassing the Roman Catholic Church in Scotland (for whom Cardinal Winning was a powerful voice) and 'Keep the Clause' which was run by Jack Irvine and his public relations company Media House. By a remarkable coincidence, Irvine had masterminded the Bank of Scotland's defence of its deal with Pat Robertson a few months earlier.

The *Daily Record* hardly advanced the credibility of its case by claiming, bizarrely, that a vote in the House of Lords on 7 February against repeal in England and Wales would 'increase the pressure ... on Dewar and the Executive to drop their plans to abolish the section in Scotland'. Unhelpfully (for the First Minister), in a vain attempt to win that vote in the Lords, Blunkett had published legally enforceable guidelines, with marriage featuring prominently.

Although Donald Dewar told the SPLP that he had been informed by Blunkett of his plans, it was obvious that this was after the event.

Meanwhile, in an undisguised attempt to gain some advantage ahead of the by-election, the Tories had used one of their opposition debates on 10 February to discuss the retention of clause 2a, and the introduction of statutory guidelines. Unsurprisingly, they were soundly defeated (by eighty-eight votes to seventeen) on the main motion and similarly on the guidelines, with all three other parties resolutely holding to their principled positions. But the debate received scant media coverage, prompting Wendy Alexander to express her frustration. 'I think it's a pity that a very high-quality debate, which was conducted in a spirit of tolerance and was an opportunity to dispel some of the fears and misinformation surrounding the issue, didn't get a wider airing,' (*Sunday Herald*, 13 March 2000).

Around this time, Alexander herself had been the victim of some highly personalised and sexist attacks from tabloid newspapers, and this led to many Labour colleagues – male and female – rallying to her defence. The *Daily Record* had likened her, curiously, to Margaret Thatcher, which the Glasgow Kelvin MSP Pauline McNeill described as 'a retrograde step for other women who want to come and play an influential role in politics. Fortunately she had a lot of support in the Labour group and it's important we don't allow women politicians to be treated like this,' (interview, June 2000).

Despite the resounding vote in the debate on 10 February, reports began circulating within the group that three cabinet members, Tom McCabe, Jack McConnell and Henry McLeish, were seeking ways of introducing guidelines in an attempt to respond to some of the criticism from the 'Keep the Clause' campaign (one of the tabloids dubbed them 'the Big Macs', although among those in the SPLP who did not support what the three were alleged to have been attempting, they were more bitingly termed 'the cheeky burgers').

At the weekly meeting of the SPLP on 23 February, several members asked for clarification of the reports and only McConnell was prepared to state that he had not been involved in any such activity. Malcolm Chisholm drew applause when he aimed criticism at the three, particularly in terms of media leaks, and there was a real sense of anger and foreboding that some back-tracking was about to take place. Wendy Alexander, clearly aware of what was to follow, made an emotional speech ostensibly accepting the need for a change of position, although it was not difficult to read between the lines and detect her true feelings. This was reinforced when she then left the meeting (struggling, it seemed to me, to hold back tears) and was not there when Donald Dewar arrived to report that a revised set of guidelines was indeed to be issued. This was actually something of a red herring as it had always been the intention to issue new guidelines when the amendment was brought into effect, although this had not been effectively communicated by Wendy Alexander to the media or the public at large. The new wording, which we were told would not refer to marriage, would emphasise the value of 'stable family life'. It was to be announced by the First Minister at the following day's debate on the introduction of the Ethical Standards in Public Life Bill.

In his role as Education minister, Sam Galbraith had taken over as lead minister from Wendy Alexander, at least as far as public pronouncements and comments were concerned. He supplemented Donald Dewar's contribution and gave an assurance that the guidelines would not promote one lifestyle ahead of others and that marriage would not be mentioned so as to avoid stigmatising the children of unmarried parents. For most members, myself included, this was unacceptable, and I argued that, if any ground were to be given, it would neither buy time nor succeed in getting the 'Keep the Clause' people to back off. I made the point that when, in such situations, your opponents are given any hint you are weakening your position, they know they have you on the run and will continue forcing you backwards until eventually they push you over the edge. I argued that, if this concession were to be made, it would still not be enough for Souter, Winning or the *Record* and they would soon be back for more.

Others spoke in similar terms but some group members were clearly feeling the heat in their constituencies. Karen Gillon reported that feelings were running high and had been clearly communicated to her. An ardent backer of the repeal of clause 2a, she nonetheless made the point that consideration had to be given to what she termed 'our natural supporters'. It was an appeal for understanding of the dilemma faced by the Executive and it was noticeable that her contribution had the support of others whom I had not expected to waver on our commitment. I disagreed with them, but respected their courage in being prepared to be counted on this aspect of the issue.

That said, it was clearly a minority view at what was the most torrid SPLP group meeting I had experienced. Donald Dewar said the new guidelines were a necessary 'containing measure' and would enable the issue to be taken out of the limelight. If there was a single Labour MSP who believed that would happen – particularly with the by-election approaching – then I did not encounter them.

Group loyalty prevented any member speaking out, but the following day widespread support was forthcoming for remarks attributed to one of the LibDem MSPs, Mike Rumbles. To say that our partnership colleague is not generally held in high regard by Labour members is something of an understatement, but his comments that 'kowtowing in fear of the tabloid press is a fatal mistake and if they [the Executive] think this issue is going away now they could not be more mistaken,' (*The Herald*, 24 February) could have emanated from many an SPLP backbencher. Events, unsurprisingly, proved both him and us correct.

That very day, the Tories were launching their campaign for the Ayr by-election. Predictably, ignoring the Parliament's achievements, their candidate John Scott claimed that other Scots had not 'embraced' the Parliament 'just for it to become embroiled in rows about homosexuality and foxhunting,' (*The Herald*, 24 February). This did not, of course, prevent him making it clear clause 2a would form a central plank of his campaign; I was gratified, on a personal level, that he left the other matter undisturbed.

*29 **February 2000:** Meeting with other MSPs and the Equality Network, the organisation which has been co-ordinating the gay and lesbian campaign for repeal. I was struck by the determination which they showed, refusing to back down in the face of serious intimidation suffered by some of their members.*

The effect which clause 2a had on the by-election campaign is examined in Chapter 5; suffice it to say that Ayr did not exactly take the heat out of the issue. During the campaign, it should have surprised nobody that the debate over repeal of the clause had resulted in an increase in homophobic attacks in Scotland. Strathclyde Gay and Lesbian Switchboard recorded 20 per cent more calls to

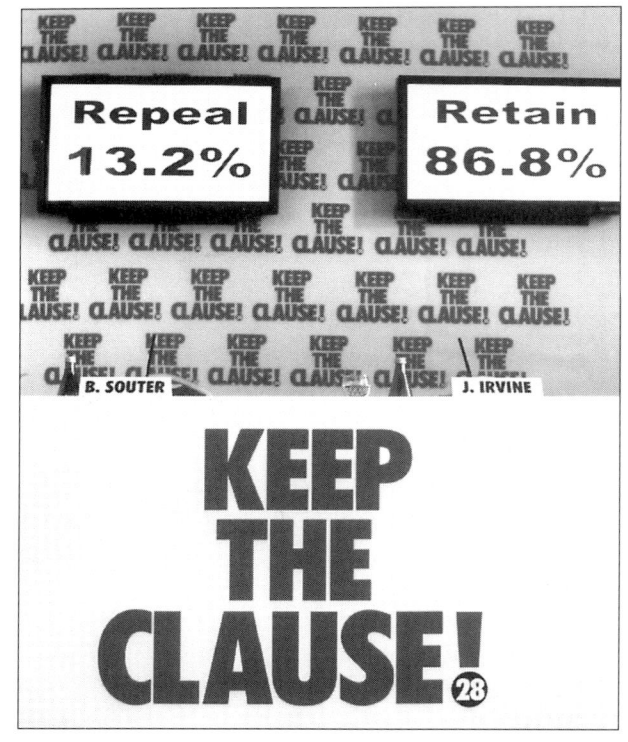

*30 May 2000: The contrast between the organisations for and against clause 2a
(source: The Herald)*

their helpline during the campaign. An Edinburgh doctor was beaten unconscious with a baseball bat after leaving a gay night club in the city where, the Scottish Executive announced in February, attacks on gays were four times the national average. But it was not just the capital which witnessed such intolerance, with attacks also reported in the Highlands and Aberdeen.

The 'Keep the Clause' billboards were identified as a source of the blame. Certainly, Keith Cowan of Outright Scotland was in no doubt about the link: 'Some of the language used in the posters is contributing to a culture in which gay people are seen as legitimate targets.' He believed that it was less likely victims would even report incidents 'given the culture which exists, where it is almost acceptable to harass gay people in that way' (*The Scotsman*, 7 March). In the same edition of the paper, the 'Keep the Clause' campaign's David Macauley, while 'regretting' incidents of violence, denied any such link and claimed, 'We are not opposed to homosexuals. We are not responsible for the actions of others.' Well, perhaps not directly.

Meanwhile, Brian Souter clearly did not like it when, the following month, he was on the receiving end of protests and verbal abuse as he entered church in Perth, but the by-election had buoyed him to the extent that he was prepared for the next stage of his campaign. There were, however, contradictory accounts of what form this might take.

On 26 March, *Scotland on Sunday* reported that those in charge of the campaign 'now accept that the clause will be repealed and campaigners are to focus on attempting to persuade the Executive to draft legally enforceable, strict guidelines.' Had that been the case, logic would have dictated that the campaign be re-named, but three days later it emerged that the original focus remained undiminished as Souter unveiled his grand plan: a £1 million postal ballot of every household in Scotland. The aim, he stated, utilising a phrase with which Donald Dewar was not unfamiliar, was to 'demonstrate once and for all what the settled will of the Scottish people is,' (*The Scotsman*, 28 March).

The First Minister responded in typically measured tones: 'I think it would be very odd if social progress depended on private individuals,' adding that it was 'a matter for leadership and for a decision made in Parliament,' (*The Herald*, 29 March). Nonetheless, the issue came to dominate the headlines over the following days, with the

Daily Record apoplectic that the Electoral Reform Society (ERS) had declined to run the ballot. In plumbing new depths of intolerance, it berated the ERS and suggested in an editorial that the decision was down to the organisation's governing council 'one of whose members is the openly gay Labour MP Stephen Twigg,' (29 March).

This caused universal outrage among MSPs to whom I spoke that day. It took my breath away, even though it appeared in a newspaper which, earlier in the campaign, had felt the need to tell its readers that Wendy Alexander was still unmarried at the age of thirty-six (good grief!) and Susan Deacon had never found it 'necessary' to get married, despite being a mother (while no comment was made on the domestic arrangements of any male member of the cabinet). Welcome to the new Scotland?

Prime Minister Tony Blair had entered the debate on clause 2a when he addressed Labour's Scottish conference on 10 March, attacking opponents of repeal in terms markedly more forthright than those of any Scottish Executive minister. He re-engaged on 29 March, using Prime Minister's questions in the House of Commons to brand supporters of the clause as 'anti-gay bigots', adding that 'Keep the Clause' campaigners were using the issue of child protection to mask homophobia. This produced a response from Jack Irvine on behalf of 'Keep the Clause' to the effect that Blair had been 'insulting' and 'shows a profound misunderstanding of the issue'. Strangely, Irvine had felt no such outrage when his comrade-in-arms, Cardinal Winning, described homosexuality as 'a perversion' in January.

The Ethical Standards in Public Life Bill had its stage one debate in the Parliament on 27 April. Opening for the Executive, Wendy Alexander spoke of the need for clause 2a to be removed from the statute book to prevent Scotland being 'dragged back to an intolerant past'. In what was clearly a carefully crafted speech, delivered with a confidence which suggested she had recovered from the low period when criticism seemed to have been directed at her from all sides, she attacked the Souter-funded campaign, describing it memorably as 'a campaign very expensive to mount, but with a cheapness all of its own'. It was a relatively low-key debate, at the end of which the Parliament agreed to the Bill's general principles by 103 votes to sixteen (all Tories) with five abstentions.

The previous day, Souter confirmed details of his private ballot, to be conducted by ICM Research, following the refusal of the Electoral Reform Society to become involved. It was dogged by accusations of an outdated electoral roll and the uneven distribution of ballot papers, some people receiving multiple copies while their neighbours received none. The ballot initially posed a dilemma for those unwilling to legitimise it by participating. Should they register their vote in favour of repeal or leave the field open to those against, citing the boycott as the reason why the 'yes' voters were in the majority? The latter option ultimately prevailed and most people I came into contact with (MSP or otherwise) did not vote.

The sands shift

> **11 May 2000:** *At around 6.00 pm, as I was leaving the office to head back to Glasgow, I got a call from Robbie Dinwoodie of* The Herald. *He asked what I thought of the Executive's 'new move on Clause 2a'. I knew nothing about it and was stunned at his news of an announcement by Sam Galbraith that the new sex education guidance for schools was to be put on a statutory footing.*

Not a hint of this reached me in the Parliament that afternoon, nor in the office after it and, caught unawares, I declined to give Dinwoodie the quote he wanted. It emerged that the announcement had been made by Galbraith to the media at 4.30 pm, while the chamber was full. Aware that Wendy Alexander was on Executive business in the USA, it occurred to me that her absence cannot have been incidental to the timing. It subsequently emerged she had been told (although not consulted) by phone what was to happen.

The distinction between guidance and guidelines did not seem to me to be one which could be easily made, far less sustained; Labour colleagues seemed resigned to some further concession, although the feeling was that it must be 'thus far and no further'. Johann Lamont, whom I had expected would share my concern, was sufficiently relaxed about it to speak in support of the move on BBC Radio's *Good Morning Scotland* the following day: 'To be honest, it was a meaningless shift; parents needed to be reassured and they wouldn't have understood had we resisted it,' (interview, August 2000).

But Gordon Jackson, the member for Govan, did express unease to me about the lack of consultation with the SPLP, commenting, 'I thought they'd learned the lesson two weeks ago', a reference to the Executive backing down, following SPLP pressure, on the Warrant Sales Bill. Janis Hughes, MSP for Rutherglen, who had maintained an unswerving position in support of repeal, was more concerned about the fact that the SNP were crowing to the media that this was the line they had been advocating for some weeks. As she put it to me, 'Salmond was on his knees after his disastrous debate (on independence) yesterday, compounded by coming second-best to Wallace at questions today, and what do we do: hand him the perfect pick-me-up'.

The timing was explained by the need to submit a suitable amendment for submission to the Education committee, which was considering the bill at stage two at its meeting on 15 May. This necessitated members of the committee (including the SNP) being told in advance of the introduction of 'guidance' in order to bring them on board. That achieved, Sam Galbraith then sought to inform as many other Labour members as possible of the change before it was announced. He had only limited success and I found myself in the majority of backbenchers who heard about it from journalists.

The Herald called the issuing of statutory guidance 'a climbdown that we regret', predicting that 'the forthcoming duty on local authorities to consult parents on the shape and form of their sex education could well be a recipe for anarchy,' (editorial, 12 May). Two days later, *Scotland on Sunday* suggested Wendy Alexander had paid 'a high price for failing to listen', adding more sympathetically, 'we hope the government cave-in did not come too late to save [her] political career'.

The first opportunity the SPLP had to discuss the matter was the normal weekly meeting on 17 May in Glasgow. Sam Galbraith was apologetic as he talked us through the events. He failed to give Hugh Henry an answer as to why the issue had not been raised at our meeting the previous week, though in truth he did not need to. What rankled as much as anything was the fact that most SNP members knew before many Labour members, including some ministers. Nevertheless, I emerged from the meeting conscious of the fact that it was the manner in which the message had been conveyed (or not) which was centre stage, rather than the message itself. It was clear that most of the SPLP were scunnered with clause 2a and, like a bad dream, simply wanted it to be over; but there were still five weeks until the stage three debate.

When the result of the Souter poll appeared, it predictably demonstrated a six-to-one majority in favour of retaining the clause (on a turnout of 34 per cent). This failed to advance the debate, with Souter claiming 'a denial of this result would be a denial of democracy,' (*The Herald*, 31 May 2000) and Wendy Alexander dismissing the outcome: 'Less than one-third of Scots back his position, and I think that is because as time went on, many became less and less comfortable with cheque book democracy,' (*Daily Record*, 31 May 2000).

Despite continued denials (as late as 1 June, an Executive spokesperson was quoted in *The Scotsman* as saying, 'I can tell you the answer is "no" from the Education Minister, and he is quite insistent on that,') there was widespread, if reluctant, acceptance within the SPLP that 'marriage' (in some form) would be included in the guidelines. The Education committee had rejected an amendment to the bill from Labour backbencher Michael McMahon which would have included it, but the Executive was committed to adopting the recommendations of the McCabe committee, which it had established with the remit to produce the guidelines. Given the presence of the main churches on the committee, there was little doubt as to the outcome.

By way of light relief, and there was precious little of it in evidence throughout this debate, if I had not already appreciated that the clause 2a debate had been running for far too long, then it hit me when in discussion with an SPLP colleague (who must remain nameless, for reasons which will become apparent) about the McCabe report. I expressed my certain belief that 'marriage' would be included to which he replied, 'With Tom running it, there's no doubt about that.' Thinking he was joking, I laughed, but it soon emerged that my fellow MSP was under the impression that the committee had been chaired by the Minister for Parliament and not, as was the case, by Mike McCabe, director of education for South Ayrshire Council. I didn't have the heart to break the news.

The final debate on the issue was due on 21 June, when the Ethical Standards in Public Life Bill reached stage three. The McCabe report was due for publication on 15 June and, at less than an hour's notice, a special meeting of the SPLP was called. Anxious on this occasion to ensure we were all informed, Sam Galbraith wanted to brief us on the content of the report. Except that he didn't. He couldn't. Instead, he announced that he had not yet seen it and so did not know its content, but it did include marriage, albeit in an 'acceptable' form. He took some questions, there was scarcely a murmur, and we all left. Had the announcement been made in, say, February, the SPLP would have been in uproar. But February seemed an awfully long time ago . . .

It is also true to say that, had Wendy Alexander announced way back on 30 October, that clause 2a would be repealed, but that guidelines containing the McCabe committee wording would be introduced, those of us welcoming the repeal would scarcely have blinked an eye. But that is not to accuse the Communities minister of lack of foresight. Nobody could possibly have anticipated what the subsequent eight months would bring; nor would anyone want to witness a repeat.

The stage three debate itself on 21 June was a low-key affair, even during Brian Monteith's amendment seeking to insert marriage on to the face of the bill. Many people (including, no doubt, some MSPs) discovered for the first time what the Ethical Standards in Public Life Bill was actually about and were possibly surprised that the repeal of clause 2a involved only a minor part tacked on at the end. Could such an apparently insignificant few words really have caused such a furore across the length and breadth of Scotland? It seemed barely credible, although that feeling had certainly been no stranger to me at various stages during the campaign. But now clause 2a was consigned to the dustbin and it was over, or was it?

Learning the lessons

The repercussions of the repeal of the clause are not yet clear and it remains to be seen what the new moralists will now do. Drawing a line under what it termed 'a sorry, tawdry affair that has reflected badly on the new Scotland', *The Herald* editorial of 17 June called for 'Souter and his backers to recognise that it is time to move on. Chequebook democracy does not work, particularly when it is bolstered by mendacity.' But *will* Souter and his cohorts move on, and if so, to what?

In an editorial, the *New Statesman Scotland* aptly described

Scotland under the microscope

Scotland's political landscape after the clause's ultimate demise: 'Like it or not, this unpleasant mess says something unpleasant about Scotland. Instead of using a new institution to build a better and fairer society... we find it tarnished and hijacked by the advocates of a retrograde morality which we are forced to accept is still part of us. It is, frankly, a shaming spectacle,' (12 June 2000).

The clause 2a debate acted as a clear warning that the new Scotland is not as new as some – particularly those of us involved in its political life – would like to believe. The ease with which a campaign was whipped up against the repeal of clause 2a, based on downright lies about the teaching of homosexuality in schools, carries a warning and not just to politicians. What does it say about tolerance in Scotland at the start of the twenty-first century?

Sam Galbraith, the Education minister who was very much in the firing line on the repeal of clause 2a, signified his disappointment at the intolerance which the debate surrounding it exposed: 'I thought these attitudes had gone. The clause was seen as silly, outdated and of no use – because it had no practical effect. Yet suddenly it exploded into an inferno. Who would have thought the proposal would generate a £2 million campaign of opposition?' (interview, June 2000).

Labour deputy whip Duncan McNeil is of the view that Sam Galbraith was not alone in the Executive in failing to anticipate the furore. 'We didn't evaluate the political risks of repeal and this led us into dangerous waters. We empowered the moral right and in a small country we saw how powerful it can be, particularly when it has financial backing and the support of the popular press.' He feels the Labour Party, chastened by the battering which its MSPs and the Executive took in the clause 2a debate, will react with caution. 'Following on from the repeal of the clause, I can see there being a tendency for the Executive to stay with core issues – this is what I believe the party membership is asking for,' (interview, June 2000).

Patricia Ferguson believes that the clause 2a repeal would not have achieved such prominence had it been UK-wide legislation: 'We got it right in the end, because the legislation has gone and it's good that Scotland has led the way. It's a great shame that it became such a big issue, but MSPs are more accessible and the media pays more attention to the Scottish Parliament than to the House of

Commons. For that reason the issue built up in a way that simply has not happened in England and Wales,' (interview, August 2000).

I endorse that assessment and would suggest that a further aspect of it is the much greater influence of the Roman Catholic Church in Scotland than in England or Wales. Cardinal Thomas Winning has long seen it as part of his role to engage in the political process. Often, this has served the Labour Party well because traditionally a large majority of Scotland's Catholics have supported the Labour Party and the respective agendas on social issues have been fairly close.

The link between the two might explain why some Labour MPs and MSPs were openly supportive of Winning's position in the clause 2a debate. Perhaps they believed they were acting as conduits for the continuance of good relations between the Church and the party. On the other hand, they might have been engaged (intentionally or not) in legitimising the monocultural Scotland which is most rooted in some of Labour's central belt heartlands.

Whether the repeal of clause 2a will materially affect Labour's support among Catholics is yet to be tested. I suspect it will not, but well-established assumptions made about their electoral loyalty require to be re-assessed anyway, for two reasons.

First, as Labour's agenda has shifted over the past decade from one of welfarism and a redistributive ethos to more of an enabling one, both the SNP and the Scottish Socialist Party are seeking to fill what they regard as the vacant ground thus created. Scotland's dispossessed either see voting at all as a waste of time or regard the SNP and the SSP as legitimate alternatives to Labour. This, of course, applies to those of all religions and none, but it is disproportionately the case in terms of Catholics of working age as a whole, of whom a higher percentage are still concentrated in manual occupations.

However, that imbalance is being redressed, which leads to the second reason. A majority of Scottish Catholics aged eighteen to fifty are now employed in non-manual occupations (57 per cent, compared to 59 per cent of non-Catholics) and are now firmly established (increasingly at senior levels) in business, academia and the professions. For many of them, the Labour Party *may* remain their party of choice, but it is now less naturally so.

The consequences are that Labour can no longer take the electoral support of Scotland's Catholics for granted. Cardinal Winning is astute enough to have recognised this and is using his church's influence with the Labour Party to attempt to shape the political agenda. The church, aided by the ability of the so-called 'moral right' (which by no means constitutes a majority of Scotland's 700,000 Catholics), is now becoming more vocal, better-organised and more willing to take up issues. The reaction by extremist groups to Health Minister Susan Deacon's funding of birth control clinics is an example of this. While the Catholic Church would have no truck with violence or intimidation, it nevertheless allowed one of its spokespersons, Fr Tom Connelly, to denounce Deacon as 'a nutcase' over the issue. Such intemperate language (and, as previously mentioned, Cardinal Winning has resorted to it himself) does not exactly convey a message that tolerance and understanding of people who are (by whatever definition) 'different' is to be encouraged in Scotland 2000.

Since the Parliament came into being, the view of Scotland as an inclusive, mature, tolerant society has been challenged. On 1 July 1999, a moving fanfare written by the composer James MacMillan for the official opening of the Scottish Parliament had left a lasting impression on the watching nation. Two months later, MacMillan made an impression of an altogether different kind when he used a lecture at the Edinburgh International Festival to allege that Scotland was a land of 'sleep-walking bigotry' and that the continued existence of Catholic schools was threatened by the creation of the Scottish Parliament. This, and the vigorous debate which it stimulated, prompted Professor Tom Devine of Aberdeen University to commission eighteen other contributions on the subject, which were published as a collection under the title *Scotland's Shame?* (which had also been the title – minus the question-mark – of MacMillan's lecture). Rather disappointingly, this failed to reach a judgement on MacMillan's claims, with Devine himself concluding that 'no final agreed position is yet possible on the question of anti-Catholicism in modern Scottish society'.

Nevertheless, it is necessary to record that Scotland does not conform to the tolerant, inclusive society which many who live here confidently claim it to be. The incidence of racist abuse, and often attacks, which are regularly reported are testimony to that and the attitude to the accommodation of asylum-seekers in the summer of 2000 has not been universally positive (indeed, in some cases it has been downright hostile).

Was it naïve to hope that the Parliament – Scotland's looking glass – would project a view of a country confident in its new-found ability to come up with the over-used notion of 'Scottish solutions to Scottish problems'? Gerry Hassan believes the idea that civic Scotland is 'a land awash with rich complex institutions and opinions just waiting to contribute to the new politics' is a myth. 'This was always romantic delusion, but the debate over clause 2a has killed it off for ever. Scottish civil society is just as full of contradictions as elsewhere, and contains a fair share of narrow and ugly prejudice and bigotry,' (*The Scotsman*, 17 July 2000).

I fear his analysis is correct, although I am unwilling to extend it to embrace the conclusion that the lack of tolerance within my country can be laid almost exclusively at the door of what Iain Macwhirter calls 'the lumpen Scot'. This creature ('predominantly, but not exclusively, male; hates gays and English; almost completely uneducatable; resorting to extreme and delinquent forms of behaviour'(*Sunday Herald*, 23 April 2000)) certainly exists. But the sort of mindless prejudice which I have encountered during the Parliament's short life just as often emanates from tongues and minds well capable of articulating a reasonable-sounding case. It is almost always prefaced by a statement such as, 'Don't get me wrong, I have nothing against unemployed people/Albanians/homosexuals/single parents/Asians . . .' then proceeds quickly downhill from there.

It may well be the case that more than half of Scotland's male population read the *Daily Record* and, given the paper's uncompromising line on the repeal of clause 2a, that could be said to sound alarm bells for our chances of developing a more all-embracing, inclusive outlook as a nation. It is to be hoped the recent change of editor will render that fear unfounded but at such times I draw comfort from the heart-warming UK-wide poll taken shortly after the 1992 general election. It revealed that a majority of readers of *The Sun* (which had campaigned relentlessly for a Tory victory) actually believed their paper backed Labour. All is not lost.

So the role of the media – or at least certain sections of it – should not be permitted to circumscribe our sense of values, our feeling of worth as a nation. We have the opportunity now, through the Parliament, to reflect positive images of Scotland, its people and its institutions and I am convinced that is what the vast majority of Scots wants their MSPs to do. If the first year has achieved nothing else, it has laid bare for us the extent of the task.

9 In committee

4 July 2000: *We completed the Social Inclusion, Housing and Voluntary Sector committee's report on housing stock transfer today, ten months and twenty meetings after it began with evidence from Wendy Alexander and her two junior ministers.*

Holding the Executive to account is one of the prime functions of the Parliament's main committees. Demonstrably, they have begun to do so with vigour and some success in the first year. That function is actually the first-named of the six given to the committees by the Consultative Steering Group (CSG) when it reported in December 1998. Although there is no actual mention of 'holding to account', the wording is unequivocal: 'to consider and report on the policy and administration of the Scottish administration'. That role is also included in two other functions: scrutinising primary and secondary legislation and proposed European Union legislation; and scrutinising the financial proposals and administration of the Scottish Executive.

The other committee functions are conducting inquiries into such matters as the Parliament may require; initiating legislation; and scrutinising procedures relating to the Parliament and its members.

Holding the Executive to account forms the major role of the eight subject committees and of four of the mandatory committees

(Audit, Equal Opportunities, European and Finance). Only the Procedures, Public Petitions, Standards and Subordinate Legislation committees are not expected to be part of that process, which is reflected in the fact that these committees each have only seven members, while the others have eleven or thirteen.

The importance which the committees place on acting as a watchdog on the performance of the Executive is reflected in the number of appearances before them made by ministers. Unlike Westminster, where it is rare for ministers to be called to give evidence at select committee hearings, Scottish Executive ministers (including junior ministers) do so on a regular basis. As an example, the Finance committee had Jack McConnell, the Minister for Finance, in attendance at no fewer than eight of our twenty-nine meetings between June 1999 and July 2000. His appearances encompassed a variety of functions, including giving evidence to committee inquiries, speaking on his budget proposals, considering the Public Finance and Accountability Bill and moving resolutions in support of statutory instruments. These are fairly typical in terms of frequency and demonstrate how the various committee functions require differing contributions from ministers. That input is supplemented by appearances by Scottish Executive civil servants, who appear on their own as well as with their ministers.

The BBC's Brian Taylor is one of the few journalists who follows the work of the committees closely. He is convinced of the impression which they have already made: 'The Executive and civil servants are chilled at developments in the committees, especially when dealing with Bills. At the House of Commons ministers are part of the committees considering legislation but at Holyrood they are just interested onlookers. They can seek to influence but ultimately they can't control them, nor can civil servants. They must win their case, and that's the importance of the new politics,' (interview, September 2000).

Not all MSPs accept the emphasis which committees have been forced, usually through pressure of legislation, to give to their Executive watchdog role. The SNP's Christine Grahame, a member of the Justice and Home Affairs committee, claimed that the amount of time which that committee was being forced to give to legislative work was excessive: 'Whether it is deliberate or accidental is irrelevant. I am not there to be a reviewing body for the Executive,' (*The*

Scotsman, 5 April 2000). This seemed a strange claim to emanate from a member of the main opposition party, but it was echoed by her colleague and fellow-committee member Michael Matheson who said, 'I am concerned that an issue such as budget scrutiny is being squeezed in. We have a responsibility to investigate issues and initiate our own legislation and that is just not happening,' (*The Scotsman*, 5 April 2000).

These remarks to some extent reflected the fact that the Justice and Home Affairs committee had been extremely busy dealing with legislation passed to it, including the Abolition of Feudal Tenure, Adults with Incapacity and the Abolition of Poindings and Warrant Sales bills. Nonetheless, Matheson seemed not to have appreciated that the procedure for scrutinising the budget proposals over the period of a year was one of the most innovative aspects of the Parliament, and that the Budget Bill was arguably the most important bill which the Parliament will consider in any year.

Andy Kerr, convener of the Transport and Environment committee, also felt the Budget Bill arrived at an inconvenient time. 'It seemed like a distraction from normal committee business; there were other things to do.' He further questioned the form in which the budget proposals were received, a criticism echoed by most of the other committees (and the Finance committee itself): 'The departmental reports arrived late and were untidy; sometimes data was untraceable. There was a lack of clarity as to what the Executive were doing and what the committees were supposed to be doing,' (interview, June 2000).

Michael Matheson was right in identifying the fact that other demands on it had prevented the Justice and Home Affairs committee considering the initiation of its own legislation, although in doing so they were not alone: no committee managed to find the time to do so in the first year of the parliament.

This demonstrates that predictions of the committees' ability effectively to combine the investigative and scrutiny roles of Westminster's two types of committees were somewhat premature. If anything, the committees are becoming victims of their own success, with several overstretched as a result of the work being allocated to them from various sources.

Sarah Davidson experienced the committee system from the inside as a senior clerk. 'Across the board, the workload has been heavier than had been anticipated when the mechanics of the Parliament were being planned. This impacted on the support staff, particularly the clerks, and it impacted unevenly. My committees (Audit and Finance) had tightly proscribed remits but others were much wider and they became over-ambitious in what they sought to achieve,' (interview, September 2000).

Streamlining the structure

24 May 2000: There was a strong reaction at today's meeting of the SPLP in response to proposed changes to the committee structure. The question being asked afterwards was why this had not been handled better, so soon after the discord over the warrant sales issue.

That the workload on the committees (and consequently on its members) was proving heavier than had been anticipated was recognised when the four main parties in the Parliamentary Bureau began to consider means of streamlining the structure. Part of the plan was to reduce the number of MSPs who would be required to serve on two committees, both by reducing the number of committees and their size. It also involved the suggestion that the Justice and Home Affairs committee might be split in two and that the Equal Opportunities committee might be dissolved, its remit instead being transferred to all committees in what was termed a 'mainstreaming exercise'.

A number of SPLP members spoke out strongly against the proposals, contained in a paper circulated by Tom McCabe. It was the product of discussions at the Bureau and was clearly labelled a discussion paper, but Tom appeared taken aback at the strength of opposition. A further proposal – which I was among those opposing – was for the Local Government and Social Inclusion, Housing and Voluntary Sector committees to be merged. This would have meant combining two of the Parliament's busiest committees (both met weekly, and occasionally twice weekly), each with eleven members, into a new super-committe with only nine members. The workload of such a hybrid simply did not bear thinking about.

The proposals had also generated much opposition within the other parties. This was illustrated the following week at a meeting of the Conveners' Liaison Group (CLG), which comprises the conveners of all sixteen Parliament committees. There was considerable resentment that proposals for fundamental change in the remit and make-up of committees should have been issued without reference to conveners. One of the proposals was that the Public Petitions committee should be disbanded and its role handed to the CLG. If this was meant to sweeten the pill for conveners, it failed as the group asserted its outright opposition to the disappearance of the Petitions committee. Instead, the CLG decided to initiate its own review over the summer of 2000, including an assessment of what clerking and other support resources were necessary to ensure the efficient running of the committees and the speedy production of the official report of their proceedings.

The message from the trenches had been received at HQ and at an SPLP meeting in June Tom McCabe presented revised proposals from the Bureau. These provided for subject committees to increase in number from eight to nine (with Justice and Home Affairs becoming separate committees) and for a reduction in the number of mandatory committees from eight to seven, with a new Procedures and Standards committee being formed. All committees were to be reduced in size, with the effect for Labour backbenchers that only thirteen of us would be required to serve on two committees, a substantial reduction from the existing level of thirty-four (out of thirty-nine).

The proposals were endorsed by the SPLP and the understanding was that the new structure would be introduced the following autumn. However, as Parliament resumed after the 2000 summer recess this was far from certain, both the LibDem and SNP business managers having being told by their members to think again. Nor would the Tories be of any assistance, since their business manager, James Douglas Hamilton, had not even supported the proposals at the Parliamentary Bureau: 'The proposals did not come from us; the Tory group are not pressing for change,' (interview, July 2000).

But the Labour group did, as assistant whip Duncan McNeil confirms: 'Suggestions for change came from the members themselves, especially those on committees with a heavy workload. I think the jury is still out on the committee numbers, but we will be monitoring the situation,' (interview, June 2000).

Kenny Gibson of the SNP believes the changes proposed would not be beneficial. 'The committees have established their autonomy and they must retain it. I would be concerned, if the numbers on each committee were reduced, that this would reduce the spread of views and restrict the ability of the committees to scrutinise legislation and hear evidence,' (interview, August 2000).

The question of autonomy was also stressed by Labour's Johann Lamont. 'The test often set of being an effective backbencher is the extent to which we are able to distance ourselves from our party. That is not something which should be judged solely on the ability of backbenchers to "rebel". The test applies in committees, where members don't have to follow a party line. It's easy for the opposition parties to dress up a contrary view as holding the Executive to account, when in fact party politics are being pursued. If committee members are to scrutinise the Executive they can only do so on the basis of their members being independent-minded. The SNP don't aid that process by having their spokespersons on the relevant committees. I believe only Labour and Liberal Democrat members have demonstrated genuine independence of their own leadership,' (interview, August 2000).

The committee system has now had a year in which to bed down, and Mark Irvine believes they have done so to good effect. 'The real success story has been the parliamentary committees, which play a crucial role in how Holyrood works. They are the engine room of a new politics,' (*New Statesman Scotland*, 5 June 2000). Douglas Fraser is more sceptical, however: 'The impact so far has not been stunning, but there is a slow burn effect. This is where novelty [in the Parliament] has offered the most difficulties,' (*Sunday Herald*, 30 April 2000).

Irvine described the committee system as a 'triumph of consensus, not combat' and to a large extent that has been the case. The intention of the CSG was that MSPs should discard party loyalty along with their coats at the committee room door and, because the membership of the committees mirrors the parties' representation in the Parliament, there is no natural majority. In theory, there is a Labour/LibDem majority on each, but the partnership does not extend to the committees and there has been no shortage of occasions when not only did the two parties not vote together, but members of the same party voted differently.

It would be naïve to suggest that party interest is entirely absent in committees, but it is certainly not taken for granted. When the

Finance committee first met, members naturally gravitated to party colleagues and sat together. At the following meeting, I suggested as convener that seating should be in alphabetical order, to reinforce the impression that as a committee we were acting on behalf of the Parliament as a whole in our work. This was agreed and the arrangement has endured.

I am not aware of another committee which has adopted it and the only other committee of which I have experience is Social Inclusion, Housing and the Voluntary Sector, where it does not operate. That is not to say that members have set seats which they occupy each time the committee meets, but certainly the Labour and SNP members do sit with party colleagues. To some extent, this signifies the fact that the committee is more overtly party political than the Finance committee and this is just one way in which I have found the two to be in contrast. I doubt that Jack McConnell would claim he has an easy ride when giving evidence to the Finance committee (with three party finance spokespersons plus the SNP's Treasury spokesperson on the committee, he is certainly questioned knowledgeably) but he is received courteously. The same cannot always be said in respect of the Social Inclusion committee, where considerably more robust questioning has greeted the Communities Minister and some non-Parliament witnesses, particularly from SNP members.

Equally, divisions in the Finance committee are rare, and are not always based on party lines. Having said that, one of those divisions involved my use of the casting vote. It concerned the controversial issue of the Barnett formula, which decides the basis on which increases to the Scottish-assigned budget are allocated by the Treasury. This has become a party political issue, with the SNP determined that the formula should be reviewed to make it more beneficial to Scotland. The contrary view – which is certainly the Labour Party one – is that we do rather well from Barnett as long as the UK economy is growing (which it is likely to do for the foreseeable future) and that, were the formula re-examined and subjected to a needs assessment involving the whole of the UK, Scotland could only lose as a result. The issue when the committee was split evenly (one member being absent) was whether we simply received briefings on the issue or moved straight to a full inquiry.

My casting vote was in favour of the former, although I was aware that this left me open to charges of party bias.

The Health and Community Care committee deals with sensitive, often controversial, issues, but has usually done so on a non-partisan basis according to its convener, Margaret Smith. 'There has been only one party political incident in the committee all year, when the minister, Susan Deacon, was being questioned on the Arbuthnott report (on the allocation of health resources throughout Scotland). Otherwise, opposition has been constructive, even on an issue like the Private Finance Initiative where its effectiveness, rather than the principle, has driven our examination of it,' (interview, July 2000).

Be that as it may, it is simply impossible for party views to be expunged entirely from the committee rooms. The best that can be hoped for is that members will, as far as possible, exercise their best judgement on issues and in my experience that is achieved. Speaking for my own party, there is no whipping in operation at committees, although given that Executive legislation is likely to be in tune with most Labour and LibDem members, perhaps that is not too surprising.

As was always anticipated, there are examples of committees taking decisions which are not in line with Executive policy and one of these was the Social Inclusion, Housing and Voluntary Sector committee's housing stock transfer report. For six months from November 1999, the committee took evidence from a plethora of organisations on the Executive's controversial proposals to transfer housing stock from councils to locally-based housing associations. When the committee had finished taking evidence and making visits, we considered various drafts of the report to be presented to the Parliament. Each draft ran to around 100 pages and many hours were given over in committee, considering them line by line.

21 June 2000: I have rarely seen such anger as I witnessed today in the Social Inclusion committee. Margaret Curran's knuckles were white as she reacted to Fiona Hyslop's attack. Great drama, and Margaret was justified, but thankfully the committee was in private session.

When the penultimate version of the draft committee report was being discussed in June, Fiona Hyslop, the committee vice-convener

26 June 2000: Raised tempers. Margaret Curran (right) and Fiona Hyslop clash at the Social Inclusion Committee (source: Parliament Broadcasting Unit)

and the SNP's housing spokesperson, claimed that the convener, Margaret Curran, had submitted a raft of amendments designed to make the report less critical of the Executive position. She was supported by her colleagues Lloyd Quinan and Alex Neil, and the accusation caused great resentment among other committee members. The claims were utterly false because what Margaret had done was no more than had been agreed at the previous week's meeting. All other committee members (Labour, LibDem and Tory) backed the convener, following which the three SNP members walked out of the meeting.

It is no exaggeration to say that, while those of us remaining were outraged at this behaviour there was also a sense of dismay that the committee – and by extension the Parliament itself – had been tarnished by the whole episode. The following day's media reports confirmed these fears but the next meeting failed to resolve the matter, which Fiona Hyslop announced she would be referring to the Procedures committee. It was an unedifying spectacle and an unpleasant experience, one which I hope the Parliament will not often witness again. But it did illustrate that there will be occasions when party interests override the general aim of the committees to work for the Parliament as a whole.

Reporting the committees

When the committee's report on housing stock transfer was published in July 2000, it offered only qualified endorsement of the Executive's proposals. Yet the media coverage focussed more on the SNP's minority report than on the substantial recommendations of the report itself. This was intensely frustrating for those of us who had spent so much time and effort on complex issues which could have a dramatic effect on the standard of living of many Scots in the years ahead.

Press coverage of the report's publication illustrated the extent to which, after the first year, even the broadsheet newspapers have failed to appreciate fully the work of the Parliament's committees.

Quite apart from missing the big picture in terms of the report's contents, the article relating to it published by *The Herald*, almost unbelievably, carried the headline 'Executive committee backs transfer of council housing' (14 July 2000). Most of the school pupils whom I have shown round the Parliament appreciate that the work of the committees is quite separate from that of the Executive. It was an appalling blunder by a paper which should have known better.

During the year, other committee reports became the subject of media attention. Unlike their Westminster equivalent (where select committee reports are rarely debated and equally rarely lead to government action), reports in the Scottish Parliament carry considerable weight and are presented to the Parliament as a whole. They are not generally endorsed with a vote, although this is the case when they are the subject of a debate in the chamber. Twelve half days each year are made available for debating committee reports and these are allocated by the Conveners' Liaison Group. Whether or not they are debated, where reports make recommendations for Executive action, it is expected that these will be taken into account by the Executive. Should they decline to implement the recommendations, this could lead to a vote in the Parliament, where MSPs' loyalty to party as opposed to committee would be tested. This has not yet happened.

The premature appearance of committee reports has also become an issue. In February 2000, the Education, Culture and Sport committee's report into the national arts companies (which included the controversial funding crisis at Scottish Opera) was a victim of this but the most notable incident occurred in December 1999. The Health and Community Care committee published its report on the Arbuthnott committee's recommendations. It was critical of the targeting of resources and, by extension, of the Scottish Executive and was the subject of an unfortunate leak (the source of which was never identified) two days before it was due for publication.

Executive ministers, who had not been given sight of the report, responded to journalists on its alleged contents and this further concerned the committee's convener, Margaret Smith: 'Ministers at Westminster have a policy of not commenting on leaked reports and I was dismayed that that was not followed by the Scottish Executive; it seemed to do nothing to dissuade anyone motivated to leak reports in the future' (interview, July 2000).

She won support for this argument at the Conveners' Liaison Group, which attempted to enshrine in a protocol which it was drawing up with the Executive an undertaking that neither a minister nor any of his/her staff would comment on a leaked report. The Executive responded that it could not refuse to do so once the information was in the public domain and there followed a stand-off lasting several weeks before a modified wording was agreed, which was rather less robust than the conveners had wanted.

A report of the Finance committee, of which I am convener, also led to some controversy when it was published in June 2000. The report was the conclusion to stage one of the new budget process, which is spread over a full year and involves consulting with each of the Parliament's subject committees. Their role is to scrutinise the Executive's spending proposals at three stages, utilising the expert knowledge which they have built up in their own subject areas. As an indication that the process is fluid and still developing, during the first year the Finance committee, responding to representations from the women's group Engender, asked each committee to look at gender impact when considering the spending plans.

The Finance committee prepared its report to the Parliament from the comments which it had received from other Parliament committees of the spending proposals for 2001–2. In fact, very little was said about the figures contained in the proposals, most of the comment relating to the form in which the information had been made available and the consequent difficulty of committee members in making a properly-informed response.

This led to the Finance committee presenting a report which was critical of the consultation process and calling for 'radical changes' to the structure, content and style of the document containing the proposals. News coverage of this – and the subsequent debate on the report in the Parliament – centred on criticism of the Executive and Finance Minister Jack McConnell. Although factually correct, this missed two points. First, it illustrated the fact that committees were prepared to be constructively critical and did so on the basis of acting for the Parliament as a whole. This was surely at its most meaningful when a Labour-chaired committee did so. Secondly, this represented the first manifestation of a revolutionary new system of transparency in budget planning, which was light years ahead of the House of Commons model. Again, this was thought barely worthy of comment, by the same editors and journalists who accuse the Scottish Parliament of making 'no difference'.

Setting standards

> *23 June 1999:* I *was lobbied for the first time as an MSP today. The Friends of the Victoria sent a fifteen-strong delegation to the Parliament to tell Glasgow members in no uncertain terms that the hospital must be saved.*

As was to be expected, the committee which has attracted most media attention has been Standards. Much of the committee's efforts over the first year were directed at the important task of drawing up the Code of Conduct which regulates MSPs' behaviour inside and outside the Parliament, but it also carried out two inquiries involving controversial issues.

The most noteworthy concerned what has come to be known as 'Lobbygate', when newspaper allegations were made in September 1999 about access provided by certain ministers to Beattie Media, a public affairs and public relations company. This was an incident waiting to happen from the day the Parliament opened its doors so perhaps it was of some benefit that it was dealt with at an early stage of the institution's development.

I know from personal experience (for two years I was a director of a public affairs company in Edinburgh) that lobbying excites great interest, much of it fuelled by ignorance of what is actually involved. In fact, lobbying is a perfectly legitimate activity which is to be found in and around every democratic legislature worldwide. One of the strengths of the Scottish Parliament is that it is open and accessible to Scotland's people and its organisations, in many different forms, and one of the Parliament's biggest successes thus far has been its attempts to encourage people to connect with it.

Any MSP will admit that, on a daily basis, he or she receives unsolicited communications by telephone, e-mail, letter or in person from a wide range of individuals and organisations seeking to influence the work of that member or of the Parliament itself. No matter the form such contact takes, it constitutes lobbying. Some believe that because certain companies act on behalf of clients, their approaches are less legitimate or even illegitimate. My view is that the activity does have to be regulated but, providing those lobbying do so in an open and transparent manner, making it clear at all times on whose behalf the lobbying is being carried out, then the basic tests of legitimacy are met. Ultimately, what importance or weight an MSP attaches to information or advice, in whatever form, delivered to him or her is entirely a matter of individual judgement.

It would be misleading to suggest that is the opinion of all MSPs, but the majority view will become known in the autumn of 2000, when the Standards committee publishes its report on lobbying companies. The report will be informed by a questionnaire which all MSPs were invited to complete and will be submitted to the Parliament for endorsement as a means of regulating all such activity.

To a major extent, the Standards committee's initiative on this issue was driven by the 'Lobbygate' affair. The issue dominated the Scottish media for several days and the Standards committee immediately instigated its inquiry. Suffice to say that all those within the Parliament accused of impropriety were cleared. The major fall-out eventually concerned Beattie Media, which announced that it was shutting down its public affairs arm.

Apparently it needs to be restated that the inquiry was the committee's initiative. It was surprising to read a journalist of Murray Ritchie's experience claim (*Scotland Reclaimed*, p. 213) that Donald Dewar 'ordered an inquiry by the Parliament's Standards committee'. This suggests that the Executive has the power to set committee agendas; nothing could be further from the truth and were it not so, the very basis on which the independence of the committee structure has been established would be fatally undermined.

Tricia Marwick, a member of the Standards committee, says it was 'a searing experience; it was as if we were under siege from the media. The CSG had not set up a procedure for investigating complaints and the committee was working in the dark. Our decision to put everyone on oath was an important moment because it gave the inquiry *gravitas* and made people take it seriously.' For her, the conduct of that inquiry stands out as a defining moment in the Parliament's first year: 'There is often a deliberate blurring by the Executive between the Scottish Parliament and the Scottish Executive; during Lobbygate we dealt with that, with the Parliament shown to be supreme,' (interview, June 2000).

That the inquiry was carried out at all – far less that it took place in the full glare of publicity – was testament to the modern, responsive and effective procedures of the Scottish Parliament. When a similar case was highlighted, concerning ministers and their advisers, in the UK Parliament in the summer of 1998, no House of Commons inquiry followed.

The Standards committee's other notable inquiry was rather close to home, in that I myself was the subject of it. In October 1999 I was reported to the committee by the Tory MSP Ben Wallace, a bitter opponent of my Protection of Wild Mammals Bill. Wallace claimed that assistance which I had received in the legal drafting of the bill, plus the administrative support which was provided to enable me to reply to more than 1,000 letters relating to it, constituted a breach of the Scotland Act. The allegation was that the assistance amounted to 'remuneration'.

In both cases, these activities had been paid for by the Scottish Campaign Against Hunting with Dogs, the umbrella organisation backing me in taking the bill through Parliament. In neither case had I received any personal gain and indeed, without that support, it would have been impossible for me to introduce, far less progress, the bill. Wallace must have been aware of this, but his aim appears to have been to win a Standards committee ruling against me, making my position untenable and leading to the bill (which at that time had not been formally introduced) being abandoned. After receiving my seven-page submission, the committee did not deem it necessary to invite me to give evidence, declaring that I had done nothing improper, but advising me to add the support which I had received to my entry in the register of members' interests.

Reviewing their experiences of the year, MSPs across the parties speak of the effectiveness of the committees. LibDem Donald Gorrie, who is also an MP, says, 'They have done some really good work and stuck to their guns against the Executive, unlike in the House of Commons. The Local Government committee got good concessions from the Executive on the Ethical Standards Bill, on rights of appeal for councillors and extending the provisions to many quangos,' (interview, July 2000).

Labour's Maureen Macmillan agrees, although she says some committees are still 'searching for a role'. A member of the European committee, she commented: 'It has a remit so huge that it is struggling to find its way on some issues and it has tried to do too much. Inevitably, reserved issues arise and it is difficult to say no,' (interview, June 2000). Her colleague Pauline McNeill echoes this, saying 'their workload is infinite. In the Health committee [of which she is a member] there are so many dimensions. Each issue opens new doors and we want to deal with it thoroughly. So much evidence is available and there is a queue of people waiting to give it,' (interview, June 2000).

James Douglas Hamilton (a former Tory Scottish Office minister and now also a member of the House of Lords) is able to contrast past and present experiences. 'Having no revising chamber was one aspect of the Scots Parliament which concerned me. But committees are more powerful than in the House of Commons and they have used that to good effect in the first year,' (interview, July 2000).

Kenny Gibson, an SNP member of the Local Government committee, says it has achieved genuine cross-party consensus. 'Until dealing with amendments to the Ethical Standards in Public Life Bill, we had not had a vote in the committee's first thirteen months, despite contentious issues like the McIntosh report (on the relationship between the Parliament and local government) being discussed. And our committee has certainly engaged with civic Scotland, because we have visited fifteen local authorities in our first year,' (interview, August 2000).

Scottish MPs have also been impressed with the performance of the committees. Brian Donohoe believes, 'the committees are working well, and you can see that. They have made a useful start to the process of examining the Executive and should be complemented on it. It's quite different in the House of Commons, where shaping legislation is only possible in standing committees; in the Scottish Parliament it's possible for all committees,' (interview, July 2000).

Never one to go with the flow, Tory Brian Monteith believes, 'the success of the committees has been exaggerated. There is a fundamental problem: having the dual role of both legislation and inquiries is difficult. The Justice and Home Affairs committee does not have adequate time to scrutinise the Executive, while the Education, Culture and Sport committee [of which he is a member] is dominated by education; culture and sport are dealt with only when there is a crisis,' (interview, July 2000).

The Liberal Democrat convener of the Health and Community Care committee, Margaret Smith, believes the committees have done 'an incredible job in terms of scrutiny, compared to Westminster. But we're seriously under-resourced: my committee has half a researcher to assist us in scrutinising a budget of more than £5 billion' (interview, July 2000).

The conveners stand their ground

> **27 June 2000:** *After a year of arguing our case with the Parliamentary Bureau, today saw a triumph for the Conveners' Liaison Group in winning official status as a body within the Parliament.*

During the year, and without attracting much media attention, an additional Scottish parliamentary committee was established. As mentioned previously, the Conveners' Liaison Group had been formed to enable the sixteen conveners to meet when necessary to consider issues of mutual interest concerning the operation of the committees. However, it established a fortnightly schedule of meetings and soon developed a life and a status of its own.

The committee had been set up by the Presiding Officer, Sir David Steel, with one of his deputies, George Reid, as convener. I was not the only group member to suggest that a committee comprising exclusively conveners ought not to have too much trouble electing one of our own to convene it, but this was resisted by the Presiding Officer and eventually we relented. This was at least in part because of the fact that Reid has a manner which makes him ideally suited to the role, and he has proved not just a firm and fair chair of our meetings but has also been demonstrably effective behind the scenes on behalf of the group and our agenda.

That latter role was necessary because the Conveners' Liaison Group had to fight determinedly to gain official recognition within the Parliament's standing orders and to shake off the 'liaison group' tag. Initially, the party business managers resisted such status being granted, perhaps fearing that a committee of conveners, anxious to have a say in the conduct of the business of Parliament, could challenge their own authority in this area. Eventually, this was precisely the role given to the new committee when its formal status was agreed in June 2000. This happened when, following a protracted exchange of missives delivered between the two bodies by George

Reid, the group delegated Trish Godman and John McAllion to argue the case with the Parliamentary Bureau.

That they were successful illustrates not just that the committee conveners wield considerable influence but, perhaps more importantly, that the business managers do not maintain an inflexible approach and are willing to reach an accommodation when a persuasive case is made to them.

When the group achieves formal status as a Parliamentary Body (standing orders preclude it being known as a committee), it will add to the powers which it had already assembled. These are more extensive than is generally appreciated and include decisions on which committee reports are debated in the parliament; whether or not committee requests to meet outside Edinburgh are appropriate; and vetting committee requests for a share of the Parliament's research budget. The new committee will also decide which committee will take the lead in the processing of bills (hitherto the responsibility of the Parliamentary Bureau), circumscribe the role of committee reporters who are appointed to carry out investigations into specific subjects, and take on responsibility (again from the Bureau) for building links with civic society.

The very establishment of the conveners' committee is a refreshing example of how flexible the Scottish Parliament is prepared to be in responding to exigencies by declaring, basically, that if there is a more effective, more inclusive means of doing our business, then let's do it that way.

Challenges

One area in which the committees have not been as successful as had been anticipated concerns their ability to get out of Edinburgh. The Consultative Steering Group proposed that:

> committees should be encouraged to meet and to take evidence outside Edinburgh, particularly when the subject matter might affect people staying in a particular area of Scotland, and that in a number of cases committees should have their permanent base somewhere other than Edinburgh.

I am not aware that the idea of a permanent base away from the capital has been seriously considered, nor that it is necessarily a practical proposition. However, in terms of the committees' general mobility, there is considerable scope for improvement.

There are certainly constraints on doing so, the most notable being time. With the Parliament meeting on Wednesday afternoon and all day Thursday, this leaves only Tuesday within the normal 'parliamentary week'. If travel time (one way) for a visit exceeds three hours, then the meeting will require an overnight stay. This does not represent a barrier in terms of cost, but it does make it difficult in terms of both MSP and staff time, particularly the latter. For a committee to meet requires not just clerking support but the official report, sound engineers and attendants. All are already fully stretched without setting foot outside the parliamentary campus, and it places obvious restrictions on committees meeting in Edinburgh if support staff are in transit when needed.

In the first year, a major factor in the lack of committees venturing into the wide blue yonder was financial considerations, although ironically, this did not involve a shortage of resources. On the contrary, for the period ending in March 2000, the budget for committee travel was underspent by almost £100,000. Had the same amount been overspent, there can be little doubt newspapers would have taken great delight in highlighting MSPs' 'profligacy' (it would probably have been called junketing if overnight stays were involved). That is, at least subconsciously, probably one reason for committees being disinclined to travel. Chastened by the reaction to the allowances issue, many MSPs are extremely reluctant to give the media further excuses for negative reporting where expenditure is involved.

Such considerations certainly featured in the Social Inclusion, Housing and the Voluntary Sector committee when we were scheduling the work programme for our inquiry into drug misuse. The committee's special adviser for the inquiry had suggested that Dublin's parallels with the main cities in Scotland meant that useful lessons could be learned from seeing and hearing about them. Originally, the committee delayed a decision, then decided not to go because we were not convinced it could be justified. That justification was as much an evaluation of what the media reaction could be as the validity of what committee members might have gained from being in Dublin. Later, when our second special adviser emphasised the potential value of the visit, the committee reconsidered and decided that it should, after all, go ahead – but for two days, in the recess and with only the convener plus one member from each of the four parties being allowed to go.

Such caution contrasts starkly with House of Commons select committees, which travel regularly around the world, almost exclusively when the Parliament is in session and always with the full committee. That includes the Scottish Affairs select committee, yet you would search in vain to detect any Scottish newspaper criticism of such activities. That is not to suggest that House of Commons committees should not travel, merely an attempt to illustrate that the Scottish Parliament does not enjoy the benefit of any doubt.

When that Dublin visit took place in August 2000, it was only the second occasion on which a committee of the Scottish Parliament had travelled outside the country. The other was a visit made by the European committee to Brussels in March 2000; given that committee's remit, it might quite legitimately have been expected to make additional visits during the year.

Public expectation has been – and remains – that the Parliament should not be restricted to Edinburgh. For those outwith the central belt, there is the further hope that it will be prepared to indulge in more than day trips in order to connect with the electorate. The record so far does not suggest that will be the case to any significant extent and neither do scheduled developments.

There were only ten committee meetings outside Edinburgh in the Parliament's first year, in Stirling, in Glasgow, in Galashiels and in Inverness. This left swathes of the country untouched and much of Scotland's population denied the opportunity to attend a committee meeting and see their Parliament in action in their own area. It should be stressed that many committees have held visits as part of inquiries, but while these usually involve meetings with local authorities, colleges, the business sector, trade unions, community groups or the voluntary sector, they do not constitute a formal meeting and are open only to those people directly involved in meeting the parliamentarians. Often such meetings involve only some members of a committee. For example on one day, as part of the drug misuse inquiry, the Social Inclusion, Housing and Voluntary Sector committee split into three separate groups which visited Aberdeen, Ayrshire and Glasgow. This makes sense and is of considerable value in informing a committee's work, but it should not be seen as an alternative to holding formal meetings outwith the capital.

The omens for this happening are not portentous. Readers of *The Herald* on 12 June 2000 were presented with a front-page story entitled 'Holyrood to spread its wings from Edinburgh'. Was this the big breakthrough dawning? Would the parliament, fired with the success just the previous month of its sojourn in Glasgow, recreate that warm embrace by visiting Inverness, Dumfries, Stornoway or Dundee? Well, no. Did it then signal an ambitious programme of scheduled committee meetings in Scotland's smaller and farther-flung centres of population, including the islands? Wrong again. In fact, the first paragraph revealed all you needed to know about the wingspan of the Holyrood eagle: 'The first steps have been taken which could lead to a permanent presence in Glasgow for MSPs, with the City Chambers playing host to parliamentary committees.'

It was later confirmed that there would indeed be regular Monday meetings in the City Chambers on a scheduled basis, beginning in the autumn of 2000. Representing a Glasgow constituency, I am naturally delighted at any boost which the city receives either in terms of status or financial spin-off. And I certainly welcome any occasion on which a committee to which I belong meets in the dear green place (quite apart from the consideration that it provides me with an extra hour in bed that morning). But I cannot imagine that MSPs from outwith Glasgow will share the attraction and for Scots living outwith the central belt it makes not a bit of difference in terms of accessibility to their Parliament.

At the time of writing, the only other suggestion as to a semi-permanent base for parliamentary committees is another central-belt venue, Stirling Council chambers. This falls far short of the original plan to make the Parliament accessible to Scotland in its widest sense. Determined attempts must be made to connect the Parliament to the highlands and islands, the Borders and our third and fourth cities; if that means that more support staff have to be employed, then that must be done. If newspapers want to attack the Scottish Parliament for reaching out to its people, then they will soon become the laughing stock many of them have been trying to label the Parliament.

It is more than a little ironic that the Scottish Parliament which was 'adjourned' in 1707 did not have a permanent base and used to rove the country meeting in several different locations. How embarrassing if, with the rather better travel and communications available to the modern version, it should prove to be more static than its predecessor.

If we do not overcome the hurdles that seem to be impeding the Parliament's mobility, then we will fail the people of Scotland. Suggesting that only the main centres of population are suitable for hosting the committees runs counter to the vision of an outward-looking legislature with which they were presented. Such timidity also flies in the face of the 'can-do' philosophy apparent in so many other instances since the Parliament was established.

Not only can we do it, we *must* do it. Let the media lead that campaign by demanding that the necessary resources are made available for it to become a reality. And when it does, let them get on their bikes to report to Scotland what its Parliament really does on a day-to-day basis.

> **6 June 2000:** *Problems arose concerning the Finance committee's inquiry into European structural funds. Gordon Brown has declined our request for him to give evidence; we shall reiterate the invitation, with a fall-back of a Treasury official attending.*

One final aspect of the work of the committees also requires clarification before a settled pattern can emerge. Perhaps the most important characteristic of the committees' operation is the frequency with which they call Scottish Executive ministers to give evidence. This contrasts with the House of Commons where permanent secretaries (the top civil servant in the department) appear and speak with authority for their department. They do so on behalf of the government and essentially are asked the same questions which select committee members would put to the minister were he or she there. Instances when UK government ministers appear at select committees are rare and that may explain their reluctance to do so at Scottish Parliament committees.

There have been only two instances where a committee invited a UK government minister to give evidence. Both concerned a linked inquiry being undertaken into European structural funds by the Finance and European committees. Each committee invited the Chancellor of the Exchequer, Gordon Brown, to appear and answer questions on the Treasury's interpretation of the Barnett formula as it affects the disbursement of EU funds within Scotland. The Chancellor declined both, directing the committees to the Scottish Executive Finance Minister, Jack McConnell, who, he said, could adequately reflect policy in that area.

Neither committee accepted this. The European committee sought instead to have the Secretary of State for Scotland, John Reid, appear while the Finance committee reiterated its belief that the Chancellor was the most appropriate source of the information which it sought. The Chancellor again declined and it was not possible either for a Treasury official to give evidence to the committee, despite the fact that a senior official from his department had done so for the committee's previous inquiry.

John Reid made his position clear when giving evidence to the Scottish Affairs select committee at the House of Commons on 21 June 2000: 'I have no intention of speaking to the (European) committee... I'm accountable to this parliament.' However, he did temper this by saying also that while his attending a Holyrood committee 'would not be the norm... there are no principled objections.' Later, this drew the riposte from SNP leader Alex Salmond that Reid was 'trying to block the work of the Scottish Parliament,' (*The Scotsman*, 22 June 2000). This rather missed the point, because what John Reid was saying was that he did not see it as his role to attempt to influence the Scottish Parliament one way or the other. Or, as he put it in his evidence at the same committee meeting, 'what cannot happen is that this Parliament regards itself... as the masters or the ministers of the Scottish Parliament or *vice versa*.' That was alright as far as it went, but it ignored the fact that Communities Minister Wendy Alexander had travelled to the House of Commons just a few weeks earlier to give evidence to the Scottish Affairs select committee's inquiry into poverty.

There is a lack of consistency on this matter which needs to be resolved. As convener of the Finance committee, I can say that we were unanimously of the opinion that our inquiry into EU funding could not be completed without Treasury evidence. The committee eventually had to accept this in writing, while the European committee completed its report without any UK-level input, a conclusion which was less than satisfactory.

Sooner or later, this tug-of-war will re-occur. For instance, as part of a future poverty inquiry, the Social Inclusion, Housing and Voluntary Sector committee will likely wish to consider the effect which the proposed review of housing benefit might have. Although housing benefit is a reserved issue, the committee has already discussed the possibility of inviting the Social Security Secretary, Alistair Darling, to give evidence. That prospect has an intriguing nuance in that the Parliament is based in Darling's own constituency...

How might this delicate issue be resolved? Perhaps through the protocols which exist between the two legislatures, with a provision that while the assumption would be that it should not be necessary for UK ministers to attend Scottish Parliament committees, there would be cases where this was appropriate. The arrangement would be reciprocal. Such issues are enthusiastically reported, and if some form of understanding is not reached, the matter will become a source of rancour between Edinburgh and London, to the advantage of neither.

At the end of the first year of their operation, the view of most observers is that the work of the committees is perhaps the Parliament's greatest achievement. Most MSPs would admit to having gained greatly in knowledge and expertise as a result of their experience, which will have its benefit in subsequent years as these skills are utilised to ensure the Executive is held to account.

When there will prove to be sufficient time for the committees to enter the only door so far unopened – that of initiating legislation – remains to be seen. Perhaps the Executive will hope they do not do so with great gusto, such is the existing pressure on legislative timetabling (not to mention the policy uncertainty inherent in that role). However, if the committees themselves are rationalised, then fewer members having to serve on two committees could mean that these committees would meet more often, thus increasing their capacity for setting their own agenda, as opposed to having it largely circumscribed by Executive legislation.

I hope, too, that the people of Scotland will increase their engagement with the Parliament in general and the committees in particular. The Petitions committee has been inundated with public petitions arriving from many individuals as well as organisations. Clearly, this aspect of the Parliament's accessibility has quickly become understood, together with the knowledge that the Parliament has an obligation to consider them, while Westminster does not.

Mind you, there could and should be a greater public presence at committees when they meet (albeit mainly in Edinburgh), as there should be a greater demand for committees to make themselves more available and accessible throughout the country. Perhaps these are issues which the Civic Forum might take up and encourage. The Parliament voted funds of £300,000 over the next three years for the Forum to enable it to become established and it is beginning to develop its profile. If the demand which I believe exists from across Scotland is articulated clearly and in a variety of accents, then it will not be possible for the Parliament to turn a deaf ear. Civic Scotland is clearing its collective throat and MSPs should receive the message loud and clear.

At the outset in May 1999, I believed the committees would become the engine room of the Parliament. With the benefit of experience, I hold that view even more strongly and I keenly anticipate the further development of their role as the driving force of Scotland's new democracy.

10 / And now what?

> *1 July 2000: Speaking at a Study of Parliament seminar in the committee chambers it almost escaped my notice that this was the first anniversary of that day. Was it just one year? It seemed as though enough has happened to fill five.*

My mother often claimed that an early school report card of mine contained the ambivalent assessment 'He is trying'. Whether or not the story is apocryphal, I suspect that, given the course of events, most MSPs would not regard a similar appraisal of the Parliament's first full year as overly harsh.

It has been said that a parliament has three major functions: to introduce legislation which improves the life of the people who elected it; to scrutinise the executive and ensure it is acting responsibly on behalf of those people; and to provide a forum for the discussion of public issues. If these constitute valid measures, the Scottish Parliament's often unsteady maiden voyage has been negotiated with some success. But it *is* only one year and any success requires qualification.

BBC political editor Brian Taylor had anticipated that the Parliament would succeed. 'I felt it would become "big league" politics so I'm not surprised that, despite negative media coverage, it has already developed into a significant institution. I also expected it to overtake the Commons in importance, but I've been seriously surprised at the extent and speed of its eclipse of Westminster in Scottish terms,' (interview, September 2000).

That the Parliament's year zero has been a rollercoaster should surprise no-one – every subsequent year will mirror these fortunes, at least in general terms. The most notable of the events – those which have marked the highs and lows – have had a double-edged effect on the Parliament. On the one hand, they invite criticism and highlight divisions between (and occasionally within) the parties; on the other, they demonstrate that the Parliament is dealing with issues of substance and in doing so can produce distinctively Scottish legislation.

The end of the Parliament's first year brought a welter of reviews and assessments, the general consensus of which seemed to be that it had seen a reasonable start made to the repatriation of politics. The *Sunday Herald*'s conclusion was realistic: 'Many could claim the Parliament has achieved a little. That is all that could have been expected of it,' (editorial, 30 April 2000).

For what it is worth, that pretty much sums up my own view of the political landscape four months later. However, I am reluctant to accede to the apparent need to categorise the Parliament as a success or a failure so quickly. There is no sense in rushing to judgement. Meaningful assessments cannot be made over a period less than the first four-year session; arguably, they should be delayed until the end of the second, by which time the people of Scotland will have many tangible benefits on which to base their opinions.

So much has happened in such a short period that, if nothing else, the Scottish Parliament has already demonstrated that its very existence generates political activity and interest on an unprecedented scale in our country. Had I been offered, on the day that the Parliament sat for the first time in May 1999, a vision of the future showing precisely where it would stand in July 2000, I am in no doubt I would have said, 'I'll settle for that as a start.'

The first year has seen the Parliament legislate with gusto; a total of eleven bills completed their progress on a wide range of subject areas, and for most of these sufficient time would never have been found at Westminster. At least as many are planned for the second year and that is likely to be the pattern as the Parliament becomes established. That level of legislative activity cannot but materially affect the lives of people living in Scotland for the better.

Of course, one of the features which most distinguishes the Scottish Parliament from the legislature which spawned it is that initiating legislation is not restricted to the Executive. Although establishing their primary role of scrutinising Executive bills was the committees' priority, they will soon begin to develop their own legislative function. To do so effectively will almost certainly require a consensual approach, so as to achieve all-party support. This could lead to strains between the partnership parties and their own members on committees. What if committees decide to sponsor legislation that the Executive does not want or cannot support? In such a situation would the independence of committee members withstand the test of loyalties between party and Parliament?

Another possible scenario concerns committee priorities. Imagine for a moment that a committee becomes frustrated at being unable to initiate its own legislation because of the weight of Executive bills being referred to it. The committee might then decide to say to the Executive, 'Sorry, we cannot consider your bill X at the moment because we have decided to give our own bill priority.' The Executive – using its control of the Parliamentary Bureau – might retaliate by refusing to schedule parliamentary time for the committee's own bill. That would not exactly lead to a constitutional crisis, but it could provoke a trial of strength which would pit Executive against Parliament and would, to put it mildly, prove interesting. It might also serve the secondary, and necessary, purpose of illustrating to sections of the media that the two are not one and the same.

Dramatic though such confrontations would be, it is more likely that committees will identify gaps in legislation and seek to fill them. The hope would be that this would win Executive support, but should that not be forthcoming, the committee concerned would be perfectly justified in continuing.

Former committee clerk Sarah Davidson identified possible developments in the legislative process: 'It will be interesting to watch how non-Executive legislation develops. Once a member has decided on a subject for a bill, he or she might consider whether it would be more practical to take it forward as a Member's Bill or through a committee as a whole. Equally, one member of a committee could be given the responsibility of piloting a piece of committee legislation through its various stages, which would make it almost indistinguishable from a Member's Bill,' (interview, September 2000).

The *Daily Record*'s Dave King recognised a distinctive mood within the committees. 'The members act in a more consensual way than in the chamber, even when discussing the same issue. The new politics are only partly developed, but the seeds are there in the committees. And as the committee members hone their skills of interrogation, the committees have the potential to develop to the level of Senate committees in the USA,' (interview, September 2000).

Turning to the second test, an argument that the Executive *is* being held to account could be sustained. If not to any great extent in the chamber, there is clear evidence that it has happened in the Parliament's committees. Amendments to legislation such as the Census Amendment Bill and the Ethical Standards in Public Life Bill – not to mention the continued existence of the Abolition of Poindings and Warrant Sales Bill – are among the most obvious examples. In respect of the manner in which the Sheridan bill was reprieved, I endorse the assessment of columnist Ian Bell: 'The Westminster committees, forever bolting the stable door after the horse has fled, would never have supplied the moral ammunition capable of stopping the executive in its tracks,' (*Scotland on Sunday*, 30 April 2000).

As the expertise of committees, both in their subject areas and in their ability to maximise their powers increases, so too will their overall effectiveness – individually as well as collectively. Be scared, Scottish Executive, be very scared (well, be on your mettle, at least).

The third of the parliamentary functions concerns acting as a crucible for debate on matters of broad public interest or concern. In a sense, every matter discussed by the Parliament qualifies under this heading, but I would assess this in terms of debates which engage with and/or respond to public opinion. There has been no shortage of controversial issues; indeed, they have been the feature of the first year. But this can be a double-edged sword, because they expose a divergence of views over priorities. The most contentious issues of year zero were the repeal of clause 2a; the abolition of tuition fees; the 'Lobbygate' affair; and my proposal to ban the hunting of wild mammals with dogs. These and many other issues have provoked debate in the media and across Scotland; on some the majority were with the Parliament, on others they were not.

This emphasises the fact that, while the Executive must remain in touch with opinion across Scotland, they cannot allow government by referendum. Nor should they draft, or alter, policy in response to media campaigns. Attempts at both were made during the first year, happily without success. But who can deny that the Scottish political scene is not more vibrant than was the case prior to devolution? People may not always welcome being force-fed political issues but the issues are there and the debate around them – outside as well as inside the Parliament – is accessible. The 'off' switch is always within reach for those who prefer not to engage.

A number of commentators have stated their belief that the Parliament has not yet caught the imagination of the Scottish public, that it has not broken out of the *cul de sac* occupied by the so-called 'chattering classes'. There is some truth in this, although I believe it to be exaggerated. The amount of media coverage given to events in or connected with the Parliament is considerably greater than was the case prior to home rule, and it is much greater than the political coverage available to inhabitants of England's regions about the delivery of healthcare, education or housing in their areas. Without wishing either to revisit the ground covered in Chapter four, or to resort too much to the blame culture for which I criticise political opponents, the media does have a responsibility to report events accurately. What concerns me most about the tabloid press is that it often appears to hold its readership in contempt, believing they are incapable of interpreting events, as a result of which they have to be told what to think.

My experience is that, while the average person does not have a great interest in politics (which is certainly not a sign of inadequacy), he or she does have a firm grasp of events which interest them. I suspect more people in Scotland are politically aware now than has ever been the case, for which devolution is primarily responsible. If I could have a single wish granted, I would probably opt for the media as a whole, and the tabloid newspapers in particular, to be required simply to present events unadulterated and invite their readers to interpret or dig down to whatever level of interest they have. Need that be hopelessly idealistic? I suppose it must.

One of the most intriguing aspects of the Parliament's first year has been the fault lines that have begun to appear. To a significant extent these have formed, not as many had anticipated, on a unionist-separatist basis, but on an urban-rural divide. Issues such as the farming crisis, job losses in the Borders, land reform, fox hunting, and feudal tenure have been cited as evidence of a gulf between town and country, the central belt as opposed to the Highlands and islands, or industrial versus rustic Scotland.

This is unfortunate for two reasons. First, because it is a false dichotomy, suggesting there are just two Scotlands. People in Aberdeen and Dundee can be heard railing against a perceived 'central-belt bias' just as loudly as those in Alness or Duns. Meanwhile, Glasgow complains about the level of health resources which it is allocated compared to Edinburgh; the Borders claims the Highlands and islands do better in terms of job creation initiatives; the fishing industry would like to have the level of support given to farming; and so on.

Secondly, it simply is not true to suggest that urban Scotland can benefit only at the expense of rural Scotland, or *vice versa*. The Parliament has a Rural Affairs committee, providing a focus which did not exist previously. The committee has scrutinised legislation and taken evidence on issues about which rural communities and organisations representing them were concerned; it has undertaken a study into rural unemployment and made recommendations which the Scottish Executive is acting upon. Meanwhile, the other committees have remits which are patently nationwide and they carry out their work accordingly.

The Parliament is much better able to adopt a pan-Scotland approach than was the case when political representation consisted of seventy-two MPs at Westminster. MSPs not only have more time to concentrate on more issues, they encompass a wider spread of political parties with more of a local focus. Meanwhile, with the work of MPs continuing, Scotland has the best of both worlds.

That said, it would be misleading to suggest that there is not also a unionist-separatist divide within the Parliament. While the SNP's ultimate aim is clear (although internally tactics and priorities may vary), the other three main parties are committed to ensuring that the Parliament flourishes within the United Kingdom. Although the Tories increasingly find themselves part of an informal opposition coalition with the Nationalists in the Parliament chamber (to their mutual embarrassment), they remain adamant that they would not vote to bring down the partnership. This is confirmed by their business manager, James Douglas Hamilton: 'In a vote of confidence, or even if at some point in the future the SNP were to become the biggest party, the role of the Tories would be to maintain the union; that is non-negotiable,' (interview, July 2000).

Columnist Iain Macwhirter has caricatured the Parliament in Jekyll and Hyde terms, claiming it demonstrates a 'constitutional schizophrenia which corresponds rather well to our national ambivalence towards Scottish identity and national life,' (Hassan and Warhurst, p. 17). The contrast he draws is, on the one hand, a confident start made by the Parliament as it introduces a range of legislation for which time was never found at Westminster; on the other, the characterisation of the typical MSP as a time-server from the darkest recesses of Scottish (Labour) local government.

That theory ignores not just the fact that the essential ingredient of Scottish (Labour) local government – untrammelled power – is notable by its absence at Holyrood but also that the long-awaited legislation of the Parliament's first year was framed by, scrutinised by, amended by and ultimately turned into law by these same time-servers. In fact, I would argue that the evidence suggests a more accurate description of the Parliament's elected members would be 'time-travellers', such is the dramatic advance represented by the Parliament which they form, not just on local government, but on the previous governance of Scotland.

As the Parliament's first year drew to a close, there was some media comment about the stress experienced by Scotland's new parliamentarians. Logically, this centred on those who had school-age (or younger) children, for many of whom the family-friendly policy was an important factor in their deciding to seek selection as a candidate. Ken Macintosh won the marginal seat of Eastwood for Labour. 'It's been very, very hard. There is as much work as you want to give it – you could work twenty-four hours a day, seven days a week. The difficulty is making time for your family. When you're elected to public office, part of you is public property.' Macintosh's constituency is mainly urban, but the LibDem Jamie Stone, who represents Caithness, Sutherland and Easter Ross, often covers 500 miles a week in addition to travelling to and from Edinburgh.

Unsurprisingly, he finds it exhausting. 'I'm not girning about it. This is what I signed up to. But I never expected the volume of stuff coming at you to be quite as heavy as it is.' Fiona Hyslop of the SNP is a list member for the Lothians and lives in Linlithgow. Nevertheless, with two pre-school children, she says, 'Although the Parliament is family-friendly, the problem is the stuff that comes with it – the party politics or the evening and weekend meetings. People expect to see you; you're accountable, and rightly so,' (all quotes, *Sunday Herald*, 16 April 2000).

The source of the stories on stress was a survey carried out by Salford University, which also looked at members of the House of Commons and the National Assembly of Wales. Interestingly, the conclusion was the same for all three, with Dr Ashley Weinberg, who conducted the survey, commenting, 'The common theme is lack of support in what they do in the constituency. A lot of what was planned for the [Scottish] Parliament was about the way it works, but not about the many demands facing them in their constituencies. It seems it takes more than better hours to make the job more family-friendly,' (*Sunday Herald*, 16 April, 2000).

Despite having two children below school age, Johann Lamont's feelings of stress emanated not from her work in the Parliament (where she speaks as frequently as any Labour backbencher) but in the constituency: 'I had no experience of running an office and what that involves – being a boss, allocating work, managing budgets. Dealing with casework was also new to me and I felt it was crucially important to get that right,' (interview, August 2000).

Her colleague Margaret Curran (a single mother with two sons) is determined that the demands of the job will not diminish the impact of women in the Parliament. However, she believes, 'We have to have a ruthlessness in favour of the family. All the evidence shows it's not just in the interests of women with kids. It's in the interests of good decision-making. We should accept we're not superhuman. We want ordinary balanced people there, not just those who feel they are the governing elite, as a lot of men seem to think they are,' (*Sunday Herald*, 16 April 2000).

The hours when the Parliament sits are certainly an issue, not least because of the difficulty in getting through the business in the time currently available. But any increase – say by introducing a Monday afternoon or a Wednesday evening session – would need to be balanced with the effects caused not just to family life but to work in and relationships with members' constituencies.

In establishing the Parliament, one of the aims was to bring government in Scotland closer to its people. To a considerable extent, the institution and its members have been successful in reaching out to the public. In a speech delivered on the first anniversary of the Parliament's official opening, the Presiding Officer, Sir David Steel, said, 'I think we have lived up to the Parliament's aspirations of openness, accessibility and accountability. In my thirty-five years in the Houses at Westminster, I have never seen such effective scrutiny of government and its agencies, nor the ready accessibility of the Parliament to so many bodies.'

His comparisons are certainly valid, although greater effort is required to take the Parliament's committees to areas of our country outwith the central belt, and resources should not be used as an excuse for restricting the extent to which we do so. Nevertheless, the first year has seen the Parliament firmly established as part of our national psyche. Not even its most persistent adversary would deny that it is here to stay.

It is the basic function of this book to convey a view of how the Parliament looks from the inside. The temptation to balance what the inhabitants (elected and unelected) had to say for themselves with some perspectives on how it appears from outside was resisted: that is for others to undertake. But I did make two exceptions. The first concerned MPs, who provided a Westminster perspective. The other was the Civic Forum, which is the body charged with the responsibility of articulating the views of Scottish civic society on the effectiveness of the Parliament. After one year, its director Donald Reid sees 'evidence that even where people have felt dissatisfied with new policy proposals, or with the Scottish Executive, they are satisfied with the Parliament as an institution. It is wrong to expect the "new Scotland" to be delivered in one year, but nevertheless the Parliament has made a substantial start'.

That could be said to equate to a B-plus, which as a report card for a year spent on a learning curve so steep that one member jumped off, and others retain a rather tenuous hold, is not too bad.

The central focus of the first year has been the partnership between the Labour Party and the LibDems. Derided by the opposition parties from the day it was formed, it has nevertheless succeeded at its most basic level: survival. That of course represents only the first lap of four; can it stay alive for the remainder of the race? Patently, it is in the interests of both partners that it does and I could find no MSP from any party willing to predict its collapse, despite the fast-moving agenda within the Parliament and its unpredictable nature.

Margaret Smith summed up the view from the junior partner: 'I expect it to go the full four years, although it could founder if there is no progress on achieving a more proportional voting system for local government. That's very important to us; one of the party's fundamental political principles is that of equity, of everyone's votes counting. The wording of the Partnership Agreement on PR is not as tight as we would have liked, although that's more of a problem for Labour than for us. My own view is that if a fairer system is not introduced for the next local government elections, then it must be in place for the one after that,' (interview, July 2000).

Should that turn out to be the price of maintaining the partnership, for Labour's Andy Kerr it would be too high: 'In reality, for Labour the principle [of PR] is politically unacceptable to a majority both of MSPs and of the party membership.' But ultimately he believes that hard politics would come into play: 'If the leadership of the two parties want it to run the full course, then it will. It's as simple as that,' (interview, September 2000).

Although it will doubtless need to withstand more stormy weather, I do expect the partnership to survive until 2003, as anticipated when the agreement was signed in May 1999. Out of necessity, an accommodation acceptable to both parties will be reached on the voting system for local authorities.

They would probably be unwilling to admit it, but I suspect the opposition party leaders share the expectation that the partnership will endure. Yet, whether driven by envy or frustration, they seem incapable of fully coming to terms with the fact that coalition government is the central feature of life in Scotland's redrawn political landscape. If either the Tories or the SNP were ever to get their hands on the reins of power, it could only be as part of a similar arrangement – perhaps even jointly. It was rather dispiriting to read John Swinney – albeit at the time involved in the SNP leadership contest – disparaging the LibDems as 'nothing more than Labour's voting fodder. They have been exposed as unprincipled power-seekers, completely in thrall to Labour, and everyone who voted for them at the last election must now be wondering why they bothered,' (*The Herald*, 1 September 2000).

The SNP might like to believe they hold the copyright on principled power-seeking, but when electors cast their votes in May 1999, they presumably did so in the hope that it would enable the party of their choice to influence directly how Scotland was governed. LibDem voters in May 1999 had that hope fulfilled, unlike those who voted for the SNP. That's democracy.

Assuming the partnership does last, it is interesting to speculate as to how its conflation of the two parties might affect the perceptions of the people of Scotland. There is likely to be a UK general election in 2001; there will certainly be a Scottish general election in 2003. Will either Labour or the LibDems – or both – suffer as a result of their cohabitation at Holyrood?

In terms of Westminster, Denis Robertson Sullivan, the LibDems' Scottish Treasurer, foresees problems for his party: 'In electoral terms, it's a negative (being in the partnership). LibDem voters will see it as being the right thing to have done, but we are less likely to win new voters as a result of it. I don't envisage a loss of seats, but I do anticipate our share of the popular vote across Scotland decreasing slightly.'

Commenting when the clause 2a debate was at its height, Michael Connarty voiced the fears of a number of his Labour colleagues in the House of Commons when he urged a strategy of 'joined-up politics' in the period until the UK general election. 'Our (MSP) colleagues have to realise that many Scots do not distinguish between Westminster and the Scottish Parliament. They only look at how Labour is performing in both places. MPs are next in the firing line and, unless things change, we will pay for their mistakes,' (*New Statesman Scotland*, 12 June 2000).

Looking ahead to 2003, Sullivan was again pessimistic. 'It will obviously depend to some extent on what happens at Holyrood in the intervening period, but assuming we come though it without major disaster, I foresee a similar situation to the general election. The difference will be that in 2003 a drop in our overall vote could cost us a list seat or two, which would be an ironic twist. Being in government should encourage a growth in support, especially if the partnership continues to deliver on its programme.'

Duncan McNeill's main opponent in 2003 will be the Liberal

Democrat cabinet minister, Ross Finnie. 'We may be political allies in the partnership in Parliament, but we remain political opponents in the constituency. Both of us understand that and, come the election, so will the electors,' (interview, September 2000).

But Margaret Smith felt her party had reasons to be cheerful: 'There are up and down sides, but more of the former. As a party, we've grown up quite a lot in the past year and, being in government, we can point to things we have achieved. Ending tuition fees is the clearest example but motorway tolling was dropped after we said, "we're not having it". And the Freedom of Information Bill will be much better than the version south of the border, because Scottish LibDems exerted pressure and overcame Labour's timidity,' (interview, July 2000).

Her colleague Donald Gorrie identified the other kind of PR as the priority for the Liberal Democrats: 'How we do in 2003 will depend on the extent to which we as a party publicise our achievements. We have been responsible for more in terms of the partnership than we are given credit for in the media and we have to work at improving that. Some of our leaders get twitchy about us criticising Labour but I don't see the problem with that; we have to maintain some distinctiveness. The voting system gives people the opportunity to split their votes between parties, so there's no reason why we should necessarily lose out. But we could,' (interview, July 2000).

As Donald Dewar prepared to enter hospital for an operation to replace a heart valve in the spring of 2000, he received the following advice from the *Sunday Herald*: 'The First Minister should take time to recover but also to think, to listen and to talk; to find a bigger, bolder, longer-term vision for Scotland than he has yet found,' (editorial, 30 April 2000).

An allegation aimed at the Scottish Executive and the partnership parties, particularly Labour, is that there is an absence of a vision, of a big idea, which would characterise the administration and leave a lasting legacy on the face of Scotland. That charge was first laid when the Executive outlined its inaugural legislative programme in June 1999 and has resurfaced on a regular basis since. It is not unfair to say that no grand strategy has been in evidence, but I would argue that should not be held against the man at the helm within the Executive, First Minister Donald Dewar.

And now what?

Regarded by many as the Father of the Nation, that moniker, although overused, is nonetheless apt. More than anyone else, Donald Dewar personifies Scotland's new political settlement. His role in driving the Scottish Constitutional Convention as it popularised the vision of the Parliament as an achievable political aim; his period as Shadow Secretary of State for Scotland, during which the foundations for home rule were put in place; his pivotal role in the referendum of 1997, achieving an outcome of huge significance; his piloting of the Scotland Bill through Westminster to form the Act which paved the way for our first democratic Parliament; his brokering of the mould-breaking partnership with the Liberal Democrats; and his election by the Parliament as the first First Minister.

To question whether anyone else could have undertaken these roles (far less whether they could have carried them out as effectively) is to miss the point: Donald Dewar *did* achieve positive outcomes at every stage, increasingly carrying the people and the institutions of Scotland with him as the march to the Parliament gained an unstoppable momentum. The establishment of Scotland's Parliament was Donald Dewar's vision. *That* was his big idea, that was his mission – and it was accomplished. If that achievement does not warrant the title 'Father of the Nation', then nothing does.

Having achieved the goals which he set for himself and his country, is it not unrealistic – and perhaps even unfair – to expect that the man who bears the responsibility of his position as First Minister, should also be expected to be the architect of the post-devolution grand plan? At sixty-three, Dewar is entitled to say (although he never would), 'It's been a long race and I've done my bit; who will now take up the baton?'

I anticipate that, relatively soon after the next UK general election, Donald Dewar will announce his decision to stand down as First Minister and Labour's Scottish leader. That would facilitate the election by the party of a successor, probably in the spring of 2002. The new First Minister would then have a year in which to consolidate his or her position, while developing and presenting their vision for Scotland as the focal point of the Labour Party's campaign for the 2003 Scottish Parliament elections.

That is mere speculation, but it is shared by several Labour colleagues in the Parliament, and not a few of its political journalists. It should not be taken as a diminution of Donald Dewar, or his status; rather the opposite. It seems to me the unfolding of the next stage of the Parliament's development is the appropriate time for a new hand on the Labour tiller, one from the post-Westminster political generation.

That perception represents just one view and carries no more weight than any other. It is also based on an assumption (always a dangerous thing) that Labour's leader will be the First Minister as the Scottish Parliament's second session dawns in May 2003. Time, and the people of Scotland, will tell.

Before this assessment of year zero was completed, the Parliament's second year (logically year one, I suppose) was well underway. The pace of Scotland's political agenda shows no sign of slackening: since the cut-off of 6 July 2000 which I imposed, the SNP has elected a new leader; £5.7 billion was added to the Parliament's budget for the next three years; the Scottish Qualifications Authority has plunged the examination system into chaos; and a fuel crisis has brought the country almost to a standstill, and that was just up to the end of September!

It is that kind of political dynamism that makes the Scottish Parliament such an exciting and vibrant environment to be part of. It may not (yet) be the most accomplished legislature in the world nor even one of the most effective, but it is *our* Parliament and any mistakes we make will be our own – there is no longer anyone else to blame. It would be odd if mistakes had not been made and indeed they were. But mistakes are forgivable, providing lessons are learned from them and they are not repeated. Equally, we can take credit for our successes, of which the first year also produced its fair share.

Metaphorically as well as literally, the new Holyrood site has provided a solid foundation on which to construct the new governance of Scotland. Progress up the learning curve is discernible and will continue. Hold tight!

Postscript

Around 9 o'clock on the evening of 10 October 2000, I learned from Ceefax that Donald Dewar was in hospital, critically ill and on a life support machine. The resumé of his life and career which followed read for all the world like an obituary, leaving little doubt as to his prospects of recovery.

In such traumatic situations, it is normal to have etched in your memory precisely where you were when you heard the news. I can, of course, but much more prominent in my mind are the last words that I exchanged with Donald. MSPs were leaving the Scottish Parliament chamber at the end of First Minister's Questions on 5 October and I happened to emerge from my row as he was moving past it, up the sloping passageway towards the door. We had just witnessed John Swinney's debut as leader of his party. Doubtless he had hoped for a winning start to his weekly jousts with the First Minister; if so, he had suffered a disappointment. 'Glad to see you've continued with Swinney where you left off with Salmond' I casually remarked to Donald as we moved together towards the exit. Perhaps in recognition of our shared passion for football he remarked 'Ah, but as you know, you're only as good as your last result'.

Tragically, as it transpired it was indeed his 'last result' in that chamber and the memory of our brief encounter will live with me forever.

The formal announcement on 11 October that his life had ended brought with it a sense of complete disbelief which was replicated in the reaction of each MSP colleague with whom I spoke. Donald had been such a colossus, he had been so central to the whole Scottish Parliament project that the prospect of us, the Parliament, the Labour Party, Scotland as we knew it continuing without his dominant presence was quite surreal.

Two days later, Parliament was recalled from its autumn recess for a special session to allow tributes to be paid to the First Minister. The Labour members gathered prior to it to be informed of arrangements for the funeral. My recollection is of the pallor common to each and every face. Few spoke, and those who did had great difficulty in doing so. As we walked from Parliament HQ to the Assembly Hall as a group – exactly as we had done on the day of the Parliament's first session in May 1999 – one colleague remarked that she was trying to convince herself this would turn out to have been merely a bad dream; when Parliament resumed after the recess, Donald would be in his place, as normal.

Minutes later, when all members had taken their seats, that innocent reference to Donald's place acquired added poignancy. His seat, at the centre of the front row, had been left empty, adding physical emphasis to the gap that his death represented. I found that eerie, ghost-like and quite disconcerting; it brought me as close to tears as any other moment that day.

There were speeches only from the party leaders, with Henry McLeish representing the Labour Party. It was noticeable that both John Swinney and David McLetchie referred to Donald Dewar as 'our' First Minister and their words, compassionate and heartfelt, were utterly convincing.

Sadly, though predictably, the days before the funeral were filled with media speculation as to the succession. Only after his death did anyone appreciate the requirement – inserted in the Scotland Act by Donald himself – that the post of First Minister be filled within twenty-eight days of a vacancy arising; failure to do so would result in the Parliament being dissolved and a new one being elected. The purpose of such a clause in the Act was to prevent unnecessary delay following a general election in the formation of an administration. With typical perspicacity, Donald had been determined to avoid a protracted and unseemly wrangle, inviting adverse publicity to the institution. How ironic, then, that his own passing should provide the first test of its rigour.

The funeral on 18 October was an occasion worthy of the man who had done more than anyone else to deliver Scotland's parliament. The ecumenical ceremony in Glasgow Cathedral was followed by a procession through his beloved city, past fellow Glaswegians lining the route to pay their last respects, to a private family service. Doubtless Donald himself would have disapproved of the whole thing, regarding it as too worldly by far. Those assembled knew that day that the world itself was a poorer place by far.

Le roi est mort; vive le roi! The law provided twenty-eight days in which to appoint a new First Minister, but only sixteen were required. On Saturday 21 October, following a forty-eight hour campaign, Henry McLeish gained 44 votes to Jack McConnell's 38 in the Party's electoral college to become Labour's new Scottish leader. Five days later the Parliament elected him as Scotland's First Minister.

It is no disrespect to Henry McLeish to offer the view that the first First Minister has been succeeded, not replaced. Quite simply, Donald Dewar was irreplaceable. But the Parliament is his legacy and should those of us privileged to be part of it require a motive for ensuring its ultimate success then his memory surely provides it.

Bibliography

Cavanagh, M., Shepherd, M., McGarvey, N. (2000), *New Scottish Parliament – New Scottish Parliamentarians?*, Political Studies Association, Conference Paper.

Devine, Tom (2000), *Scotland's Shame?*, Edinburgh: Mainstream.

Hassan, Gerry and Chris Warhurst (eds) (2000), *The New Scottish Politics: The First Year of the Scottish Parliament and Beyond*, Edinburgh: The Stationery Office.

Ritchie, Murray (2000), *Scotland Reclaimed: The Inside Story of Scotland's First Democratic Parliamentary Election*, Edinburgh: The Saltire Society.

Taylor, Brian (1999), *The Scottish Parliament*, Edinburgh: Polygon.

Index

Italic page references refer to photographs.

Aberdeen Evening Express, 63
Abolition of Feudal Tenure Act, 111, 164
Abolition of Poindings and Warrant Sales Bill, 100–8, 154, 164, 190
accessibility, 37, 122, 124, 174, 185–6, 195
Ad Hoc Liaison Group, 113–15
additional member system (AMS), 2, 4, 112–13, 116
Adults with Incapacity Act, 111, 164
Alba, Carlos, 44
Alexander, Wendy, 13, 17, 25, 55, 69, 105, 129, 152, 153, 154, 162, 184
  and clause 2a repeal, 140, 143, *144*, 147–8, 152, 155, 156
allowances issue, 14, 21–3, 42–3, 113, 180
Arbuthnot committee
  leaking of recommendations, 97, 172
  report on allocation of health resources, 169, 172
Assembly Hall, The Mound, Edinburgh, *10*, 15, 30, 139
asylum seekers, 117, 121, 127, 160

Audit committee, 20, 89, 163, 165
Auditor General for Scotland, 89
Ayr by-election (Scottish Parliament), 65, 67–71, *70*, 76, 146, 149

Baillie, Jackie, 13, 101, 102, 106, 110
Bain, Andy, *Snash*, 52–3
Bank of Scotland, link-up with Pat Robertson, 141–2, 146
Barnett formula, 20, 168, 184
Barrie, Scott, 67, 103, 104
BBC, News 24, 51
  Radio 4: PM programme, 44
BBC Radio Scotland, *Good Morning Scotland*, 3, 103–4, 125, 153
BBC Scotland
  Reporting Scotland, 103
  Scottish Six (early evening news programme), 125
Beattie Media, 47–8, 174, 175
Bell, Ian, 190
bills, 24–6, 32, 188–90
Black, Robert, 89
Blair, Tony, 13, 56, 63, 71, 98, 131
  and clause 2a, 56–7, 152
  and devolution, 129, 133
  government, 4, 40, 80, 94

Blunkett, David, 129, 146–7
Boyack, Sarah, 7, 13, 105
Breslin, Fr John, 143
British-Irish Council, 126
Brogan, Ben, 62
Brown, Alice, 50
Brown, Gordon, 130, 183–4
Brown, Nick, 130
Brown, Robert, 116
Brown, Tom, 59, 142, 143
budget, Scottish Parliament, 168, 173
Budget Bill, 54, 164
building, new Scottish Parliament *see* Holyrood Building Project

Callaghan, Jim, 13
Campaign for a Scottish Parliament, 5
Campbell, Alistair, 56–7
Canavan, Dennis, 2, 14, 55
Cathcart constituency, xii, 22, 120, 121, 145–6
Census (Scotland) Amendment Bill, 98–100, 190
Chalmers, Philip, 98
Chisholm, Malcolm, 19, 61, 119, 122, 147
Church of Scotland, 143
  Church and Nation Committee, 46
  General Assembly, 108
Civic Forum, 186, 195

civil service, 94, 163
Clarke, Martin, 40, 44, 59, 60
clause 2a repeal issue, 47–50, 53, 56–7, 59, 60, 70–1, 72, 129, 140–61, 190
  'Keep the Clause' campaign, 72–3, 98, 144–7, 151, 152
  postal ballot, 151–3, 155
  relative resources of organisations for and against, 150
Clerk of the Parliament, 16
Code of Conduct for Members, 117, 174
committees
  autonomy question, 167–9
  committee structure, D'Hondt system, 16–18
  effectiveness of, 176–8
  function, 162–5
  mandatory, 162–3
  proposed changes to structure, 165–9
  reporting the, 171–4
  scrutiny of bills, 162, 188–90
  subject, 162–3
  Westminster compared with Holyrood, 123, 177
  work outwith Edinburgh, 179–83
Commons, House of see House of Commons
Commonwealth Parliamentary Association, 127
Connarty, Michael, 71, 197
Connelly, Fr Tom, 159
Conservatives, 1, 2, 14, 31, 75–6, 147, 192–3
  first Scottish Parliament by-election win, 73
  government (1979–97), xi, 28, 140
Consultative Steering Group (CSG), 15, 29, 34, 81, 162, 167, 175, 179
  Expert Panel on Media Issues, 41
conveners of committees, 16–17, 166, 178–9
Conveners' Liaison Group (CLG), 97, 165–6, 172–3, 178–9
Countryside Alliance, 51–2
Courier and Advertiser (Dundee), 39
Cowan, Keith, 151
Cox, Peter, 60
Craigie, Cathy, 68, 112
Cross-Party Working Group on a Replacement Diligence to Poinding and Warrant Sales, 107–8
Crow, Michael, 62
Cubie, Andrew, 81, 82
Cubie report (1999), 80–4, 129
Cunningham, Roseanna, 55
Curran, Margaret, 104, 110, 169–70, 170, 194
Curtice, John, 71

Daily Mail, 54, 57
Daily Mirror, 39
Daily Record, 39, 40, 42–4, 46–7, 55, 56, 57, 59–60, 61, 142, 143, 146–7, 152, 160
Daily Star, 39
Daily Telegraph, 54
Darling, Alistair, 185
Davidson, David, 20
Davidson, Ian, 71, 117
Davidson, Sarah, 20, 164–5, 189–90
de Bruin, Barbre, 131
Deacon, Susan, 13, 96, 105, 152, 159, 169
debates
  interventions, 31–2
  outwith the devolved agenda, 126
debt collection, warrant sales as, 100–8
Deputy First Minister, 9, 14, 135
Devine, Tom, 159
devolution, 38–9, 111, 133, 191
  Blair and, 129, 133
  Gordon Brown and, 130–1
Devolution Minister, 15
devolved issues see issues, devolved
Dewar, Donald, 3–10, 10, 13, 17, 24, 40, 46, 48, 56, 69, 71, 72, 84, 92, 98, 104, 132, 175
  character, 3, 97
  and clause 2a repeal, 70, 146–7, 149, 151
  death, 203–4
  elected as First Minister, 14
  as 'Father of the Nation', 199
  and FMQs, 34, 35
  illness, 35, 101, 105–7, 135, 198, 202
  and the new Scottish Parliament building, 85, 86, 87, 89
as Shadow Secretary of State for Scotland, 128, 199
  special advisers, 94–5
  speech at opening of Scottish Parliament, 139
Dickson, Malcolm, 72
Dinwoodie, Robbie, 58, 104, 153
directorates, 16
Disability Living Allowance, 117
domestic policy, 24
Donohoe, Brian, 63, 118, 119, 177
Doran, Frank, 63–4, 118
Douglas Hamilton, Lord James, 73, 74, 116, 122, 126, 166, 177, 192–3
Dover House, London, 128
drug misuse, 131, 180, 181
dual mandate, 122
Duncan, Michael, 92

Economist, The, 25
Edinburgh, 10, 15, 30, 85, 128, 139
  work outwith, 179–83
Edinburgh Evening News, 55
Education, Culture and Sport committee, 154, 155, 172, 177
Elder, Dorothy Grace, 43, 110
elections
  Scottish Parliamentary (1999), 39, 138
  Scottish Parliamentary (2003), 197
  UK general (1992), xii, 38
  UK general (2001), 137, 197
Electoral Reform Society, 152
Engender, 173
England, knock-on effect, 128–9
Enterprise and Lifelong Learning committee, 17, 18
Equal Opportunities committee, 99, 163, 165
Equality Network, 149
Ethical Standards in Public Life Bill, 70, 111, 148, 152, 155–6, 176–7, 190
euro, 126
European committee, 17, 163, 176, 183–4
  visit to Brussels, 181
European Parliament, 108
European structural funds, 183–6
Ewing, Winnie, 11
examination system crisis, 200

Index

Executive Policy Unit, 95–8

Fabiani, Linda, 93
farming crisis, 192
Ferguson, Patricia, 5, 119, 157
feudal tenure, 24, 111, 164, 192
Finance committee, 18, 19–20, 54, 89, 130–1, 163,165, 168, 173
  inquiry into European structural funds, 183–6
Finnie, Ross, 6, 7, 54, 129–30, 198
First Minister, 14, 198–200, 203–4
  official residence, 95
  and Secretary of State for Scotland, 132
First Minister's questions (FMQs), 33–5, 136
Fitzpatrick, Brian, 2, 98
foreign affairs, 126
Forsyth, Michael, 127–8
Foulkes, George, 127
fox hunting, 192; *see also* hunting with dogs
Fraser, Douglas, 40, 50, 61, 64, 167
Free Church of Scotland, 143
Freedom of Information Bill, 75, 198
Friends of the Victoria, 174
fuel crisis, 200
Fyfe, Maria, 24, 62–3, 109, 118, 119

Galbraith, Sam, 6, 122, 148, 153–6, 156, 157
Gallie, Phil, 67, 69, 143
Galloway, George, 55, 71
gay rights, 140
General Register Office, 99
genetically modified contaminated seed, 129–30
Germany, 113, 116
  Reichstag building in Berlin, 93–4
  SPD and Greens, 8
Gibbons, John, 93
Gibson, Kenny, 13, 42, 120, 126, 166, 177
Gillon, Karen, 148
Glasgow, 2, 22, 181
  City Chambers, 94, 182
  City Council, 126
  Scottish Parliament in, 108–11, 129, 182
Glasgow Evening Times, 55, 56, 62
Godman, Trish, 103, 179
Goldie, Annabel, 113

Gordon, Robert, 93
Gorrie, Donald, 6, 7, 8, 23, 24, 83, 85, 86–7, *87*, 90–1, 122, 176, 198
Govan constituency, 1, 2, 132–3
graduate endowment fund, 82–3
Grahame, Christine, 163
Grant, Rhoda, 21
grants, student, 80, 82
Grice, Paul, 16, 113
Guide to the Scottish Parliament, A, 16

Hamilton, Duncan, 55–6
Hamilton South by-election (Westminster), 65, 66–7
Hardie, Alison, 57
Hardie, Keir, 100
Harper, Ross, 2
Hassan, Gerry, 160
Health and Community Care committee, 19, 169, 172, 177
health issues, 119, 131, 169
Henry, Hugh, 68, 154
Herald, The, 55, 56, 57–8, 59–60, 62, 63, 104, 129, 134, 142, 154, 156, 172, 182
Hernon, Ian, 62
Highlands and Islands, 120, 121, 151
Holyrood Building Project, 20, 23–4, 47, 84–94
  costs, 87–91
  siting of, 85–6
Holyrood Progress Group, 20, 92
Home Robertson, John, 33, 60, 116
Hood, Jimmy, 4
hours, working, 29, 31, 122–4, 194–5
House of Commons, 27, 29, 50, 62, 123
  age profile, 11, 12
  ministers in committees, 163
  role of Scottish MPs in, 117–18
  select committees, 181
  standing committees, 123, 177
House of Lords, 122, 146
housing benefit system, 126, 185
housing issues, 25, 118, 119, 120
housing stock transfer, 162, 169–71, 171–2

Hughes, Janis, 19, 67, 103, 154
hunting with dogs, 50–4, 143, 176, 190–1; *see also* fox hunting
Hyslop, Fiona, 13, 169–71, *171*, 194

immigration issues, 109, 117, 118
independence, SNP's debate on the future of, 35
Independent Television Commission (ITC), 64
international development, 127
Irvine, Jack, 52, 146, 152
Irvine, Mark, 167
issues
  devolved, 109, 118, 119, 121
  grey areas, 121, 126
  reserved, 109, 118, 125–7, 176–7
ITN, 51

Jackson, Gordon, 2, 91, 92, 100, 154
joint ministerial committees, 130–1
Jones, Peter, 25
judicial review, 110
Justice and Home Affairs committee, 100, 163–4, 165, 166, 177

Kerr, Andy, 13, 18–19, 70, 71, 101, 164, 196
King, Dave, 40, 42, 44, 190
Kirkpatrick, Janice, 93
Kirkwood, Archy, 113, 114
Kvaerner shipyard, Govan, 132–3

Labour Campaign for Electoral Reform, 5
Labour Party, 38
  government, xii, 4, 40, 80, 94
  Labour Co-ordinating Committee, 27
  relations with SNP, 21
  and the Roman Catholic Church, 158–9
  in Scotland, xi, 1, 4, 38, 77, 154
  Scottish conference (2000), Blair's visit, 56–7, 71
Labour-Liberal Democrats partnership, 3–10, 79, 134–7, 195–7
Lamont, Johann, 12, 28, 56, 106, 153, 167, 194

land ownership bill, 24, 26, 192
leaked reports, 97, 114, 172–3
legislation, 16, 124, 188–90
  the first legislative programme, 20, 24–5
  proper scrutiny, 32–3
  timetabling, 32–3
legislature
  distinctiveness of Scottish, 28–9
  protocol between Holyrood and Westminster, 185–6
Liberal Democrats, 1, 30–1, 66–7, 74–5, 197; see also Labour-Liberal Democrats partnership
Livingstone, Marilyn, 104, 135
'Lobbygate', 47–50, 132, 174, 175, 190
lobbying, 174–8
local authorities, 141, 177
local government, 119, 193
  proportional voting system for, 8, 53, 84, 196
  relationship with Scottish Parliament, 177
Local Government Act (1988), Section 28, 140
Local Government committee, 18, 100, 165, 176, 177
Local Government (Scotland) Act (1986), 140; see also clause 2a repeal issue
Lords, House of see House of Lords

McAllion, John, 4, 19, 106, 179
Macaskill, Kenny, 125
Macauley, David, 145, 151
McAveety, Frank, 13
McCabe committee, 155–6
McCabe, Mike, 155–6
McCabe, Tom, 7, 17, 18, 22, 69, 91, 102, 104, 105, 113, 147, 155, 165, 166
McConnell, Jack, 13, 28, 48, 49, 50, 101, 147, 163, 168, 173, 184, 204
Macdonald, Lewis, 93, 118
MacDonald, Margo, 55, 87, 87, 88, 90
Macintosh, Ken, 89, 193
McIntosh report on relationship between Parliament and local government, 177
MacKay, Angus, 13, 99

McKenna, Ron, 60
Maclean, Kate, 19, 68, 98, 99, 103
McLeish, Henry, 6, 15, 17, 29, 101, 104, 132, 135, 147, 203
  elected as First Minister, 204
Macleod, Angus, 72, 94
Macleod, Catherine, 59–60, 62, 129, 131
McLetchie, David, 5, 14, 31, 43, 47, 75–6, 203
McMahon, Michael, 155
MacMahon, Peter, 25–6, 58
MacMillan, Andrew, 92
MacMillan, James, 159
MacMillan, Maureen, 21, 110, 120, 176
McNeil, Duncan, 6, 61, 104, 106, 131, 134, 157, 166, 197–8
McNeill, Pauline, 5, 13, 61, 104, 106, 147, 177
Macwhirter, Iain, 10, 47, 49, 50, 58–9, 82, 92–3, 96, 107, 110–11, 160, 193
Mail on Sunday, 55
Major, John, 94
Manson, David, 93
Martin, Paul, 42
Marwick, Tricia, 5, 35, 61, 85–6, 107, 175
Matheson, Michael, 164
Maxton, John, 120, 140
medal issue, 45–6
media, 38, 50–9, 96, 142, 147, 152
  negative coverage, 187, 191
  role in clause 2a affair, 160–1
  see also press
Media House, 52, 145, 146
Members' Business, 126
Members of the Scottish Parliament see MSPs
Michael, Alun, 3
Milburn, Alan, 131
Millan, Bruce, 85
Miller, Rita, 70, 70, 72
ministers
  cabinet, 14
  evidence at committees compared with Westminster, 163, 183–4
  junior, 14
  role in issues distribution, 121
  special advisers at Westminster, 94
Ministry of Agriculture, Fisheries and Food

(MAFF), 129–30
Miralles, Enric, 85, 91
Moffat, Alastair, 62
Monteith, Brian, 6, 42, 55, 81, 156, 177
Moore, Michael, 7
Morrison, Alasdair, 13
MPs
  and MSPs relationship, 113, 117–24
  role of Scottish in House of Commons, 117–18
  stress, 194
  working week, 122–3
MSPs
  age profile, 11–14
  as all equal in rights and status, 114
  also MPs, dual mandate, 122
  with columns in newspapers, 55
  constituency, 1, 116–17
  e-mail addresses, 37
  list, 1, 2, 21, 116, 120–1
  relationship between constituency and list, 42, 112–17
  stress, 193–4
  web sites, 37
  women, 11, 28, 110–11, 123–4
  women subject to media abuse, 55–9, 96, 147, 152
  working hours, 29, 31, 122–4, 194–5
  see also Code of Conduct for Members
Munro, John Farquhar, 8
Murphy, Paul, 133–4

National Assembly of Wales, 3, 11, 131, 194
nationalism, 28
Neil, Alex, 77, 170
Neil, Andrew, 40, 57–8
Neill Committee on code of conduct for MPs, 50
Nelson, Dean, 47, 50
New Parliament House, Edinburgh, 128
New Scottish Politics, The (Hassan and Warhurst), 93
New Statesman Scotland, 62, 156–7, 167
newspapers, 39, 46
  MSPs with columns in, 55
Noble, Gill, 130–1
Northern Ireland, devolution in, 133

Index

Northern Ireland Assembly, 131

Observer, 47
'cash for access' allegations, 132–4
Oldfather, Irene, 115, 119
open question time, 33–4
opinion polls, 65
Osborne, Sandra, 71–2
Outright Scotland, 151
Owen, David, 13

pairing constituencies, 11
parliament, functions of a, 187
Parliament Hall, Edinburgh, 139
Parliamentary Bureau, 16–17, 44, 115, 165, 166, 178–9, 189
Parliamentary Questions (PQs), oral and written, 34, 36
Partnership for Scotland, A, 3–10, 79, 81
aims, 9
on PR, 196
partnership government, Labour-Liberal Democrats, 3–10, 79, 134–7, 195–7
party business managers, 178–9
Paterson, Lindsay, 83
Peacock, Peter, 21
pensions, 126
Plaid Cymru, 3
poindings, 100–8
policy issues, 118
poverty, 131, 184–5
Presiding Officer, 14, 32, 35, 87
press, 39–45, 46
political, 25–6
see also newspapers
Press Complaints Commission (PCC), 46–7, 55
Press and Journal, 39, 63
Prime Minister's questions, 29–30, 34
Procedures committee, 33, 36, 166, 1163
Programme for Government, A, 9
proportional representation
for local government, 8, 53, 84, 196
Protection of Wild Mammals (Scotland) Bill, 50–4, 176
Public Finance and Accountability Bill, 163

Public Petitions committee, 19, 163, 166, 185

quangos, 176
questions *see* First Minister's questions (FMQs); open questions; Parliamentary Questions (PQs); Prime Minister's questions
Quinan, Lloyd, 170

Radcliffe, Nora, 74
Raffan, Keith, 8, 20
Rafferty, John, 17, 95, *95*, 96–7
departure, 97
recess issue, 43–5
referendum (1979), 28, 38
referendum (1997), xii, 15–16, 38, 39, 138, 199
regional assemblies, 133
Reid, Donald, 195
Reid, George, 32, 92, 113, 178–9
Reid, John, 48, 127, 128, 132–3, 134, 184
Reid, Kevin, 48, 132
Relationships between MSPs: Guidance from the Presiding Officer, 116–17
religion, question in the census, 99
religious discrimination, in the Act of Settlement, 126
reports of Parliament committees, 171–4
reserved issues *see* issues, reserved
Ritchie, Murray, 56, 57, 58, 89, 130, 175
RMJM, 92
Robertson, George, 66
Robertson, Pat, link-up with Bank of Scotland, 141–2, 146
Robison, Shona, 110
Robson, Euan, 91
Roche, Barbara, 109
Roman Catholic Church, 143–4, 146
and the Labour Party, 158–9
Roman Catholic schools, 159
Royal High School, Calton Hill, Edinburgh, 85
Rumbles, Mike, 74, 91, 149
Rural Affairs committee, 192
Russell, Mike, 22, 45–6, *45*, 86, 115

St Andrew's House, Edinburgh, 85
Salmond, Alex, 14, 34, 35, 47, 56, 77, 89, 93, 136, 154, 184
Schlesinger, Philip, 41
Scotland Act, 4, 15, 118, 176, 199
Scotland on Sunday, 59, 151, 154, 190
Scotland's Parliament (white paper 1997), 29
Scotland's Shame?, 159
Scotsman, The, 40, 48, *52–3*, 57–8, 70, 73, 104, 114, 142, 155, 160, 164
Scott, John, *70*, 73, 149
Scott, Tavish, 13, 93
Scottish Affairs, 83
Scottish Affairs select committee, 181, 184
Scottish Assembly, 27
Scottish Campaign Against Hunting with Dogs (SCAHD), 51, 176
Scottish Constitutional Convention, xii, 9, 28, 199
Scottish Council of Voluntary Organisations, 37
Scottish Daily Mail, 55
Scottish Episcopal Church, 143
Scottish Executive
and committees, 162–3
components of, 14
and Scottish Parliament, 175
Scottish Grand Committee, 85, 127–8
Scottish Greens, 2
Scottish Media Group (SMG), 62, 63–4
Scottish National Party *see* SNP
Scottish Office, 132
Scottish Parliament
assessment of first year, 186–200
comparison with House of Commons, 29–34
new building, 84–94
number of seats, 2
opening, 10–14, 27, 138–40
'reconvening' of the 1707 adjournment, 11, 182
and Scottish Executive, 175
unionist-separatist divide, 192–3
Scottish Parliamentary Corporate Body, 86–7, 88, 90

Scottish Parliamentary Labour
    Party (SPLP) *see* Labour
    Party, in Scotland
Scottish Parliamentary Press
    Association (SPPA), 40
Scottish Qualifications
    Authority, 200
Scottish School Boards
    Association (SSBA), and
    Keep the Clause cam-
    paign, 144–6
Scottish Six issue, 125
Scottish Socialist Party (SSP),
    2, 66–7, 74, 76–8, 158
    and SNP, 77–8
Secretary of State for
    Northern Ireland, 133
Secretary of State for
    Scotland, future of role,
    132–4
Secretary of State for Wales,
    133–4
separatism *see* unionist-
    separatist divide
Sheridan, Tommy, 2, 13, 55,
    100
Sinn Fein, 131
Smith, Margaret, 7, 74, 169,
    172–3, 177–8, 196, 198
SNP (Scottish National
    Party), 1, 38, 76, 77,
    110, 124–5, 158, 196–7
    budget issue, 168
    columns in newspapers, 55
    debate on the future of
        independence, 35
    election of new leader, 200
    relations with Labour, 14,
        21
Social Inclusion, Housing and
    Voluntary Sector com-
    mittee, 17, 18, 19, 100,
    162, 165, 168, 169–71,
    170–1, 180, 181, 185
social inclusion agenda, 76
Souter, Brian, 71, 72–3, 98,
    144, 156
    postal ballot, 151–3, 155
South Ayrshire council, 67, 70
South Lanarkshire council, 66
special advisers, 94–8
speeches, standard of, 33
Spencely, John, 89, 90
Spencely report, 89
Standards committee, 48, 50,
    117, 132, 163, 166,
    174–8
    report on lobbying

companies, 175
Standards in Scotland's
    Schools Bill, 32
standing committees, at
    Westminster, 123, 177
standing orders, 13, 16
Steel, Sir David, 7, 46–7, 51,
    74, 88, 90, 91, 113, 115,
    122, 178, 195
    appointed as Presiding
        Officer, 14
Stephen, Nicol, 7
Stewart, Brian, 92
Stone, Jamie, 193–4
Strathclyde Gay and Lesbian
    Switchboard, 149–51
Straw, Jack, 63, 109, 110
student tuition fees *see* tuition
    fees issue
Sturgeon, Nicola, 2, 116
Subordinate Legislation
    committee, 163
Sullivan, Denis Robertson, 7,
    8, 197
Sun, The, 39, 57, 160
Sunday Herald, 40, 59, 61, 115,
    160, 167, 188, 194, 198
Sunday Mail, 55
Swinney, John, 20, 77, 196,
    202, 203

Tagliabuie, Benedetta, 92
Tait, Robert, 58
Taylor, Brian, 40, 102–3, 130,
    163, 187–8
television, 41, 62, 63
Thatcher, Margaret, xi, 28,
    140, 147
Thomson, Callum, 20
transfer of powers from
    Westminster, debates, 20
Transport and Environment
    committee, 19, 164
Treasury, 168, 183–4
tuition fees issue, 6, 8, 9, 10,
    79–84, 129, 190, 198
Twigg, Stephen, 152
Tynan, Bill, 66
Tyson, Mike, issue, 63–4,
    109–11, 125, 126

Ullrich, Kay, 115
unionist-separatist divide,
    192–3
urban-rural divide, 192

Victoria Hospital, campaign
    to save, 174

violence against women,
    109–11
voting
    first-past-the-post system, 4
    proportional, 5, 75, 83, 196
    two-vote system, 4, 13

Wales
    devolution in, 3, 133
    knock-on effect, 128–9
Wallace, Ben, 52, 69, 176
Wallace, Jim, 3–10, 7, 10, 84,
    99, 101, 109
    as deputy First Minister, 9,
        35, 74, 105–7, 135–6,
        136
    fronts First Minister's
        questions (FMQs), 136
    as Justice Minister, 75
Warner, Gerald, 59
warrant sales, abolition issue,
    25, 100–8, 154, 164, 190
Weinberg, Dr Ashley, 194
Wellington, Sheena, 139–40,
    139
Welsh, Ian, resignation, 11,
    67–8, 146
Welsh Assembly *see* National
    Assembly of Wales
Westminster
    relationship with
        Holyrood, 109–10,
        117–24
    transfer of powers from,
        debates, 20, 62–4
    women at, 11
Whitefield, Karen, 99
Whitehead, Maire, 2
Whitton, David, 89, 96
Wilson, Allan, 112, 115
Wilson, Andrew, 5, 19, 24, 35,
    55, 131
Wilson, Brian, 85
Winning, Cardinal Thomas,
    143–4, 146, 152, 158–9
Wishart, Ruth, 122
women
    impact on Scottish
        Parliament, 194
    MPs, 11
    MSPs, 11, 28, 110–11,
        123–4
    media abuse, 55–9, 96, 147,
        152
    violence against, 109–11
Wright, Andrew, 93

Young, John, 46